DATE DUE

The Second Great Emancipation

The Second
Great Emancipation

The Mechanical
Cotton Picker,
Black Migration,
and How They Shaped
the Modern South

Donald Holley

THE UNIVERSITY OF ARKANSAS PRESS
FAYETTEVILLE • 2000

Designed by Ellen Beeler

⊚ The paper used in this publication meets the minimum requirements of the American
National Standard for Permanence of Paper for Printed Library Materials Z39.48–1984.

Library of Congress Cataloging-in-Publication Data

Holley, Donald, 1940–
   The second great emancipation : the mechanical cotton picker, Black migration, and how
   they shaped the modern South / Donald Holley.
      p.   cm.
   Includes bibliographical references and index.
   ISBN 1-55728-606-X (cloth : alk. paper)
      1. Cotton farmers—Southern States—History—20th century. 2. Afro-American agricul-
   tural laborers—Southern States—History—20th century. 3. Farm mechanization—Social
   aspects—Southern States—History—20th century. 4. Cotton-picking machinery—
   Southern States—History—20th century. 5. Migration, Internal—United States—
   History—20th century. 6. Afro-Americans—Employment—History—20th century.
   I. Title.

   HD8039.C662 U644 2000
   338.1'63'0975—dc21   00-026140

For Helen and Bailey,
my daughter and granddaughter

Contents

Illustrations

Figures

Tables

Preface

If it were not for the mechanical cotton picker, you might be picking cotton right now in the middle of a hot, dusty field in Arkansas instead of reading this book. You are not doing so because machines now perform one of the most backbreaking forms of stoop labor ever known. The transition from hand-picking to machine picking resulted in enormous improvements in the lives of everyone who depended on cotton for a living.

I assume that you, the reader, will join me in not crying over lost innocence or a mythical rural culture sacrificed to progress. You must be reading these lines because you are concerned with how the Cotton South shook off its historic legacy of plantation agriculture and entered the modern world of agribusiness.

The invention of the mechanical cotton picker, or more generally the transition from hand labor to machine labor in the Cotton South, was one of the major developments of twentieth-century agriculture, with spillover effects into migration, civil rights, and politics. The collapse of the South's infamous plantation system during World War II created an opportunity for positive change if some means could be found to enable cotton growers to farm without hand labor. From the beginning of southern agriculture, hand labor, cheap labor, and having enough of both when they were needed had always been the dominant worry. The mechanization of agriculture took place decades earlier in the Midwest, where farms were larger, more productive, and farmers more prosperous. In California and other western states, growers mechanized early because they were not handicapped by inefficient labor arrangements and took advantage of a more productive physical environment. While these regions turned to mechanization, southern farmers remained mired in inefficient, backward methods and bound to the classic one-mule, fifteen-acre farm. Indeed, the entire region locked itself into a system that required poverty, ignorance, and limited opportunity in order to control the labor needed to chop and pick cotton. The South could not break the grip of this system until the inefficient structures themselves were swept away, but that could not take place without mechanization, which in turn required a dramatic technological breakthrough. Cotton was the last major crop to make the transition from hand to machine labor. The centerpiece of this transition was the mechanical cotton picker.

The First Great Emancipation freed the slaves. The Second Great Emancipation freed the Cotton South from the plantation system and its attendant evils—cheap labor, ignorance, and Jim Crow discrimination. These changes all derived in large part from the development of the mechanical cotton picker, a dominant force for social and economic change in the South after World War II.

This book tells the story of the South's transition from labor-intensive to capital-intensive agriculture, a transition that was both inevitable and necessary for the Cotton South to achieve social and economic modernization. The focus is on the Mississippi River Delta, the rich alluvial flood plain that embraces parts of Arkansas, Louisiana, and Mississippi. This region, between 1930 and 1970, was the first part of the old Cotton Belt to mechanize cotton production.

The story of the cotton picker is more than the story of a machine. The mechanical cotton picker symbolizes how far modern agriculture has taken the Cotton South from the era of mules and tenants. The development of the mechanical cotton picker is part of a fascinating story of how the pre–World War II South of poverty and sharecroppers became the modern, urbanized South of the 1990s. This story embodies the following elements:

- The breakdown of the plantation system, with its hierarchy of tenants and one-mule farms
- The saga of a lone, eccentric inventor, John D. Rust, whose genius threw the Cotton South into a panic during the Great Depression
- The development work of International Harvester Corporation, which over twenty-five years poured $4.5 million into a successful effort to perfect a commercially viable mechanical picker
- The migration of 7 million people, black and white, who fled the South after 1940 in search of better jobs, better schools, and improved living conditions
- The civil rights movement of the 1950s and 1960s in which black people threw off the constraints associated with Jim Crow, a form of labor control
- The transition from labor-intensive to capital-intensive agriculture, the basis of modern agribusiness

While the mechanical cotton picker alone did not cause these momentous changes, none of them could have occurred without the facilitating effect of the mechanization of cotton.

The traditional system of cotton culture, with its vested interests and institutional inertia, had held back the South economically since the Civil War, and this system had to be destroyed before agriculture could break away from hand labor and take advantage of more efficient methods of production. The future of American cotton as an industry depended on discarding the ancient, inefficient methods used for a century and a half.

My interest in these matters goes back to my early years when I lived in Osceola, Arkansas. I was there during the 1950s, when Mississippi County, which boasted that it was the largest cotton-producing county in the nation, was in full transition to agribusiness. I recall seeing people in the fields chopping cotton, and machines as well as people picking it. I did not then fully understand all of the forces of change that were converging in the Cotton Belt, and today that era has passed into history. The tenant cabins that once lined country roads are all gone now, and many of the region's former residents have Illinois and Michigan zip codes.

My work on the Farm Security Administration enabled me to get in touch with the history of the Mississippi River Delta as a historian, not just an amateur observer. Like many people who grew up there, I cannot forget the hot, sticky weather, the long straight roads with the sudden ninety-degree turns, and the open fields that stretch into the distance. When I look across this landscape, I still wonder what this great alluvial land was like before the turn of the twentieth century; and I am awed by the labor that it took to clear and drain these bottomlands and create one of the most productive agricultural regions in the world.

While I am a historian, not a farmer, I have always had great sympathy for farmers and an interest in how they do their work. This is especially true since people my age have seen the Cotton South undergo a major transition in our own life time—a transition as dramatic and important as the one that occurred during the Civil War and Reconstruction. This transition ended only about thirty years ago, and it is so easily overlooked because it happened "right here," all around us. How it all happened is the story that this book tells.

Since I have worked on this book for a decade or more, I have a long list of people to thank. I am grateful to staff members at the National Archives; the Smithsonian Institution Archives; the National Museum of American History in Washington, D.C.; the State Historical Society of Wisconsin at Madison; the Deere and Company Archives at Moline, Illinois; Mitchell Library at Mississippi State University at Starkville; and the Delta State University Archives at Cleveland, Mississippi.

More specifically, I am grateful to Gilbert Fite, whose earlier work on agricultural mechanization first showed me that this topic might be practical. At an early stage of this project, he offered helpful suggestions. I will always be grateful to William F. Droessler, head librarian at the University of Arkansas at Monticello, for assistance of all kinds and reassurance over the years. He read the manuscript several times and saved me from many egregious errors. Sandra Dupree and Linda Forrest of the UAM library endured my overbearing requests for interlibrary loan assistance. Other people supplied important information and insights that became part of the story: Stanley Ayres of Leland, Mississippi; John B. Currie of Wilmot, Arkansas; Pete Daniel, a curator in the National Museum of American History in Washington, D.C.; J. T. and Steve Frizzell of Star City, Arkansas; Jere Nash Jr. of Greenville, Mississippi; and G. E. Powell of Pine Bluff, Arkansas.

I must also thank the UAM Research Committee for numerous grants that enabled me to travel to the National Archives and to examine the International Harvester collection at the State Historical Society of Wisconsin and the Deere and Company Archives.

The dedication is to Helen Holley, my daughter, and Bailey, her daughter and my granddaughter, both of whom will wonder why a book about mechanical cotton pickers, of all things, is dedicated to them. It was just their turn, and they had to wait a long time for "their" book.

Chapter 1

Mules and Tenants: Hand Labor in the Cotton South

In 1793 Eli Whitney, while visiting on a cotton plantation near Savannah, Georgia, assembled a model of a machine that separated the seeds from the fibers of short-staple cotton plants. Cottonseeds had previously been removed by hand, a laborious process that held back production. Whitney claimed that his cotton en*gine*, or gin, replaced the labor of ten men when it was hand cranked, or fifty men if operated by horse- or waterpower. This simple device dramatically increased cotton production and created immense wealth.[1]

Because of Whitney's gin, cotton, slavery, and plantation agriculture defined life in the Old South. As the frontier moved westward, pioneer farmers carried cotton and slaves into the lower South, stretching the Cotton Belt from the Carolinas to Texas. Except for the cotton gin, however, cotton production remained virtually unmechanized and dependent on hand labor. Whitney's invention energized the spread of cotton and revitalized slavery, an institution that had previously been in decline; but cotton farmers were unable to duplicate the productivity gains that the McCormick reaper created in the Midwest.

While the cotton gin was the invention that created the Old South, the modern South is the product of the mechanical cotton picker. A century and a half after Whitney, the South experienced another major technological innovation that created revolutionary change. The cotton picker, which went into commercial production after World War II, generated great fear and trepidation. The cotton gin had set off a series of events that produced the antebellum South, bolstered slavery, and contributed to the Civil War. The potential effect of the mechanical cotton picker was seen as equally prodigious. This new machine symbolized a revolution that would eliminate hand labor from the cotton harvest and free the region from its dependence on labor-intensive agriculture. The effect on the region's sharecroppers was implicitly disastrous. Since many croppers were black, this outcome seemed especially fearful. At the same time, cotton was the last major crop to achieve full mechanization, enabling cotton farmers to work more efficiently and earning them greater prosperity.

The story of the mechanization of cotton goes back to the nineteenth century and the region's mule-and-tenant economy. It begins with the Cotton South's plantation system, in which sharecroppers and tenant farmers produced cotton with nothing more than hand tools. As with the South's political and economic history, the region's agricultural history is conventionally divided at the Civil War, with prosperity in evidence prior to the war and depression afterward.

Despite their continued reliance on hand labor, antebellum southern farmers enjoyed "flush" times as the per capita income of the region soared above the national average.[2] Cotton planters cleared the alluvial river bottoms and expanded the cotton kingdom. The Old South contained the classic conditions that produced plantation agriculture. Around the world, plantations have arisen in undeveloped areas where a staple crop is grown on a large scale. A plantation economy was one in which farmers produced a crop for highly competitive national or international markets but labor was subject to constraints.[3] In other words, plantations required the use of cheaper labor than was freely available. By definition this labor was premodern, inefficient, and oversupplied.[4] A labor surplus overcame its inefficiency and reduced costs. The plantation system emerged and prospered in the antebellum period—a prosperity based on the high price of cotton and a growing slave population.

The farm equipment used in the Cotton Belt consisted only of simple tools like a plow, harrow, seed planter and fertilizer distributor, a team of mules with their harnesses, and hoes. A wagon was also needed, as well as other hand tools, including axes, rakes, and shovels—nothing more. Ginning was the only mechanized process in cotton farming.[5] Similarly, cotton production required little or no skill, and workers devoid of any motivation grew it successfully. Slaves, sharecroppers, and poor whites have all set records in cotton production.

After 1865 the transition from slave to free labor produced sharecropping; but the upheavals of the Civil War and Reconstruction created no fundamental changes in cotton production techniques. In the late nineteenth century, plantation labor evolved into a pattern that lasted until World War II. Cotton remained a crop of mules and tenants. The Cotton South did not need to mechanize because labor was abundant and cheap.

Cast of Characters

The organizational hierarchy of postbellum southern plantations acquired its familiar cast of characters by 1880.[6] At the top was the planter, or owner, who usually acted as manager. A large plantation might have "riding bosses" who supervised other workers, especially day laborers. Tenants came in several classes, starting with the "renter," who supplied all operating capital as well as the labor necessary for making and harvesting his crop. Cash tenants rented land for a fixed cash amount and bore all the expenses of production and retained, minus their rent, the entire crop. Some tenants, called "standing-rent tenants," paid a portion of the crop instead of cash as rent. A cash tenant usually did not receive close supervision. In plantation districts renters were rare, but a planter sometimes rented out a few acres to supplement his income.

Next was the "share tenant," who supplied his own work stock, simple tools, and seed; he paid a fourth of his cotton and a third of his corn as rent. They were also rarely found in the large plantation districts. In the Yazoo-Mississippi Delta they were referred to as "fourth tenants."

Occupying the next-to-the-lowest rung on the agricultural ladder was the sharecropper who furnished his own labor and that of his family in return for half of the crop. In most states the cropper was legally not a tenant at all, but a worker who was paid half of the crop he grew for his labor.[7] The cropper also paid half of the cost of the seed; poison, if used; fertilizer; and ginning charges. But sharecroppers, also known as "half hands" or "half tenants," did live rent-free in cabins located on the plantations. Most croppers had low motivation to work hard, to work efficiently, or to improve the property; so the South was stuck with the worst possible system for labor efficiency. If tenants, as in most cases, were furnished supplies of food and clothing, then their furnish amounted to payment in advance for labor. Payment was also not directly tied to the number of hours worked. Thus the nature of the system fostered shiftlessness, indolence, and wastefulness. Plantation owners contracted with all tenants on an annual basis in an effort to ensure picking labor, forcing them to choose small family-based tenancies over labor-saving machinery.[8]

Wage laborers, or "wage hands," were the only class of agricultural labor who worked for cash wages. Blacksmiths and hostlers, who worked with horses and mules, were paid by the week or month. Other laborers received a daily wage for the days they worked, or they were paid per acre hoed or per hundred pounds of seed cotton picked. They were hired as needed during peak labor periods. Their wages, however, placed them on the lowest rung of the agricultural ladder. Regular wage hands might live on the plantation, but seasonal wage hands were transported back and forth daily from nearby cities and towns during the chopping and picking seasons.

The plantation labor force was not one that called for skilled and educated workers, nor one that offered any motivation to use machines to work more efficiently. The typical southern cotton worker was not truly employed full time. A study of cotton farming in Mississippi showed that cotton farmers were idle for a quarter of the year.[9] Periods of intense work were followed by slack times with little to do.[10]

The average cotton plantation in 1934 included a labor force consisting of families whose labor arrangements varied from wage hands to sharecroppers, share tenants, and renters, with each tenant family living on its own unit (fig. 1.1). The tenant cabins were dispersed over the plantation as each family lived

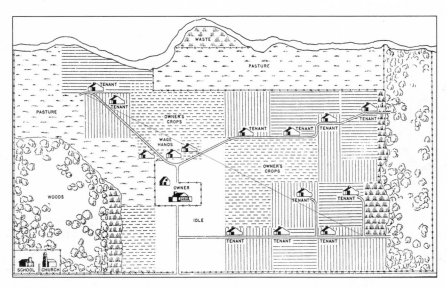

FIGURE 1.1. Layout of an average cotton plantation, with eleven tenant families (eight sharecroppers, two share tenants, and one cash renter) and three families headed by wage hands, 1934. Source: T. J. Woofter Jr., *Landlord and Tenant on the Cotton Plantation*, Research Monograph 5 (Washington, D.C.: Works Progress Administration, 1936), xxxii.

separately on their assigned acreage. The plantation owner also maintained his own land worked by wage hands.

The relationships between landlords and various classes of workers formed mirror images: the more landlords supplied, the less workers received. The more labor security landlords were willing to pay for, the less flexibility they had. The fewer assets workers owned, the more of the cotton their landlords claimed (table 1.1).

Both landlords and tenants had their own reasons for favoring various labor arrangements depending on changing conditions (table 1.2). The general rule was that when labor became scarce, planters tended to use more sharecroppers because sharecroppers committed themselves for the entire season; but when labor was plentiful, the demand for wage laborers increased. For labor, farming on shares was a means of escaping from close supervision and enjoying greater independence. Sharecroppers also earned more than wage laborers. Landlords favored wage labor if labor was in oversupply because it gave them the maximum control over the management of workers. Share tenants were more independent and motivated since they supplied their own equipment, had more resources invested in the crop, and paid landlords a smaller share.[11]

The Cycle of Cotton Culture

"To start raising cotton," a pundit wrote in 1933, "you first select yourself a twenty-acre piece of land in a place where there will be no frost for seven months. You clear the land of timber, underbrush, or last year's cotton stalks. You get yourself a wife, two or three children, a mule, a plow or two, a distributor for fertilizer and seed, a harrow, and a hoe." Anyone can raise cotton, he continued. "It requires little brawn, less brain. About all that is essential is a gambling disposition and immunity to sunstroke. . . . It requires intelligence," he emphasized, "to know when to *stop* growing cotton."[12]

The cotton season contained three peak-labor periods: plowing in the spring, thinning and weeding in the summer, and picking in the fall. The annual tasks followed a seemingly unvarying pattern, and these tasks all involved simple hand labor.

The cycle of cotton culture formed the dominant rhythm in southern life. The first of three peak-labor requirements involved the preparation of the seedbed. On the best farms, the cotton season began in the late fall and winter, when the old stalks were plowed under to rot and add humus to the soil.

TABLE 1.1. Systems of Tenure: Relationships between Landlords and Tenants in Southern Cotton Farming

	METHOD OF RENTING			
	Sharecropping (Croppers)	Share Renting (Share Tenants)	Cash Renting (Cash or Standing Tenant)	Wage Labor
Landlord furnished	• Land • House or cabin • Fuel • Tools • Work stock • Seed • One-half of fertilizer • Feed for work stock	• Land • House or cabin • Fuel • One-fourth or one-third of fertilizer • Labor • Work stock	• Land • House or cabin • Fuel	• Hourly, daily, weekly or monthly wage
Tenant furnished	• Labor • One-half of fertilizer	• Feed for work stock • Tools • Seed • Three-fourths or two-thirds of fertilizer	• Labor • Work stock • Feed for work stock • Tools • Seed • Fertilizer	• Labor for specific tasks
Landlord received	• One-half of the crop	• One-fourth or one-third of the crop	• Fixed amount in cash or lint cotton	• Labor
Tenant received	• One-half of the crop	• Three-fourths or two-thirds of the crop	• Entire crop less fixed amount	• Cash

Source: T. J. Woofter Jr., *Landlord and Tenant on the Cotton Plantation*, Research Monograph 5 (Washington, D.C.: Works Progress Administration, 1936), 10. See also E. A. Boeger and E. A. Goldenweiser, *A Study of the Tenant System of Farming in the Yazoo-Mississippi Delta*, Bulletin 337 (Washington, D.C.: U.S. Department of Agriculture, 1916), 6–7; David Wayne Ganger, "The Impact of Mechanization and the New Deal's Acreage Reduction Programs on Cotton Farmers in the 1930s" (Ph.D. diss., University of California at Los Angeles, 1973), 13.

TABLE 1.2. Rationale for Tenure Choices in Southern Cotton Farming

	METHOD OF RENTING		
	Sharecropping (Croppers)	Share or Cash Renting (Tenants)	Wage (Hands) Labor (Day Labor)
Why landlords favored	• More flexibility • More stable labor supply • Larger share of crop than with tenant • More authority over operation	• Less equipment expense, but landlord also gets less of crop	• Maximum control over management, greatest uniformity • No heavy furnish advances • No bad accounts (uncollectable)
Why labor favored	• Escape from close supervision (or gang labor) • More independence in operation • Needs capital or credit • Needs better land • Needs supervision to gain experience.	• More motivated, as makes use of own investment	• Labor supply more uncertain, so price of labor is higher • Wages paid by contract period, not at end of the year

Source: Claude O. Brannen, "The Relation of Land Tenure to Plantation Organization with Developments since 1920" (Ph.D. diss., Columbia University, Fayetteville, Ark., 1928).

Winter cover crops were also planted to add nitrogen, usually deficient in many soils. The winter legumes were turned under before cotton was planted in the spring.[13]

In the Mississippi River Delta—the alluvial region on both sides of the river in Arkansas, Louisiana, and Mississippi—the ground was broken between January and March. The farmer hitched his mule to the plow and turned over the earth, running the plow down each side of last year's rows, creating ridges. Next he ran a two-bladed plow down the ridges and, using a distributor, dropped fertilizer into the furrows. He then leveled off the furrows with a harrow and dropped seed on top of it.

A variation of this process was called "middle-busting," in which a plow was driven down the old cotton row, making a new seedbed ready for planting. The farmer used a simple planter that smoothed the bed as it dropped the seed.

Cotton planting usually occurred between late April and mid May. The farmer hoped for rain but not too much. Germination required soil moisture, but too much rain prevented sprouting and even rotted the seed. In some wet springs, cotton had to be replanted several times, making for an expensive crop. If the price of cotton was low, the year was already a disaster.[14]

Under ideal conditions a small two-leaf plant broke the surface of the ground within a week or ten days. After a month, the farmer had a stand of cotton—row upon row of small green shoots, each one with a few leaves. In the second labor-peak, the young cotton plants, which were planted close together to compensate for seeds that failed to germinate, were thinned and kept free of weeds. In this process the broad-bladed hoe, the most commonly used tool in cotton fields, made its appearance. Hoeing or "chopping" cotton indicated both the process of thinning the original stand to the desired spacing between plants and subsequent weeding. Since chopping cotton required a great amount of hand labor, the farmer's wife and all his children worked in the field with him. Cotton was usually chopped three times, depending on the weather and the farmer, finally leaving one plant every eight to twelve inches. The farmer also cultivated or "plowed" the cotton during or immediately after chopping to loosen the surface and destroy weeds such as cocklebur, crabgrass, and johnsongrass that would choke the young cotton plants and deprive them of moisture. Cultivation used more labor in the Mississippi River Delta than in the arid areas of the West, where weeds grew less rapidly. No thinning was done after July, but cultivation continued until the crop was "laid by" in the middle of August.

By midsummer the cotton plants bloomed, turning, in succession, cream, pink, then red. After three days the blooms withered and dropped, leaving the "squares"—three leaves folded over the bolls containing the maturing cotton. The squares developed into an oval boll that split open at maturity, revealing long white seed hairs, called lint, that covered a large number of brown or black seeds. When mature, the length of the individual fibers ranged from a half inch to two and a half inches.

Too much rain at this critical period caused a lack of boll development, but farmers worried more about drought. Cotton bolls could also fail to develop because of the boll weevil, a small insect that fed on the green leafy part of the unopened squares. Poisons like calcium arsenate were used to dust the fields, and were applied by hand.[15] Other destructive insects included bollworms and armyworms, while various plant diseases caused wilt and root rot.

Finally the time for the most arduous and notorious cotton chore arrived. The picking season, the third labor peak, began in south Texas in August and swept northeastward through the Cotton Belt, reaching the Carolinas in the fall. Picking lasted until December unless a frost hit. Picking cotton was obviously labor intensive, demanding the attention of everyone on the farm and drawing extra labor from nearby towns and villages.

Picking literally cried out for mechanization. But as late as the 1930s, the consensus view was that cotton would always be picked by hand; everyone knew that. In the Mississippi River Delta cotton bolls opened at different times, so fields were picked more than once, sometimes up to four or five times. The entire Cotton Belt mobilized for it; the pace of life picked up in anticipation. Here was an opportunity to earn cash money.[16]

In the early morning the white-flecked cotton fields were fresh and wet with dew. The plants stood about waist high—or head high in the Delta—with leaves shooting out in all directions. The bolls were concentrated in the center of the plant and as low as a foot from the ground. The open bolls—or burrs, as they were called—consisted of five compartments, and in each compartment was a lock of cotton. Hand pickers carried long canvas bags with a strap around their left shoulder and dragged the bag from their right hip. Pickers worked with both hands, pulling the fluffy locks with a single motion of the hand, passing the locks to the right hand and dropping them into the bag. As the bag filled, it formed a huge worm that dragged behind.

The work was slow, tedious, monotonous, and backbreaking as pickers walked in a stooped position to reach the lower bolls. After picking for hours they could hardly stand up straight. At noon, work stopped and pickers rested for two hours. They then picked until dark.

About 70 bolls made a pound of seed cotton, and a good day's work was considered to be 150 pounds.[17] Some men could pick 200 or even 300 pounds. If a picker gathered 150 pounds, which was usually the amount expected, he had to snatch about 10,500 bolls during a day. If pickers were paid $1 per hundred pounds, he earned $1.50 per day. It took 1,500 pounds of seed cotton to make a 500-pound bale of cotton once the seeds were removed. A crop of 12 million bales demanded the labor of about 4 million pickers over a period of forty workdays.[18]

On small, owner-operated farms, families picked as a group, and even on large plantations cropper families worked together. But plantation owners often brought in outside labor during picking season. They found day labor readily available in nearby towns and sent flatbed trucks to transport them to and from the fields on a daily basis. Sharecroppers might pick as wage labor after they had picked all of their own cotton.

Picking was skilled work, and a popular view was that black women were the best pickers, working in groups for long hours in the broiling sun. They suffered from backache, and by the late fall, when the plant had dried, the burr's sharp points scratched and nicked their fingers. When it was nearly dark, the pickers dragged their long sacks to the scales, weighed the day's work, and were paid.

The seed cotton was dumped into small wagons, trampled down, and taken to the gin. A wagonload consisted roughly of a bale or about 500 pounds of lint and 1,000 pounds of seed. In the heart of the picking season, gins ran from early morning to late at night, sometimes running around the clock. The seed cotton was sucked up into the gin through a pipe and carried on a mechanical conveyer through a cleaner, and finally to the saws that separated the lint from the seeds. An operating gin produced a continuous, deafening roar as the whirling saws stripped away the fibers. The lint was taken to the press, where it was hydraulically compressed to a density of about 12 pounds per cubic foot. Sharecroppers had no choice of gin; they patronized the one used or owned by their landlord.

Once the cotton was ginned, tenants settled up with the plantation owner, who took his share of the crop and paid the tenant his share. The landlord also deducted the tenant's share of the cost of ginning. If a furnish merchant had run an account over the summer supplying the tenant's needs for food and other supplies, that account was settled out of the tenant's share, leaving in some cases only a few dollars for a whole year's work. In bad years tenants' shares might not cover the cost of furnish, leaving them in debt.

Cash renters and independent farmers paid between five and seven dollars for ginning, but received twenty dollars per ton for their cottonseed.[19] The seed would usually cover the cost of ginning, with enough left for planting next year. These farmers could sell their cotton to a buyer of their choice, deposit their cotton in a warehouse, or sell to a cooperative. However the cotton was sold, farmers paid their bills, had a haircut, and maybe got drunk. The money was likely gone until next year.

If the cycle of work from planting to chopping and picking occurred endlessly every season, the cycle of poverty seemed equally changeless. The number of tenants increased until they operated over 60 percent of southern cotton farms by 1935, and by that time most tenants were white rather than black. Calls for agricultural reform were heard often. Some reformers stressed diversification, hoping to break away from cotton entirely, and others boldly envisioned scientific agriculture. No reform scheme produced any breakthrough. Apparently, nothing could break the cycle of poverty and hand labor and move the South into a capital-intensive agricultural economy. The introduction of tractors during the 1930s brought the first omen of change. Real change, however, lay another twenty years in the future.

Mules and tenants had mired the Cotton South in poverty. The credit system, based on the notorious crop lien, fostered overproduction, driving prices down as cotton surpluses mounted in warehouses. Since no creditor would furnish the production of any crop but cotton, diversification was impossible. Yet the main reason the South stuck to cotton was that cotton as a cash crop made the most economic sense.[20] What kept the Cotton South backward— both technologically and economically—was not cotton or even tenancy itself but the region's effective farm size. The average sharecropper operated only fifteen acres, about all that one man and a mule could handle. But fifteen acres was far too little land to justify equipment purchases.

The South's dependence on a one-crop system was a source of persistent criticism, especially as the price of cotton declined. In the late nineteenth century, cotton prices entered a long, downward slide, reaching bottom in 1894.[21] Beyond low cotton prices, lack of diversification, and increasing rates of tenancy, cotton farmers faced other problems as well. They had always fought insects, worms, and other pests. In 1892, the boll weevil brought his appetite for cotton bolls from Mexico and spread eastward, infesting the entire Cotton Belt within thirty years. This pernicious insect's impact was, however, brief in many places as farmers learned how to combat its damage, and the weevil moved on to uninfested areas.[22] In addition, American cotton once dominated the textile industry; but after the turn of the twentieth century, foreign cotton claimed an increasing share of the international cotton market while synthetic fabrics like rayon gained in popularity. Changing fashions also made cotton seem less stylish.

The South and the Midwest

If southern agriculture could have broken with its labor-intensive system, the capital-intensive farms of the Midwest represented an alternative model that the South might have followed. Agriculture in the South and Midwest has always existed in a symbiotic but contrasting relationship. Since the mid-nineteenth century, midwestern agriculture has been more prosperous and capital intensive, while the Cotton South remained poor, backward, and unmechanized.

As early as the 1830s Cyrus H. McCormick patented a reaper that came to symbolize the application of the Industrial Revolution's new techniques to agriculture. In 1847 he opened a factory in Chicago and began manufacturing reapers for use in the rich prairie wheat lands of the Midwest. While McCormick based his machine on the ideas of other inventors, he pioneered the use of labor-saving, mass-produced farm machinery, field trials, payment plans, and advertising testimonials. The mechanical reaper filled an immediate need. Wheat farmers required machines to produce the food needed for a growing nation, especially during the labor-short years of the Civil War.[23]

Originating in Great Britain, the Industrial Revolution spread to the United States in the early nineteenth century, replacing hand labor and muscle power with machines and new forms of energy. Farms as well as factories benefited from technology. The use of machines in the production of food and fiber dramatically increased the productivity of farmers and averted a bleak Malthusian future of famine, pestilence, and disease.

Before the Industrial Revolution all farm tasks were performed by hand, laboriously and slowly. Oxen and mules plowed at a plodding pace, wheat was cut with scythes, and cotton of course was handpicked.[24] The application of machinery to agriculture enabled farmers to work more efficiently, save labor, escape backbreaking tasks, and produce far more than before. But the impact of technology was not uniform. In 1850, just three years after McCormick's reaper went into commercial production, two Memphis, Tennessee, inventors patented the first cotton harvester; but mechanical cotton pickers were not manufactured and sold commercially until a century later.

On the midwestern prairies, where labor shortages forced farmers to employ labor-saving machinery, agriculture mechanized between 1840 and 1880. John Deere marketed a strong, light steel plow adapted for scouring dense, prairie soils. Other inventors improved planting with drills that forced seed into the soil as opposed to wasteful broadcast methods. Prairie farmers moved quickly to replace the hand scythe in the small grain harvest. As a complement to the reaper, J. I. Case developed a thresher that separated the grain from the straw.

Inventors sought to adapt machines for other crops with varying success. Corn proved more difficult for machine applications than wheat. While horse-drawn corn planters and shellers proved successful, corn cultivators defied complete success. Hay made the transition from the scythe to the mowing machine by the middle of the nineteenth century. Though these machines were still horse drawn, their major importance was in saving human labor.[25] As a result, midwestern agriculture was capital intensive from its earliest days, and the region's farmers were more prosperous.[26] Southern cotton farmers failed to keep pace with modern technological developments. They still performed every task by hand, from plowing, cultivating, and finally picking cotton. In the South, labor was not only abundant but also cheap, and farmers were not motivated to mechanize and operate their farms more efficiently.

Technology enabled midwestern farmers to use fewer man-hours in the production of wheat than southern farmers needed to grow cotton (table 1.3). While the advantage of wheat over cotton was apparent as early as 1800, the advent of the McCormick reaper forced down labor requirements and raised wheat production. Cotton initially required only three times more man-hours per acre than wheat, but as wheat farmers took advantage of the mechanical reaper, this ratio widened dramatically. In the nineteenth century cotton farmers used better planters, fertilizer distributors, and improved seed varieties; and as a result, labor requirements per acre fell. After 1880, however, cotton production techniques changed little; cotton's labor demands remained steady while wheat's labor needs continued to fall, with cotton requiring seventeen times more labor per acre than wheat by the 1950s. Only the widespread use of tractors after World War II reduced the man-hours required in preharvest operations. In the late 1950s cotton still required sixty-six man-hours per acre, a high labor requirement attributable to the slow adoption of mechanical cotton pickers and the lack of effective methods of weed control.[27]

Eventually cotton farmers did take advantage of the benefits of mechanization, but the initial breakthrough was not achieved in the South itself. The traditional Cotton Belt stretched a thousand miles from the Carolinas to Texas. In the twentieth century, however, the Cotton Belt itself moved westward to Arizona, New Mexico, and California.

The older cotton areas of the southeastern United States saw their production decline. These areas not only experienced soil depletion and erosion, but also never fully recovered from the boll weevil. The small size of sharecropped farms similarly posed handicaps. In the Carolinas and Georgia, farmers grew more tobacco and truck crops, and labor moved into textile mills. Spared the handicaps of the older cotton areas, the far western Cotton Belt experienced the greatest expansion in cotton land, as well as the first signs of mechanization before World War II.[28]

TABLE 1.3. Man-Hours for Wheat and Cotton Production, 1800-1970

	COTTON				WHEAT				Cotton/ Wheat Ratio per acre
	Man-hours per acre	Before Harvest	Harvest	Man-hours per bale	Man-hours per acre	Before Harvest	Harvest	Man-hours per 100 bushels	
1800	185	135	50	601	56.0	16.0	40.0	373	3.3
1840	135	90	45	438	35.0	12.0	23.0	233	3.9
1880	119	67	52	303	20.0	8.0	12.0	152	6.0
1900	112	62	50	284	15.0	7.0	8.0	108	7.5
1910–14	116	64	52	276	15.2	7.0	8.2	106	7.6
1915–19	105	62	43	299	13.6	6.6	7.0	98	7.7
1920–24	96	59	37	296	12.4	6.0	6.4	90	7.7
1925–29	96	59	37	268	10.5	5.1	5.4	74	9.1
1930–34	97	53	44	252	9.4	4.6	4.8	70	10.3
1935–39	99	47	52	209	8.8	4.3	4.5	67	11.3
1940–44	99	46	53	182	7.5	3.8	3.7	44	13.2
1945–49	83	38	45	146	5.7	2.9	2.8	34	14.6
1950–54	66	30	36	107	4.6	2.6	2.0	27	14.3
1955–59	66	25	41	74	3.8	2.3	1.5	17	17.4
1960–64	47	23	24	47	3.0	1.9	1.1	12	15.7
1965–69	30	22	8	30	2.9	1.8	1.1	11	10.3
1970	24	21	3	26	2.9	1.8	1.1	9	8.3

Source: U.S. Bureau of the Census, *Historical Statistics of the United States: Colonial Times to 1970* (Washington, D.C.: GPO, 1975), series K 445–47, 449, 450–52, 454, p. 500.

During the 1920s, cotton production increased in Texas and Oklahoma and in the cotton areas of California, Arizona, and New Mexico. These areas, and especially the semi-arid far West, grew cotton on large farm operations; and as tractors became available they quickly replaced horsepower. The western cotton growing areas used seasonal laborers, mostly Mexican migrant workers, rather than sharecroppers with annual contracts. Without the development of the mechanical cotton picker, however, the harvest still remained the primary obstacle to complete mechanization.

Nonetheless, mechanization played an increasing role as cotton moved from east to west. The semi-arid regions of the West produced low yields and low quality cotton, which was offset by large equipment drawn by teams of horses and later by tractors. The lower labor requirements, nearly a third lower per bale, was an advantage that no other cotton region enjoyed. While the western cotton areas produced a short plant, the lack of rain in Texas and Oklahoma compensated by limiting weed growth, and the level topography facilitated the use of machines.[29]

In the West, then, both environmental and economic conditions stimulated the adoption of large-scale methods, and a transient labor supply became available for the picking season. Indeed, this labor pattern began pushing eastward.

As cotton acreage declined in the Georgia Piedmont and the Alabama Black Belt, cotton production remained strong in the Mississippi River Delta, where the level terrain favored the use of tractors for preharvest operations. At the turn of the twentieth century, rich river-bottom land was still available for clearing and draining.

Long after the midwestern prairie farmers had made the transition from hand to machine labor, the old Cotton Belt, however, still resisted mechanization.[30] Even though by the 1930s tractors were used to prepare the seedbed, plant, and cultivate, the work of thinning and hoeing still required large amounts of hand labor. But it was cotton picking that demanded more tedious hand labor than anything else. Picking was the major bottleneck in the mechanization of cotton, followed by chopping. Alone, a mechanical cotton picker could not overcome all obstacles to full mechanization; but without a mechanical picker, cotton could not shake off its premodern past and emerge as a capital-intensive crop.

Chapter 2

"Too Much Land, Too Many Mules, and Too Much Ignorant Labor"

As American agriculture mechanized after the Civil War and benefited from higher production, the Cotton South sank into an enormous backwater. While slaves were emancipated, the South itself became enslaved in its own poverty and backwardness. As late as 1930 cotton was produced with the same techniques that were used before emancipation. A one-row planter and the simple hoe were the most common tools to enter the region's cotton fields.[1]

The lack of mechanization in the Cotton South stemmed from the region's poverty. Even when farmers might have been able to take advantage of new machines, they usually could not afford to buy them. To understand the South's poverty, we must examine the economic impact of the Civil War and the institutions that were formed in the transition from slavery to freedom.

Over the past twenty-five years historians have debated two major explanations of southern poverty.[2] Using neoclassical theory and quantitative data, economic historians argued that the sharecropping and crop lien systems were rational products of a free competitive market. In the half century after emancipation, freedmen made significant progress toward land ownership. Unfortunately, according to these historians, the Civil War and its aftermath so badly shattered the region's economy that the South remained desperately poor. As a result southern farmers simply could not afford to mechanize.[3]

Economic historians believed that the Civil War was so devastating that even though the southern economy recovered in the postwar period, the South could not catch up with the dramatic pace of industrialization set by the Midwest and Northeast. Future generations of southerners were impoverished because the war and the emancipation of slaves had stripped the South of its capital, making it a capital-starved region condemned to a permanent second-class position.

Another interpretation has found the answer to southern poverty in fundamental institutional and cultural flaws. In this view late-nineteenth-century America experienced a struggle between those who embraced the commercial values of hard work and those who accepted a subsistence culture of little work and minimum achievement. While the United States expanded its market economy, the South only partly developed as a modern commercial society, a shortcoming that blocked the region's efforts at modernization.

The focus on flawed institutions and values has covered both sides of the political spectrum. According to Marxist historians, sharecropping was part of a repressive labor system imposed by planters to perpetuate their own wealth and power. As a ruling class with pre-bourgeois origins, planters blocked agricultural mechanization and economic diversification in favor of a labor-intensive agriculture, dooming the South to a future of poverty.[4]

These historians contended that the Civil War changed little in the South and that after the war, planters, if not necessarily the same planters, remained securely in control of political and economic institutions. Slavery was replaced by sharecropping, a labor system that offered little opportunity for advancement. Wage slavery had merely replaced chattel slavery. Even worse, a new system of farm credit forced farmers to give liens on their future crops, making it easy for them to slip into debt. Whether Marxists or not, most scholars have seen southern farm laborers as victims of exploitation stemming from the operation of the sharecropping and crop lien systems.

Planters, however, were hardly the only group with premodern values. Other historians argued that the South's problem was not located in its leaders but in its people and their culture. Notably, political economist Ronald E. Seavoy asserted that southern agricultural workers were largely subsistence laborers, which he defined as peasants who placed "a high social value on indolence and a low social value on labor, particularly labor to acquire money."[5] Their goal was to perform the least amount of labor possible and still provide for themselves an acceptable level of subsistence. They desired nothing more. Unlike commercially motivated societies—for example, midwestern farmers—where workers performed continuous labor in order to improve themselves, too many southern workers were unwilling to perform additional labor in order to earn material abundance.

While American agricultural workers have usually not been identified as peasants, Seavoy claimed that the sharecropping system was merely an American variation of a worldwide subsistence culture. In his view, whether the local term was freedmen, poor white trash, sharecroppers, crackers, hill-billies, Cajuns, rednecks, or self-sufficient farmers, they were all in reality peasants. By ignoring available opportunities to work hard and achieve success in commercial agriculture, they were poor because they refused to expend more labor than the minimum required for subsistence.

Southern backwardness, then, derived from the flawed institutions and cultural values associated with the postwar period. Sharecropping and the crop lien locked the South into an inefficient labor system with self-destructive tendencies. The region was overcommitted to cotton, and the effective size of farm units was too small to produce a decent living. Institutional flaws kept the South economically stagnant and its farms unmechanized. Alternately, southern poverty derived from a culture that accepted the subsistence labor norms of peasants. By implication this approach played down the Civil War as the major watershed in southern history, and focused instead on World War II as the real turning point that launched the modern South.[6]

The Civil War

The argument favoring the Civil War as the cause of southern poverty can be supported by statistical evidence. In broad terms, southern states led the nation in per capita income before the Civil War; but after the war northern states surged ahead (table 2.1). The war devastated the South's economy to such an extent that it did not recover in a generation. Moreover, the late nineteenth century witnessed an acceleration of the region's decline in per capita income. In contrast midwestern states like Illinois and Iowa experienced growth at a rate faster than the national average. Even in the 1990s, more than 130 years after the Civil War, many southern states still lag behind the nation in per capita income.

In 1900 the average value of farms in the Census Bureau's west south central region was still less than half of their value in 1860 (table 2.2). By 1920 Arkansas farms exceeded their 1860 value, but Louisiana and Mississippi farms retained only a fraction of their prewar value. At the same time, the value of Illinois and Iowa farms was above the national average. As the data indicate, states in the west north central region saw the value of their farms double more than three times between 1860 and 1920.

After 1865 the average size of southern farms dropped dramatically, while in other major agricultural regions farm size remained steady or fell only slightly. The average acreage per farm in the three Mississippi River Delta states fell to less than 100 acres by 1900, but midwestern farms remained well above 100 acres (table 2.3). In fact the South's farm size did not recover its 1860 position

TABLE 2.1. Per Capita Income, United States and Selected States, 1840–1995*

	1840	Percentage of U.S.	1880	Percentage of U.S.	1900	Percentage of U.S.	1995	Percentage of U.S.
United States	$65		$95		$113		$22,788	
Arkansas	68	104.6	62	65.3	63	55.8	17,429	76.5
Louisiana	113	173.8	69	72.6	73	64.6	18,827	82.6
Mississippi	84	129.2	64	67.4	62	54.9	16,531	72.5
Illinois	47	72.3	113	118.9	134	118.6	24,763	108.7
Iowa	38	58.5	105	110.5	138	122.1	21,012	92.2

Source: National Bureau of Economic Research, *Trends in the American Economy in the Nineteenth Century* (Princeton: Princeton University Press, 1960), 97–104; U.S. Bureau of the Census, *Statistical Abstract of the United States: 1996* (Washington, D.C.: GPO, 1996), table 699, p. 453.

*Current dollars.

TABLE 2.2. Average Farm Values, 1860–1920

	1860	1870	1880	1890	1900	1910	1920
United States	$3,251	$2,799	$2,544	$2,909	$2,905	$5,480	$10,295
East north central	2,958	3,475	3,683	4,065	4,325	7,899	13,771
West north central	2,126	2,215	2,105	3,245	4,385	10,464	22,307
Illinois	2,854	2,631	3,948	5,247	6,684	13,986	25,289
Iowa	1,960	2,701	3,061	4,247	6,550	15,008	35,616
Kansas	1,179	1,892	1,697	3,357	3,718	9,770	17,122
West south central	3,876	969	958	1,421	1,509	3,317	6,316
Arkansas	2,350	648	786	950	757	1,440	3,238
Louisiana	11,818	1,916	1,222	232	1,217	1,917	3,499
Mississippi	4,453	961	912	883	688	1,218	2,903

Source: U.S. Bureau of the Census, *Historical Statistics of the United States: Colonial Times to 1970* (Washington, D.C.: GPO, 1975), series K 17, 31, 34, 37, 39, 44, 60–63, p. 463.

until 1970, more than a century later.[7] The small size of southern farms formed the most important factor in blocking efforts at mechanization.

The cotton economy showed remarkable resilience after the war. Cotton production fell dramatically in the postwar period, but Arkansas, Georgia, South Carolina, and Texas recovered prewar levels by 1880 and most other states by 1890. In other words some states needed as little as fifteen years to reclaim their 1860 production levels.[8] Statewide production figures, however, do not tell the whole story.

A more pessimistic picture emerges from county data. Postwar cotton production in the fifteen leading cotton-producing counties in the Mississippi River Delta region did not enjoy a rapid recovery (table 2.4). Only two of these counties, Arkansas's Jefferson and Phillips, matched its 1860 production level as late as sixty years after the war. While low cotton production might have reflected positive developments like diversification, it was clear that many cotton counties were not the same after the war. Low cotton production can be interpreted as an indicator of the lack of effectiveness of commercial farmers in coercing sufficient labor from peasants to cultivate commercial crops.[9]

While some areas recovered slowly, specific regions did experience significant growth in cotton production and began to rebuild their infrastructures. This recovery was especially apparent in undeveloped areas, where frontier conditions before the war offered little infrastructure for conquering armies to destroy. For example, eastern Arkansas remained largely undeveloped in 1860, and the great task of land clearing and draining wetlands occurred at the end of the century. Historian Carl Moneyhon has argued that Arkansas recovered quickly from the war, partly because of the state's relative lack of economic

TABLE 2.3. Average Farm Acreage, 1860–1920

	1860	1870	1880	1890	1900	1910	1920
Arkansas	245	154	128	119	93	81	75
Louisiana	537	247	171	138	95	87	74
Mississippi	370	193	156	122	83	68	67
Iowa	165	134	134	151	151	156	157
Illinois	146	128	124	127	124	129	135
Kansas	171	148	155	181	241	244	275

Source: U.S. Bureau of the Census, *Historical Statistics of the United States: Colonial Times to 1970* (Washington: GPO, 1975), series K 34, 39, 44, 60, 62, 63, p. 461.

TABLE 2.4 Cotton Production of Counties and Parishes in Arkansas, Louisiana, Mississippi, 1860–1920

	1860*	1870*	1880*	1890*	1900	1910	1920
Arkansas	294	223	547	622	706	777	869
Arkansas	16	11	8	6	6	4	1
Chicot	33	9	23	19	23	23	16
Jefferson	23	17	31	43	44	46	35
Marion	17	272	4	3	2	2	2
Phillips	22	16	26	27	29	29	33
Louisiana	622	316	458	593	700	269	307
Carroll**	67	18	38	26	25	12	15
Concordia	51	24	30	35	28	5	4
Madison	36	15	21	25	16	12	6
Rapides	39	8	16	23	39	5	4
Tensas	113	23	38	37	31	11	8
Mississippi	962	508	867	1,039	1,287	1,127	958
Hinds	44	25	33	34	41	31	18
Lowndes	41	14	20	15	21	15	9
Madison	41	17	19	22	27	24	19
Noxubee	40	14	23	20	24	20	9
Yazoo	51	23	43	44	53	37	20

Source: U.S. Census Office, Eugene W. Hilgard, *Report on Cotton Production in the United States*, pt., 1, *Mississippi Valley and Southwestern States* (Washington, D.C.: GPO, 1884), table 2; U.S. Census Office, *Report on the Statistics of Agriculture in the United States at the Eleventh Census: 1890* (Washington, D.C.: GPO, 1895), table 15; U.S. Census Office, *Twelfth Census of the United States, 1900, Agriculture, Part II* (Washington, D.C.: U.S. Census Office, 1902), table 10; U.S. Bureau of the Census, *Thirteenth Census of the United States, 1910,* vol. 6, *Agriculture, 1909 and 1910* (Washington, D.C.: GPO, 1913), table 4; U.S. Bureau of the Census, *Fourteenth Census of the United States, 1920,* vol. 6, *Agriculture—The Southern States* (Washington, D.C.: GPO, 1913), table 4.

*For comparability, 1860–90 data have been adjusted to equal standard 500-pound bales used in 1900 and later.

**After the 1870 census, Carroll Parish was split into East Carroll and West Carroll; combined production for these two parishes is shown for 1880–1920.

development.[10] Since the Civil War's greatest devastation occurred in the upper South, most of the region suffered light to moderate infrastructure damage except in areas of sustained military operations. Yet overall the South remained poor.[11]

In summary, evidence for the Civil War hypothesis is strong. Cotton production recovered in many southern states within fifteen years of the end of the war, though whether the recovery time was long or short depends on one's judgment. Unfortunately, per capita income and farm value showed substantial declines, both products of small-sized farms, while farm size fell lower and lower. States and subregions that were relatively undeveloped before the war were among those that produced the strongest postwar recovery.

Institutional and Cultural Flaws

The transition from chattel slavery to the new postwar world of free black labor resulted in the creation of sharecropping and the crop lien, two flawed institutions that kept the South poor and unmechanized. After emancipation, most southern whites refused to believe that former slaves would work without coercion.[12] Freedmen, however, were willing to work but only on their own terms. Emancipation unquestionably created more opportunities for former slaves than for former slave owners.

While blacks emerged from slavery impoverished, they were in a position to take advantage of their freedom. At their first opportunity, many freedmen left their old plantations in search of separated relatives—often for children and spouses. Emancipation also meant the freedom to work less. Males performed one-third less labor as free workers than they had as slaves.[13] Another widespread reaction to freedom was that black women and children refused to work in the fields. As a consequence, a smaller labor force produced slower economic growth. This reduction in labor inputs alone explained why the postwar southern farm economy stagnated compared to midwestern agriculture.

The sharp drop in the number of black workers created a labor shortage that gave freedmen their first real power in the labor market.[14] In Little Rock the *Arkansas Gazette* echoed planters' complaints about the lack of labor, fields lying fallow, and small crops. In early 1867 the *Gazette* summed up their fears:

> The question most seriously involving the prosperity of the people of this State at this time, is not negro suffrage, but negro labor. Not whether he shall vote, but whether he will work. The season is rapidly approaching when the

necessary preparations should be made by the planter for the coming crop, and now is the time to make contracts with the freedmen for the coming year. For the present, they are our principal dependence, and we must do the best we can with them until such time as an increase of white laborers shall come into our state, and enable us to do without them. Then the high estimate which they now place upon themselves will, by competition, be brought down, and the question with them will not, as now, be, "who shall I work for?" but "who will employ me?"[15]

The Cotton South's problem, however, was a shortage of willing laborers, not a physical shortage of potential laborers. Planters faced the problem of finding a way to motivate reluctant workers to grow cotton in commercial quantities. If southern agriculture survived, its need for labor somehow had to be met. The solution was tenancy and specifically sharecropping.

Farm tenancy and sharecropping have their origins in antebellum southern agriculture. Tenancy was not a new institution at the end of the war; it emerged too quickly for southern farmers not to have had previous experience with land renting. Discussing tenancy in antebellum Georgia, historians Frederick A. Bode and Donald E. Ginter wrote, "What our findings do suggest is that postbellum tenancy was not merely an *ad hoc* invention suddenly and hastily devised in the South as a response to emancipation. It had deep and substantial roots in southern society."[16] Indeed, sharecropping is a tenure arrangement that is still used around the world in poor countries as a way of sharing the risks of production costs.[17]

The traditional explanation for sharecropping has been that mutual needs brought landlords and freedmen together.[18] Landlords needed labor but did not have the cash to pay wages; freedmen needed land but lacked capital to rent land or to buy it outright. Nor did they have the capital to furnish their own livestock and tools. If this view was correct, poverty and desperation created a system that reduced the immediate need for cash by sharing the proceeds of the crop. The payment of wages, however, was fairly common even in the early postwar years.[19]

While some historians have blamed sharecropping on pre-bourgeois planters, the origins of the institution were considerably more complex. One historian has argued that it was the former slaves who insisted on sharecropping and refused to work under any other arrangement. Planters wanted to restore the gang or "squad" system of labor that was associated with slavery and still practiced briefly after the war. Another historian quipped that planters had to be dragged into sharecropping "kicking and screaming." The freedmen themselves insisted on sharecropping. If they could not secure land of their own, they were determined to rent land and work in family units without direct and constant supervision.[20]

In a version of this viewpoint historian Edward Royce contended that sharecropping emerged from a "constriction of possibilities"—that is, no one wanted sharecropping, and the institution emerged as the last choice of everyone involved.[21] In still another insight into the motives of freedmen, Ronald Seavoy interpreted sharecropping as the freedmen's price for performing sufficient labor to grow commercial crops. In other words, it was a way that they could avoid the hard labor associated with slavery and practice the low labor norms associated subsistence cultivation.[22]

For their part, planters accepted the share system because it gave labor a stake in the crop and shifted responsibility to workers who would receive a larger share if they worked hard. Workers also gained an incentive to see the crop through until harvest since they not receive their share until the end of the year. In other words they had to accept to some degree commercial values. Employers still controlled labor through the payment of wages, whether cash or shares. The fear of labor shortages continued to be an overriding concern. In the 1930s the annual labor contract was used as the primary means of guaranteeing labor for chopping as well as picking.[23] The prospect of hundreds of acres of mature cotton without labor to pick it was, understandably, frightening.

By 1880 a new plantation economy of sharecropping had fully emerged—an economy that rested on ignorance, intimidation, and coercion.[24] In cooperation with all elements of white society, planters exercised every effort to maintain control of their cheap labor supply. In 1891, for example, when blacks in Lee County, Arkansas, organized a cotton pickers strike, a posse hunted down and arrested the strike leaders; but a mob of masked men seized the prisoners and lynched them, crushing the strike.[25]

After 1890 the rise of the Jim Crow system of legal segregation coincided with the development of the new plantation economy. Jim Crow was a product of diverse impulses, but one of them was the need to control plantation labor. The South's cotton economy depended on cheap labor, which had demonstrated a tendency toward independence after the Civil War. Segregation and disenfranchisement would limit opportunities for blacks and keep them in their place, which was in the cotton fields. Jim Crow put the institutional weight of the entire region into controlling the labor supply and coercing the production of cotton in commercial quantities.[26]

The rise of lynching across the South can be interpreted as the most extreme effort at labor intimidation. The Deep South experienced 1,812 lynchings between 1882 and 1930. The top five lynching states were Mississippi, Georgia, Louisiana, Arkansas, and South Carolina, all leading cotton and tenant states. The lower Mississippi Valley states combined for 1,239 lynchings, with Mississippi assuming the lead as the state with the most lynchings in the entire region. Arkansas experienced 313 lynchings between 1882 and 1927—many victims being Delta blacks.[27] In 1919, at Elaine, Arkansas, a small Delta town in Phillips County, a race riot occurred in response to an effort to repress the Progressive Farmers and Householders Union, which had been formed by black tenant farmers to get higher prices for their cotton. The loss of life, though never established with certainty, ranged from twenty-five to one hundred blacks and five whites.[28]

The postwar agricultural institutions of the Cotton Belt settled into a pattern that lasted until World War II.[29] In the early years after the Civil War, when cotton prices were high, sharecropping was a fairly good idea. The system did offer, in theory, an opportunity to landless farmers who hoped for a bumper crop and high prices. But the system never worked in fact as it did in theory, as many farmers fell into debt. Beyond its impact on individuals, the sharecropping system produced many negative consequences for the entire region. As the decades passed, more and more farmers found themselves trapped in the system as the number of tenants grew faster than the number of farm owners. Across eleven southern states, summarized as the "South" in table 2.5, tenant-operated farms increased from 36.2 percent to 47 percent between 1880 and 1900, later peaking at 55.5 percent in 1930. Tenancy rates were highest in the Black Belt that stretched across Georgia and Alabama and in the Mississippi River Delta. In 1930 Mississippi tenancy peaked at 72.2 percent, the highest percentage in the region, Louisiana at 66.6 percent, and Arkansas at 63 percent. In heavily black counties 70 to 80 percent of all farm operators did not own their own land.

As the so-called New South fell into tenancy, it also saw the rise of a class of merchants who benefited from the new credit institutions. Before the Civil War, cotton factors procured planters' supplies, gave them credit, and marketed their cotton. As railroads penetrated interior towns and linked them to world markets in the 1880s, local merchants became the center of the cotton trade through the crop lien. As furnish merchants for tenants and sharecroppers, they amassed great economic power. When banks formed in small southern towns late in the century, merchants sat on the boards of directors. The use of crop liens enabled them to combine the roles of landlord, merchant, and

TABLE 2.5. Percentage of Farm Tenants in Southern States, 1880-1935

	1880	1890	1900	1910	1920	1930	1935
United States	25.6	28.4	35.3	37.0	38.1	43.4	42.1
South*	36.2	38.5	47.0	49.6	49.6	51.1	55.5
Alabama	46.8	48.6	57.7	60.2	57.9	67.4	64.5
Arkansas	30.9	32.1	45.4	50.0	51.3	63.0	60.0
Georgia	30.9	53.5	59.9	65.6	66.6	68.2	65.5
Louisiana	35.2	44.4	58.0	55.3	57.1	66.6	63.7
Mississippi	43.8	52.8	62.4	66.1	66.1	72.2	69.8
Missouri	27.3	26.8	30.5	29.9	28.8	34.8	38.8
North Carolina	33.5	34.1	41.4	42.3	43.5	49.2	47.2
Oklahoma	—	0.7	43.8	54.8	51.0	61.5	61.2
South Carolina	50.3	55.3	61.1	63.0	64.5	65.1	62.2
Tennessee	34.5	30.8	40.6	41.1	41.1	46.2	46.2
Texas	37.7	41.9	49.7	52.6	53.3	60.9	57.1
California**	19.8	17.8	23.1	20.6	21.4	18.0	21.7

Source: Farm Tenancy: Report of the President's Committee (Washington, D.C.: GPO, 1937), 96.

*"South" consists of the former slave states plus Oklahoma.

**Shown for comparison.

banker.[30] The emphasis on cotton derived from the fact that it was a cash crop. Cotton buyers did not buy other crops, and merchants furnished only farmers who grew cotton.

The system itself, then, pushed the South into greater dependence on a one-crop system. In periods of high prices, cotton fever spread across the South, and farmers trembled with anticipated profits. One can image a farmer with a nub pencil multiplying the number of acres he thought he could harvest times estimated yield times the current price of cotton—if that price and the weather would only hold until harvest! But even when low prices and hard times came, farmers reacted by planting more cotton since nothing else could bring in as much as a cash crop. A bumper crop, of course, drove down the price. An increasing cotton acreage also implied that southern farmers were becoming less self-sufficient as they grew less corn and food crops. The structure of agriculture in the Cotton Belt provided markets and other support for cotton to the exclusion of other crops.

While the discussion of the Civil War and flawed institutions contain valuable insights, we need to take a broader view of the South's problems. Even if the war had not occurred, the cotton economy would still have faced hard times in the late nineteenth century. After 1865 farmers watched helplessly as the price of cotton fell into a downward slide that lasted for the rest of the century. Conceivably, the decline of cotton prices was more devastating than wartime destruction. The major trend in the region's economy between the Civil War and World War I reflected the declining demand for cotton.[31] The South's prosperity would have peaked in 1860 whether the Civil War had occurred or not, and the future led in only one direction for any region tied to cotton—downward.[32]

The problem with sharecropping went beyond the usual complaint that croppers were exploited and that they lived in abject poverty. Nor was the real problem that landlords used the sharecropping arrangement as a form of labor control. Most importantly, when planters used sharecropping to ensure an oversupply of labor, they kept the region from mechanizing agricultural production. Since labor was in constant oversupply—and therefore cheap—no incentive existed to shift to machines. Nor did the need for docile labor produce workers who could adapt to new machinery or other conditions. This labor force was one that lacked skills and education, and indeed these shortcomings were built in or assumed. As a result, the Cotton South remained tied to a labor-intensive agriculture even as other parts of the country moved to labor-saving machinery.[33]

Demographics

So both Civil War devastation and the flawed institutions theory have value in explaining southern poverty. But the tenant system in itself did not cause the poverty of the South. We can test the idea of tenancy as the cause of southern poverty and of the region's lack of mechanization by comparing farm income per acre of cropland with per capita farm income.

We might normally expect both per capita farm income and income per acre to point in the same direction—that is, both positive or both negative. But that was not the case. The three states of the Mississippi River Delta generated about half of the per capita income as did the nation as a whole, but the region's income per acre of land was usually above the national average (table 2.6). "In other words," an observer noted, "the problem is not one of poor productivity per unit of land; it is rather the number of people the land has to support."[34]

The differences in per capita and per acre income in percentages of the

TABLE 2.6. Farm Income in Arkansas, Louisiana, and Mississippi, 1930–1950

	United States	Arkansas	Louisiana	Mississippi
1930				
Per capita	$314.78	$166.67	$164.47	$168.37
Per acre	$9.71	$11.65	$14.64	$13.27
1940				
Per capita	$218.74	$106.02	$105.39	$81.97
Per acre	$6.27	$6.54	$9.00	$6.00
1950				
Per capita	$963.94	$490.02	$433.86	$309.94
Per acre	$19.13	$20.83	$21.96	$16.42

Source: Computed from U.S. Bureau of the Census, *Historical Statistics: Colonial Times to 1970* (Washington, D.C.: GPO, 1975), series K 17–81, pp. 458–64.

national income were striking (table 2.7). In 1930, for example, Arkansas's per acre farm income was 20 percent higher than the per acre farm income nationwide; but the state's per capita income was 47 percent lower—less than half—than income on the nation's farms as a whole. In the same year, Louisiana produced 51 percent more income per acre with a per capita income 48 percent lower.

The discrepancy between per acre income and per capita income suggested a demographic explanation of southern poverty. In *Cotton Fields No More* agricultural historian Gilbert Fite argued that the South's problem was that the region was overpopulated for its available resources. There were just too many people trying to eke out a living on poor, one-mule farms. "While some observers may have tried to place the blame for so much rural poverty in the South on lazy and unmotivated workers," Fite declared, "the basic difficulties were much more fundamental. Southern farmers lacked what modern economists call an adequate resources base. The fundamental cause of poverty in the southern countryside was small farms and low production. . . . To put it another way, the farm population was too large in relation to the developed land resources."[35]

TABLE 2.7. Percentage of National Farm Income, Arkansas, Louisiana, Mississippi, 1930–1960

	Per Acre	Per Capita
Arkansas		
1930	20.0	-47.0
1940	4.2	-51.5
1950	8.9	-49.2
1959	43.1	-28.0
1960	44.5	-10.3
Mississippi		
1930	36.7	-46.5
1940	-4.3	-62.5
1950	-14.2	-67.9
1959	11.9	-57.3
1960	-0.4	-49.7
Louisiana		
1930	50.9	-47.8
1940	43.5	-51.8
1950	14.8	-55.0
1959	19.3	-44.1
1960	18.1	-35.2

Source: Computed from U.S. Bureau of the Census, *Historical Statistics: Colonial Times to 1970* (Washington, D.C.: GPO, 1975), series K 17–81, pp. 458–64.

The region's fundamental problems did not escape notice by contemporary observers. In 1899, for example, W. C. Stubbs, director of the Louisiana Experiment Station, told a farmers' convention at Vicksburg, Mississippi:

But some of our Northern friends may ask why, with all this agricultural wealth, we are not prosperous and contented? The reply can be formulated in a single sentence: Too much land, too many mules, and too much ignorant labor. The latter, as hewers of wood and drawers of water, roustabouts on our steamboats, cotton pickers, and saw-mill hands, etc., are the best laborers in the world. As

adjutants to the progressive, intelligent farmer, they are valuable; but as independent, progressive farmers and as growers of diversified crops they are as yet
a failure and will be for some time to come.[36]

Stubbs indicated that southern agricultural workers typically had too little
good land, produced too little, and earned too little. They could not work efficiently because they had inadequate equipment. Even when better cottonseed,
planters, fertilizer spreaders, and plows became available, many farmers were
content with existing methods. Cotton production remained a hand-labor
operation from start to finish. Nor did farmers have any incentive to use modern machinery as long as labor was cheap and plentiful. The ready availability
of cheap labor eliminated the need to seek any alternatives. Small, unmechanized farms with low productivity also suggested the existence of peasant labor
norms.

In the depths of the Great Depression William E. Ayres, superintendent of
the Delta Experiment Station at Stoneville, Mississippi, and his colleagues
researched the question of how cotton production could be made cheaper.
Their answer was that mechanization was absolutely required to lower labor
and production costs. They argued that the South's surplus farm population
and low productivity per farm was the fundamental cause of southern rural
poverty. The typical fifteen-acre-per-family unit could never be profitable.
Southern cotton farms were too small to cover the cost of reasonable living
expenses for a typical family, pay overhead expenses, or produce a fair return
on investment. The reduction of the farm labor population from 30 to 50 percent, they argued, was essential for producing a decent living standard in agriculture. "The competition of industry for labor and labor's demands for better
living conditions," they predicted, "will ultimately force planters to see the
necessity for more and more machinery in cotton production." They urged
planters to replace farm labor with practical, economical farm machines as
soon as possible.[37]

According to Ayres and his colleagues in 1931, black migration was
already a serious problem. Northern industry could not rely on foreign labor,
and black migration to northern cities would continue. As a consequence the
time was approaching, they warned, when Delta planters would have to meet
the industrial competition for labor either with higher pay or by eliminating
the need for excess labor. "The former is impossible," Ayres and his colleagues
said; "the latter is highly desirable." By the early 1930s, Ayres emerged as the
most outspoken advocate of mechanization in the Mississippi River Delta.

The best measure of overpopulation is the land-labor ratio. This ratio is the product of the number of acres in farms divided by the farm population. Farmers in the Midwest farmed more than twice the land as their southern counterparts (table 2.8). In 1930 Arkansas farms averaged 14.3 acres per farmer, with Louisiana and Mississippi falling even lower. Midwestern farmers benefited from a ratio that ranged from three to five times greater than southern farmers, as did those in California and Texas.

Small farms were predominantly a problem in cotton areas (table 2.9). Before World War II cotton farms in the Mississippi River Delta states averaged fewer than fifteen acres, with many having fewer than ten acres. In California and Texas the average cotton farm was three or more times larger.

Since the Cotton South's fundamental problem was small, inefficient farms, the popular solutions all missed the point entirely. Southern farmers, for example, tended to strike out at bankers who charged high interest rates, at supply merchants who held monopolies, and at cotton buyers who were tied to large out-of-state corporations. In the late nineteenth century, farmers formed a series of organizations, including the Grange, the Alliance movements, the Populist Party, and the Farmers' Union. They formed cooperatives to buy and sell in quantities, and they turned to politics to seek legislative relief. But in the end these solutions all failed.[38]

TABLE 2.8. Farm Population, Acreage, and Land-Labor Ratios, 1930

	Farm Population (1,000s)	Land in Farms (1,000s of acres)	Land-Labor Ratio
Arkansas	1,122	16,053	14.3
Louisiana	833	9,355	11.2
Mississippi	1,366	17,332	12.7
Iowa	981	33,475	34.1
Illinois	1,002	30,695	30.6
Kansas	709	46,976	66.3
California	2,359	124,707	52.9
Texas	622	30,443	48.9

Source: U.S. Bureau of the Census, *Historical Statistics of the United States: Colonial Times to 1970* (Washington, D.C.: GPO, 1975), series K 34, 39, 44, 60, 62, 63, 65, 79, pp. 458, 460.

TABLE 2.9. Average Cotton Farm Acreage, 1919–1959

Region	1919	1929	1939	1949	1959
United States	17.7	21.8	14.3	23.9	28.7
South	17.6	21.6	14.0	22.7	26.5
Arkansas	14.8	17.9	13.7	25.7	37.2
California	70.0	69.8	59.5	103.1	94.6
Texas	33.2	42.6	29.7	69.0	75.7
Louisiana	13.1	15.1	9.5	14.3	19.8
Mississippi	12.3	14.2	9.4	14.5	18.7

Source: Calculated from U.S. Bureau of the Census, *United States Census of Agriculture: 1959*, vol. 2, *General Report: Statistics by Subjects* (Washington, D.C.: GPO, 1962), 829, 835.

Next, southern farmers placed their hopes on scientific farming and diversification, hoping to solve their problems through science. By the early twentieth century farm journals, newspapers, and agricultural scientists called on farmers to substitute science for labor.[39] Among the best known advocates were Clarence Poe of the *Progressive Farmer* and Seaman A. Knapp of the U.S. Extension Service. They preached crop diversification, soil conservation, and farm management. Farmers, however, clung to their old ways even in the face of clear evidence that new ideas worked. But even when they used new techniques, southern farmers still did not produce the surpluses they needed to accumulate capital and raise their standard of living. And instead of increasing their self-sufficiency, they saw tenancy increase, rising over 60 percent in the Mississippi River Delta (table 2.7). During World War I southern farmers enjoyed a brief surge of record prices, and they expanded their acreage in the hope that the future would continue to offer high prices. But postwar price collapses ushered in a sharp farm depression that lasted throughout the 1920s.[40]

In a catchy summary statement economist Gavin Wright described the South as a "low-wage region in a high-wage country."[41] He meant the South was trapped in a colonial economy that kept the region poor and backward. The Third World analogy was entirely apt. After a half century of the boasted and much anticipated New South, the region still exhibited all the earmarks of a Third World country: low wages, extractive primary economy, high rates of poverty, high birthrates, and preindustrial levels of technology still tied to hand labor. The high birthrate was in itself a clear indicator of a region still in the second stage of the demographic transition.[42]

The South was the last region of the United States to experience a fall in fertility. The process of declining fertility that was always associated with economic development began in northeastern cities in the mid-nineteenth century and spread to cities in other regions. In time the transition to lower fertility spread to rural areas, again with the northeast leading the way. Even on the eve of World War II, the South had the highest fertility rate in the nation, which resulted in overpopulation, labor surplus, low wages, and the perpetuation of poverty.[43]

In 1929 the South was poor, backward, and had still not fully recovered from the Civil War; and after the Great Depression hit, economic conditions grew even worse. The Stock Market Crash and the subsequent collapse of cotton prices propelled the region's cotton economy into a crisis equal to that of 1861, with survival itself at stake. But events were already converging that would destroy the labor-intensive system of small, inefficient, poverty-ridden farms. In the end, the number of farms fell sharply, but the remaining farms were larger, mechanized, capital intensive, and labor efficient. Many forces created this revolution, but its centerpiece was a new machine—the mechanical cotton picker.

Chapter 3

Inventions and Inventors: The Challenge of Mechanical Cotton Picking

The U.S. Patent Office issued the first patent for a mechanical cotton picker in 1850. Designed by Samuel S. Rembert and Jedediah Prescott of Memphis, Tennessee, this machine was a rudimentary version of the spindle picker that a century later became a commercial success.[1] The late nineteenth and early twentieth centuries ushered in a great age of inventions ranging from electric lights and automobiles to flying machines. Many inventors accepted the challenge of the mechanical cotton picker because they knew that the one who discovered the secret of how to mechanically harvest cotton, the last major unmechanized crop, would make a fortune.[2] But most of these inventors failed.

The mechanization of cotton posed many problems. Some observers pointed to the complexity of the cotton cycle. Cotton production required a series of steps: cultivation, thinning and weeding, and finally harvesting. All three of these tasks had to be mechanized, not just one. A mechanical picker might be perfected but hand labor would still be needed to thin and weed the cotton. Cotton farmers could not adapt existing agricultural machines to their advantage. Cotton plants, for example, could not be "combined" because of the nature of the plant with its hard stems and dried leaves. While small grains could be harvested with horse-drawn equipment, the mechanization of cotton had to wait until gasoline engines were available to provide a strong, steady source of power.

Cotton plants themselves varied widely from one region to another. Mississippi River Delta cotton grew as high as six feet, while only about two feet in the High Plains of Texas and Oklahoma. Cotton, unlike wheat, could not be completely harvested all at once. In the Delta, cotton bolls, even on the same plant, opened at different times; and farmers picked a second or even third time to gather more cotton from late-opening bolls. In addition, the testing of experimental machinery could only be done during the picking season, running from September into November. There was no effective way to simulate rows of cotton plants for experimental purposes on a laboratory floor. As a result, inventors whose machines produced disappointing results had to wait another year before trying out their new ideas. Finally, the movement of the human fingers in the picking motion was impossible to capture mechanically. While these problems did not discourage the host of inventors who invested their time and money, the mechanization of cotton lagged far behind other crops in the nineteenth and early twentieth centuries.

According to data compiled by Jacob Schmookler, the average annual patent activity was lower for cotton than for corn and grain (table 3.1). From 1837 to 1957, patents for cotton harvesters amounted only to 25 percent of all patent activity in these basic crops, with most cotton-related patents being registered in the later period.[3] Long after small grains had been mechanized, cotton remained the last major crop that was harvested with hand labor.

The task of inventing a mechanical cotton picker was not only formidable but widely regarded as impossible. That cotton would always be picked by hand was conventional wisdom. For most people mechanical cotton harvesters occupied the same category as perpetual motion machines.[4]

TABLE 3.1. Annual Percentage of Patents Granted for Harvesting Corn, Grain, and Cotton, 1837-1957

	Corn	Grain	Cotton
1837–1859	9.7	8.1	2.6
1860–1879	30.4	31.6	11.1
1880–1899	48.7	57.2	25.9
1900–1919	63.0	47.1	46.1
1920–1939	32.1	19.6	21.5
1940–1957	26.4	10.4	26.1
1837–1957	34.6	28.8	24.8
Total Patents	4,182	3,482	2,550
Percentage	40.9	34.1	25.0

Source: Calculated from Jacob Schmookler, *Patents, Inventions, and Economic Change: Data and Selected Essays* (Cambridge, Mass.: Harvard University Press, 1972), 100–103.

The potential development of a cotton harvester was nonetheless a very newsworthy subject. In the late nineteenth century, newspapers often published excited but naive reports that an inventor had perfected a mechanical cotton picker. In 1894 the Jackson, Mississippi, *Clarion-Ledger* declared after a demonstration at Bentonia in Yazoo County that a machine "PICKS TEN BALES A DAY." The story claimed the trial demonstrated "that cotton can be picked by machinery—it solved the greatest of problems and will revolutionize the cotton industry."[5] There were a few remaining problems to be worked out, of course. This short article contained most of the features found in similar reports made down through the years. Besides revolutionizing the cotton industry, the machine reportedly picked at least 90 percent of the cotton, though the sample contained many leaves and stems, lowering the grade; the picker evoked comparisons with Eli Whitney's cotton gin; the machine's operating cost was less than handpicking and it gathered as much cotton as twenty-five or thirty field hands could gather. All such reports turned out to be exaggerated.[6] In 1937, an observer quipped that "A successful cotton picker has been just right around the corner for the last eighty-seven years."[7]

The requirements of a viable cotton harvester were readily apparent. In 1930 the *Progressive Farmer* noted the desire of many farmers for a dependable and cheap cotton picker. The machine would have to harvest the crop but not damage the plant, so as to allow for later pickings; be attachable to either a team or a tractor; and cost no more than a grain binder. In summary, a commercial machine would have to incorporate lightweight, small size, moderate cost, and operating simplicity.[8]

In 1931 William E. Ayres—one of the South's strongest advocates of mechanization[9]—outlined the essential requirements for a mechanical cotton picker:

- It must be economical and reasonably priced.
- It must be as simple as possible. Extremely complicated machines are undesirable. It should be sufficiently simple to permit speedy repair or replacement of parts by good farm mechanics.
- It must be capable of picking at least as rapidly as the average one-row cultivator travels or from three-quarters to one acre an hour.
- It should be able to travel over any ground which modern cultivating machinery can negotiate. . . . Picking machines must be able to lower the picking mechanism so as to get the bottom bolls, and at the same time be able to raise all the machinery to get over rough ground. . . .
- It should be able to turn around on roads sufficient for cultivating machinery.

- It must be adapted to row spacing necessary for maximum yields.
- It must carry a sufficient load of seed cotton to make discharging cotton in the middle of the field unnecessary when operating on reasonably long rows. It should have means of promptly discharging the cotton at the end of the rows.
- Machine picking must not involve cleaning the fields of grass, weeds, and vines more thoroughly than is necessary for most profitable production.
- The machine must pick in fields where the plant is still green and the staple white without stripping the leaves, breaking the stems, or damaging the green bolls.
- It must pick either wet or dry cotton. Cotton driers are being successfully used in the treatment of cotton picked while wet. . . .
- It must pick a high percentage of open cotton. Planters may have to be satisfied with somewhat incomplete picking. . . .
- It must drop as little cotton as possible on the ground. Reasonable losses will undoubtedly be more than offset by savings made possible by reduced production expenses.[10]

To these requirements, Ayres added that the machine must not allow green leaves or oil to stain the fibers or injure them in the picking process, nor materially lower the grade of the cotton.

The realization of all these requirements was extremely difficult. No wonder numerous early inventors failed.

Between 1850 and 1930, the patent office awarded 750 patents on mechanical cotton pickers operated on a variety of principles ranging from vacuum suction to threshing and static electricity, including a variety of stripping slots, fingers, chains and rolls, picking cylinders and disks, as well as a variety of spindles—smooth, burred, serrated, barbed, and clawed (table 3.2). In hindsight many proposed machines were preposterous; but even the most unlikely demonstrated the prodigious amount of work that was invested in the invention of the mechanical cotton harvester.[11]

The proposed devices for harvesting cotton can be broken down into five distinct types:

- The stripper type of harvester combed the plant with teeth or drew it between stationary slots or teeth.
- The picker type was designed to pick the open cotton from the bolls using spindles, fingers, or prongs, without injuring the plant's foliage and unopened bolls.
- The thresher type cut down the plant near the surface of the ground and

took the entire plant into the machine, where the cotton fiber was separated from the vegetable material.

- The pneumatic cotton harvester removed the cotton from the bolls with suction or a blast of air.
- Electrical cotton harvesters used a statically charged belt or finger to attract the lint and removed it from the boll.[12]

The spindle-type picker has the longest and most active history, going back to 1850. Pneumatic machines were popular failures in the early years of this century, and the belief that they might work was surprisingly persistent. The stripper idea elicited less interest than the spindle machine because the stripper's use was limited to Oklahoma and Texas. Machines based on electrical charges, the rotary principle, and the thresher idea were the least popular.

The invention of the mechanical cotton picker developed into a competitive effort that attracted a host of fascinating inventors. Arkansas inventor and all-around eccentric Charles McDermott patented one of the first thresher machines in 1874. He claimed that his machine would do the work of six men and a mule and harvest six bales a day. The operator cut down the cotton plant, threw it into the machine, and then turned a crank to strip the cotton off the plant. Apparently the machine was never tried under field conditions. In those days the patent office's criteria for issuing patents did not include the insistence that the proposed device actually perform as specified.[13] Cotton threshers could not handle the cotton stalk, which, unlike a stalk of wheat, is large and tough. In tests, threshers attempted to harvest immature bolls and clogged easily.[14]

TABLE 3.2. Patents on Cotton Harvesters, by Type, 1850–1931

	1850–1900	1901–1920	1921–1931	Totals
Electrical	2	1	1	4
Pneumatic	37	122	50	209
Spindle	190	180	84	454
Stripper	16	21	28	65
Thresher	10	6	2	18
Totals	255	330	165	750

Source: Based on data in H. P. Smith et al., *The Mechanical Harvesting of Cotton,* Station Bulletin No. 452 (College Station: Texas Agricultural Experiment, August 1932), table 12, pp. 60–72.

The pneumatic machines used suction to remove the cotton lint from the boll. The operator touched the end of the hose to a boll and sucked the lint into a tank or bag. First patented in 1859, pneumatic machines featured many types of nozzles. Typically, the pneumatic pickers consisted of a vacuum tank with attached hoses—like a huge octopus with hoses as tentacles—that a crew of men would apply to individual bolls, drawing the lint into a tank. This idea did not actually eliminate hand labor since the operator had to direct the nozzle manually to each cotton boll. The machines also sucked in dirt, leaves, and trash along with the cotton. But apparently the idea of a cotton picker operating like a vacuum cleaner was so intuitive that pneumatic machines continued to be tried as late as the 1930s.[15]

A variation of the pneumatic idea was to use a blast of air to separate the fiber from the boll. In the 1930s, A. R. Nisbet and H. G. Wendland developed the Wind-Roll picker that seemed like a strong competitor in the cotton picker sweepstakes. According to a description, "The picking element consists of a pair of mesh rollers which roll the cotton out of the bolls as the cotton plant is blown by a blast of air, first to one side against one roller and then to the other side against the second roller 20 inches behind the first. The mesh of the rollers holds the loose fiber until a half revolution has been made, when the same blast of air blows it off the cylinder. The released fiber is caught by a revolving screen and carried to a suction pipe which empties it into bags."[16]

John S. Thurman was a mechanical engineer who experimented with vacuum cleaners before turning to pneumatic cotton harvesters. In the early 1920s, the Thurman Vacuum Cotton Harvester Company of St. Louis, Missouri, marketed a pneumatic machine. He regarded the machine's hand-labor element as a selling point. "My invention," Thurman asserted, "has proved a success for the reason that it starts with, and is based on, the proposition that cotton must be picked by the human hand guided by the human eye. What I have done is to accelerate the human hand six times, picked the cotton from 10 to 25 per cent cleaner and relieved the picker of dragging a sack of cotton through the field by sacking it in the machine."[17] The machine cost $1,200 and reportedly picked three bales a day.

The Shunk Manufacturing Company of Bucyrus, Ohio, put another suction machine on the market. The Success Suction Cotton Picker, described as "the octopus of the cotton fields," rode on a four-wheel tractor with eight men walking in front, each one equipped with a suction hose. The Success machine, patented in 1914 and placed on the market in 1924, was said to clean and fluff cotton as well as pick it.[18]

As electrical devices became common, inventors tried using an electrically charged belt or finger to remove the lint from the boll. As early as 1868 this idea received its first patent. In the 1920s T. C. Stukenborg of Memphis was still working with the idea of combining an electric charge and vacuum, using a machine with brushes revolving inward at the mouth of each suction tube. The brushes were powered by electric motors and supplemented by four sets of suction and cleaning fans in an elaborate machine, but the brushes added little to its picking ability.[19] Nor is cotton attracted to an electrical charge.

While many of these early ideas seem ludicrous today, the idea of cotton picked by electricity or vacuum cleaners in the cotton fields is still amusing. The most bizarre idea was that chemical processing could transform the entire plant entirely with the cotton stalk pulped and made into paper, rayon, or other material.[20]

Of all the ideas tried, however, only two turned out to have practical value: strippers and spindles.

Cotton strippers removed the cotton from the plant by raking the plant with teeth or projecting fingers, or by drawing it between slots or revolving brushes and rollers. The first patent on this type of device was issued to John Hughes of North Carolina in 1871, but many others also tried this simple and workable idea. The stripper raked the whole plant, including leaves, stems, and trash, and produced dirty cotton with a dramatically lower grade. The stripper principle was most successful in the High Plains of Texas and Oklahoma, where cotton plants were short with bolls that all opened at the same time. Anywhere cotton grew low and thin, the stripper was an effective tool.

Early on, strippers actually saw use in harvesting a cotton crop as opposed to just experimentation. In 1914 the High Plains of the Texas panhandle produced a bumper crop, but prices were so low that handpicking was considered too costly. In desperation, farmers built crude strippers out of picket fences and used a team of mules to drag them down the cotton rows. No gin would take such trashy cotton, so they had it threshed, which removed some of the debris, cleaning it enough so that it could be ginned.[21]

The High Plains produced conditions that generated other innovative ideas for cotton harvesters. In 1926, faced with a bumper crop, low prices, and labor shortages, Oklahoma and Texas farmers with the help of local blacksmiths crafted hand-built sleds. Some farmers mounted wooden boxes on runners with steel fingers projecting out the front, or used a box with a narrow slot to catch and strip the cotton. These simple devices cost only a few dollars and harvested four or five acres a day at an estimated cost of $2.78 per bale.[22] In time improvements were made by adding cleaners, and soon major implement companies put their own strippers on the market.

These experiments in Oklahoma and Texas marked the beginning of the mechanical harvesting of cotton.

In 1930 Deere and Company developed a commercial horse-drawn, single-row stripper and a two-row machine mounted on a tractor.[23] International Harvester Corporation also produced a stripper that could be horse drawn or mounted on a Farmall tractor, with stripping units on either side for two-row operation. Local companies also produced strippers. The stripping devices varied from steel fingers to slots or rafters.[24]

In the early 1930s the Texas Agricultural Experiment Station at Texas A & M College under the direction of Harris P. Smith became one of the centers of cotton stripper research. By 1935 Aggie engineers were testing a tractor-mounted single-row stripper equipped with a burr extractor, which help to clean the cotton as it was harvested.[25]

The use of spindles to pick cotton dated back to 1850. In spindle machines metal fingers or spindles rotated as they move through a cotton plant, catching and then twisting the lint out of the bolls. The advantage of this approach was that, unlike strippers, the machine's action left the plant intact, so that unopened bolls were unharmed and could be picked later. All of the machines used in the Mississippi River Delta today employ the spindle principle.

In 1885 Angus Campbell, an engineer with the Deering Harvesting Company in Chicago, observed the tedious process of cotton picking during a trip to Texas. Taking up the challenge, he conducted his first tests with a spindle-type picker in 1889. Over the next twenty years he made an annual journey southward at picking time to test his latest modification. "At the end of every year," according to one account, "he went back North with a little more experience and a little more ridicule; for the average cotton-grower believes as firmly in the eternal supremacy of the Negro cotton-picker as he does in the infallibility of the Democratic party."[26] Campbell overlooked the ridicule, but he lacked local shop facilities in Texas that he could draw on. As a result, he was unable to make modifications and immediately try them out.

In one of his early machines Campbell used 330 spindles. According to a contemporary observer, "These fingers are ten inches long, and have at the end a brush or tip of fine wire, and set in four grooves radially is horse hair, clipped so it projects from the fingers about one-twelfth of an inch, the tip and the hairs on the side being the means of getting the cotton from the bolls." The spindles whirled and entangled the lint, pulling it from the boll. The lint was carried into a receptacle while brushes cleaned the spindles. Pulled by two mules, the machine could gather 3,000 pounds of cotton in a 10-hour day at an estimated cost of $3.00 per day or $1.50 per bale.[27]

Campbell in time adapted his picker to the gasoline engine. In 1908 he received support from Theodore H. Price, a New Orleans cotton dealer who had secured his own patent on a cotton harvester in 1904. They jointly formed the Price-Campbell Cotton Picker Corporation in 1912.

The Price-Campbell picker was a complicated and expensive device. In field tests it performed poorly, picking too little cotton, breaking too many plants, and damaging unopened bolls. But Price and Campbell were on the right track.[28] Soon after Campbell's death in 1922, International Harvester bought the Price-Campbell patents, which embodied the principles used in the machine that IH declared a success in 1942.[29]

Other inventors tried to perfect the spindle method. Hiram M. Berry, a Greenville, Mississippi, inventor, designed a picker with barbed spindles. The Berry machine was an awkward-looking device powered by an automobile engine. The picking spindles projected into the plants from both sides as the machine straddled the row, and the cotton was doffed from the spindles by a sliding sleeve. In 1925 Berry's tests attracted the attention of Deere and Company. Though Berry's work was never perfected, his son Charles R. Berry continued to pursue the idea and eventually sold his patents to Deere.

In 1897 Peter Paul Haring of Goliad, Texas, began a thirty-year odyssey in hope of building a cotton picker using curved prongs as variations of picking spindles. In early tests the Haring machine utterly failed to pick cotton; it simply knocked cotton to the ground or dropped the cotton that it did pick.[30]

Haring, however, did not give up. He bent the picking fingers into a corkscrew to enable them to grasp the cotton and then release it when their motion was reversed. In a later model he changed the picking fingers to two hook-shaped points. In 1924, with representatives from International Harvester looking on, the Haring machine picked 75 percent of the cotton and another 15 percent in a second pass during a demonstration near Fort Worth, Texas. The demonstration was a qualified success, but the officials present were not sufficiently interested to offer Haring a contract.[31] International Harvester had already purchased the Price-Campbell patents and was conducting its own experimental work on cotton harvesters. Still believing he had a marketable machine, Haring pushed ahead with plans to put a picker into commercial production, organizing the Automatic Cotton Picker Company in

1930. But he was unable to raise enough capital, and the Great Depression ended his last hope.

The road of invention was littered with the names of other men who tried to create a mechanical cotton picker and failed. George R. Meyercord, a Chicago businessman and an associate of Haring, was famous for his Gyracotn machine. Like Haring, Meyercord used curved corkscrew-like fingers.[32] An inventor known only as B. Johnson of Temple, Texas, was granted several patents on a spindle picker between 1912 and 1918. John F. Appleby, best known as the inventor of the Appleby knotter for twine binders, built spindle-type cotton harvesters in which spindles projected downward into the plants as the machine passed over them. In 1913, he was granted a patent for the first two-row cotton harvester.[33] Many other inventors tested their ideas and filed patents, but their work failed to make a lasting contribution.

By 1920 the goal of a mechanical cotton picker had still not been achieved, but the workable ideas had been narrowed down to two viable alternatives— the spindle picker and the stripper. The pneumatic idea was unworkable but presumably too good to die a quick death, and it too was still alive. Its virtues were that it was the least expensive and the least complicated. During the 1920s and 1930s the number of inventors working on some version of a mechanical cotton harvester increased, making it one of the hottest technological frontiers. In a veritable climate of invention, there was a strong sense among inventors that the solution of mechanical cotton harvesting was near. The most promising work centered on International Harvester and John Deere, two large farm implement companies, and on one lone inventor, John Rust.

International Harvester

Founded in 1902, International Harvester (IH) was a merger of McCormick Harvesting Company, Deering Harvester Company, and other smaller firms.[34] IH's strength was that the company embraced the manufacture of all major farm machinery. One of the company's first major successes was the farm tractor.

While the development of tractors went back to the nineteenth century, they tended to be heavy machines with little utility until International Harvester introduced the McCormick-Deering Farmall tractor in 1924.[35] The first all-purpose tractor, the Farmall employed the tricycle design, had suffi-cient power for land breaking, and was suitable for cultivation since it could make sharp turns by braking either large rear wheel. Other light, general-purpose tractors followed the Farmall. These machines could operate auxiliary machinery with belt pulleys from their power take-offs. Later equipped with pneumatic tires, the all-purpose tractor was a versatile agricultural machine. As expected they were more readily accepted in the Midwest, where labor shortages continue to stimulate mechanization, than in the South. Since early heavy tractors were not suited for cultivating, southern farmers continued using their mules, but after 1935 they rapidly adopted tractors. Even though implement companies manufactured tractors during World War II, the demand outpaced the supply. By the postwar period tractors were a common sight in cotton fields.

With its Farmall tractor a commercial success, Harvester began experimenting with mechanical cotton pickers. After purchasing the Price-Campbell patents in 1924, IH began a period of development that lasted twenty-five years at a reputed cost of $4.5 million. The man in charge of the project was Clarence R. Hagen, IH's chief engineer, who did the development work in Chicago but went south for field testing.[36]

Beginning in 1922 International Harvester engineers tried unsuccessfully for three successive years to make the pneumatic idea work. In the end they concluded that a man who was encumbered with handling a hose and nozzles was at a disadvantage to one who was simply picking by hand. The IH test machine consisted of a gasoline engine that ran a vacuum pump, with a two-inch suction pipe that branched out into four picking hoses. The operator held the nozzle against the open boll, sucking up the cotton. In tests at Caruthersville, Missouri, the machine proved top heavy and toppled over in the field. The power source, a three horsepower engine, was unable to maintain sufficient vacuum. The pneumatic machine picked cotton well enough, however, for Harvester to continue tests for another year, despite the fact that the company was already working on a spindle-type picker.

The company's second pneumatic picker featured several improvements, especially a stronger vacuum; and the machine was operated by the power take-off on a Farmall tractor. The machine was again tested in late 1923 at Caruthersville. Two men were required for operation, one to manipulate the nozzles and the other to drive the tractor. The results were marginal, but Harvester continued experimental work one final year.

Built in 1924, the third and last International Harvester pneumatic machine was similar to the previous model except that it was mule drawn. Final field testing was done on the Schyler Marshall plantation near Dallas, Texas, on September 15, 1924. The company set up a competition between the pneumatic picker and an experienced hand picker. As described by a company historian:

> One man, who was capable of picking from 350 to 400 lbs. of cotton per day[,] was started out on a row of cotton and at the same time the pneumatic type picker with one man handling each of the four nozzles was started down adjoining rows. At the end of ¾ of an hour the hand picker was 50 yards ahead of the machine. In other words he had picked about 25% greater distance than each of the men handling a nozzle, had a great deal cleaner sample in his bag and had picked the cotton cleaner from the stalk.
>
> This test thoroughly convinced the management that to be practical the human element had to be entirely eliminated from cotton harvesting machines. The human wrist is like a universal joint and can adapt itself to almost any position when reaching for cotton whereas the hose and nozzle is more cumbersome and unwieldy to direct against a cotton boll. This type of machine could only have one possible advantage and that would be to increase the amount of cotton that an unskilled picker could gather.[37]

Since their pneumatic machine operated by four men lost to a single hand picker in a practical field test, IH abandoned the pneumatic approach and turned its full attention to spindle pickers.

Under Hagen's direction International Harvester completed its first spindle-type picker on September 2, 1924, and tested it on the Marshall plantation near Dallas. The machine was a one-row, self-propelled machine with four picking units and rotary doffers. Following the Price-Campbell design, the spindles used in the early machine were the long, straight type.[38] The initial view was that serrated spindles were not workable because the serrations filled with gum, preventing the lint from releasing.

Hagen and his engineers also built trail-type machines that were pulled by tractors with the picking mechanism deriving power from its rear wheels.[39] Hagen allowed the spindles to enter the cotton plant without any raking action that might strip off leaves and unopened bolls. These machines required three operators—one man to drive the tractor, one to steer the picker, and one to empty the cotton bags. In testing at Wilson, Arkansas, improvements were made to eliminate the need for steering the picker. Later trail-type machines used the tractor power-take-off as their power source, but these machines were difficult to keep in the row. Hagen had an ambitious program to build twenty experimental machines when the stock market crashed in October 1929. Knowing that a period of economic depression was not favorable for the introduction of labor-saving machinery, International Harvester pared down its plans but quietly continued its picker development program.

In the early 1930s Hagen built self-propelled pickers by mounting the picking unit on a tractor, creating a simpler machine. He also began to experiment with different types of spindles. Until 1930, International Harvester used long, straight spindles; but because of difficulty in removing the cotton, Hagen tried shorter spindles with various degrees of taper.

Over the years of experimentation, however, Hagen encountered many disappointments. The short picking season and the inability to simulate field conditions in a laboratory setting required a full year before new ideas could be tested. Another handicap was the distance between his engineering and shop facilities in Chicago and their test fields in Arkansas, Texas, and Arizona. In southern cotton areas, they encountered opposition to mechanical picking among cotton farmers who ridiculed the ideas that a machine would ever replace hand labor.[40]

Hagen's two greatest challenges were to design the optimal spindle along with an effective doffer. The spindles had to have a high affinity for cotton fibers, but also had to release the cotton quickly and easily and be clean after doffing so they would continue to pick efficiently. Engineers found that less aggressive spindles gathered less extraneous matter, but more of them were required. As a result, they developed spindles that were sufficiently aggressive but limited their number to the minimum, thus lessening complications, costs, and maintenance.[41] The rotation of the spindles was reversed in the doffing motion, but this action caused excessive wear.

International Harvester also investigated machines for the small farmer and experimented with tandem models, with one picking drum ahead of the other, to achieve double picking in one pass. Variations were to pick from one or both sides of the row. With this arrangement, the plants were picked twice, with each picking drum operating independently of the other. In early configurations, trail-type machines encountered the cotton plants before the picking unit and knocked cotton to the ground. A tractor with large-diameter drive wheels achieved the greatest success since the tractor cleared the rows without disturbing the plants.[42]

After the 1939 season Hagen came up with a seemingly curious innovation: reversing the direction of the tractor for the picking operation. He mounted a picking mechanism on an International Model H tractor that operated in reverse gear. The advantages were immediately apparent. As Hagen explained, "The row of cotton plants pass through the picking throat of the machine first, and the cotton is picked before the plants contact any part of the tractor." The operator sat directly over the row where he could see well. The basket for cotton was located behind the operator and above the tractor hood.[43] Slowly, the International Harvester picker came together in a successful machine.

Deere and Company

Deere and Company of Moline, Illinois, traced its history back to John Deere, the inventor of the steel plow in the 1830s. The company emerged in the early twentieth century as a major equipment manufacturer. By the 1930s, the most important crop to Deere was corn; and the company's two-row corn picker was on the cutting edge of technology—able to leave bare ten to twenty acres of corn stalks in a day. Deere also produced combines, planters, harrows, and cultivators, as well as hay mowers and rakes.[44]

As a major competitor to International Harvester, Deere and Company decided in the late 1920s to tackle the market for cotton strippers in the high, dry plains of Texas and Oklahoma. Plains farmers were anxious to mechanize their harvest, and they were willing to experiment with new ideas. Before the advent of strippers, they hand snapped their cotton, a process of pulling the entire boll from the stalk rather than pulling the fiber from the boll. Special cleaners called hullers or boll extractors removed the heavier trash before ginning. Although snapping lowered the cotton two grades, a farm hand could snap twice as much lint cotton per day as he could pick. But the extra trash in snapped cotton remained a problem for both ginners and yarn manufacturers.[45]

After homemade strippers enjoyed success in the High Plains, Deere began development work on a commercial mechanical stripper. The first tests at Plainview, Texas, in 1927 were so successful that in the early 1930s Deere sold five hundred horse-drawn strippers in Texas and Oklahoma. With the depression worsening, however, sales stagnated as farmers faced six-cent cotton. While they were unable to purchase new implements, they also benefited from a large labor supply at low prices, thus suppressing the demand for cotton strippers.

While putting strippers on the market, Deere in 1928 started a design program for spindle pickers at the John Deere Spreader Works in East Moline, Illinois. Under the direction of Fred Thomann and Leonard Neighbor, engineers designed a two-row picker mounted on a general-purpose tractor. Using straight, wire spindles, this machine picked from only one side of the row, and results were disappointing. The next year, Deere adopted a radically different approach. This machine consisted of a "overhead reel design in which the plants were bent over and then a reel with long wire spindles rolled over the plants in that position." The spindles were sixteen inches long and penetrated the ground about a half inch. This idea, too, failed. After 1929 Deere continued to experiment with modifications of the reel design before giving up on the idea in 1931. Although a new machine was designed in 1932, Deere did no further experimental work until 1944. During the depression, however, Deere officials kept in contact with Hiram Berry of Greenville and watched his progress with growing interest. The company also used the period between 1932 and 1944 to refine its cotton stripper for use in the Lubbock, Texas, area.[46]

John Rust

John Rust, the most publicized inventor who entered the race to develop a successful cotton picker, personified the popular image of the lone eccentric inventor. Rust worked in his garage or a small shop behind his house, not in the huge research and development facilities of a large farm implement company.

John Rust attracted attention—and evoked fear—during the 1930s as the man whose inventive genius would throw thousands, even millions, of tenants, sharecroppers, and cotton pickers out of work in the midst of the worst depression in American history. Since he expressed a reluctance to impoverish an entire class of people, he became an exceptional personality whose activities were reported in the national press. His ideas were debated, tourists asked directions to his shop, and journalists requested interviews.

Rust designed the first practical, moistened spindle picker, taking advantage of the affinity that cotton fibers have for moist metal. He used the spindle principle as did many previous inventors but believed that the best spindle was long and straight, without serrations or taper. Rust's spindles were in fact steel wires. Like International Harvester, Rust believed that mechanical harvesting must get away from any imitation of human motion in picking cotton.

When he started tinkering with the agricultural machinery, Rust was only trying to relieve people of one of the most onerous forms of stoop labor.[47] As a boy he had handpicked cotton, and he dreamed of a machine that would free millions of people from this backbreaking task.

John Daniel Rust was born near Necessity, in Stephens County, Texas, west of Fort Worth, on September 6, 1892. His father, Benjamin D. Rust, was a Civil War veteran who settled in the county in the 1870s and raised a large family. His mother was Susan Minerva Burnett. Benjamin Rust taught school and farmed 160 acres of poor west Texas land. As a youngster John did farmwork and displayed an aptitude for mechanical tinkering.

John Rust was usually associated with his younger brother, Mack Donald Rust, who was born on January 12, 1900, near Breckenridge, Texas. In 1925, Mack graduated from the University of Texas with a degree in mechanical engineering. Though their paths parted, the two brothers followed similar interests.[48]

As a youngster John Rust found farmwork to be a heavy burden, and every chance he had he sneaked off to work on his latest "invention." When he was seven, he made a steam engine that could puff smoke, though he did not understand the principle of steam. He built a model airplane with a clock spring for a motor. It would not fly, but it moved around on the floor. An old man saw it and predicted that someday "that boy will invent something big."

"That man," Rust later laughed, "was the only person who recognized my genius."[49] As a young man, however, Rust experienced so many failures that he lost confidence in his ability as an inventor.

After his parents died when he was sixteen, Rust began drifting, doing odd jobs all over Texas, Oklahoma, and Kansas. His itinerant career saw him picking cotton, harvesting wheat, and working as a repairman and carpenter. During one period he went from door to door repairing doorbells. After twenty years of drifting, he turned his attention to tinkering with labor-saving farm machinery. In the early 1920s, while working in Kansas City for a small company that was trying to improve the wheat combine, he bought a drafting board and enrolled in a correspondence course to learn mechanical drafting.

Rust was intrigued with the challenge of building a mechanical cotton picker. He kept turning over an idea in his mind. Other inventors had sought to use a spindle with barbs, which would be pushed, spinning, into the cotton plant. The barbs twisted the fibers around the spindle and pulled the cotton lock from the boll. But how could the cotton be stripped from the barbs? The spindle soon became clogged with cotton lint, leaves, and other debris. A smooth spindle would present few doffing problems, but how to get the cotton fibers to adhere to smooth metal? Late one night in Kansas City, Rust suddenly hit on the answer: use a smooth, *moist* spindle. As he later recalled:

> The thought came to me one night after I had gone to bed. I remembered how cotton used to stick to my fingers when I was a boy picking in the early morning dew. I jumped out of bed, found some absorbent cotton and a nail for testing. I licked the nail and twirled it in the cotton and found that it would work.[50]

Here was the missing link in his plan to use a smooth spindle. He quit his job and went back to live with a sister in Weatherford, Texas, and worked on his idea. Rust threw himself into the task with enthusiasm. Incredibly he believed he could put a machine on the market within five years.[51]

Rust assembled the first working model of a cotton picker in his sister's garage, and tested it on ten artificial stalks set up on a board to form an artificial cotton row. The machine picked ninety-seven out of one hundred locks of cotton. He continued testing with funds invested by his family and friends in Weatherford. He encountered the usual skeptics, too. When he told a hardware clerk he was building a cotton picker, the clerk said, "Good Heavens, Rust, you can't do that! Some of the biggest implement companies in the world have been working on that for years and they haven't got anywhere yet. If they can't build a cotton picker, what makes you think you can?" Rust explained that he thought they were working on the wrong principle. He applied for his first patent in 1928, and it was issued in 1933; eventually he and his brother Mack owned forty-seven patents on picking machines and related inventions.[52] But like Thomas Edison, he found out that invention was more perspiration than inspiration.

The young inventor's work first received attention in Weatherford newspapers. The *Weatherford Democrat* announced "Weatherford Inventor Claims to Have Built a Real Cotton Picker," the paper apparently taking a cautious approach. The "Wet Spindle Cotton Picker," as Rust called the machine, could be pulled by two mules and would pick, he predicted, eight acres a day, or three or four bales. Rust called attention to the idea of using smooth spindles because spindles with teeth made the cotton difficult to remove. According to reports, he expected to have the machine ready for use in local cotton fields in the fall of 1928,[53] but Rust made a career of underestimating production deadlines.

In late 1928 his brother Mack, who had been studying at the General Electric training school in Schenectady, New York, joined him at Weatherford. John and Mack formed a good team—John the idea man, Mack the practical one who found a way to make it work.

John Rust's worry about the impact of his picker on labor derived from values he had formed during his youth. As a young man, he had absorbed the socialist ideas that circulated in Oklahoma during the teens and 1920s. He lived in several cooperative colonies and explored utopian plans for improving the world.

While in the army during World War I, Rust was stationed at Camp Stanley, Texas, where he began reading the works of Charles P. Steinmetz, a mathematician and socialist who ventured into the politics of World War I with

America and the New Epoch (1916). During his itinerant period, Rust read socialist pamphlets like *Men and Mules* by W. F. Ries and *Introduction to Socialism* by N. A. Richardson.[54]

After their initial breakthrough with moistened spindles, the Rust brothers began a migration in search of financial support. In 1930 they moved to Louisiana and worked under the auspices of a cooperative community at New Llano, and then on to nearby Leesville. While in south Louisiana, the Rust brothers attracted the notice of the *New Orleans Item-Tribune*.[55] In an interview with a reporter, John Rust patiently explained how the machine functioned, emphasizing the advantages of a wet spindle and of a smooth rather than a saw-tooth spindle. He believed that the machine would pay for itself in saving labor costs in just ten days. The *Item-Tribune* compared the Rust machine to Whitney's cotton gin and expressed the belief that a revolution was impending in the South.

In 1931 the Rust machine became the first mechanical harvester to machine pick a bale of cotton in a single day. In 1932 the Rust brothers founded the Southern Harvester Company, a corporation with headquarters in New Orleans. Continuing to test their machine, they operated it near Lake Providence, Louisiana, in the fall of 1932 and moved there with the backing of local planters. At the Delta Experiment Station near Stoneville, Mississippi, in 1933, they set another record, picking five bales of cotton in one day. W. E. Ayres, superintendent of the station, endorsed the Rust machine as "a better cotton picker than the first Model T Ford was a car."[56] At the Southern Engineer's Convention at Memphis in January 1934, motion pictures of the Rust machine in operation created a stir; and that spring the Rust brothers relocated to Memphis, the center of the Cotton South, still in pursuit of financial support. That fall they tested their latest machine across the Mississippi River in Arkansas cotton fields.

Rust's move to Memphis had the support of the Memphis Chamber of Commerce and local investors. The Rust brothers formed the Rust Cotton Picker Company with $1 million in capital and rented an old service station on Florida Street in an area south of downtown.[57]

In the spring 1935 Rust announced that his picker would go into production within a year. "She's ready," he announced with a grin, warning that the sharecropping system would have to be abandoned.[58] But 1935 and 1936 came and went as John and Mack Rust continued to work on their picker, still believing the machine was on the verge of mass production.

John Rust remained at Memphis for the next fifteen years. During this period he continued to experiment with improvements in his cotton picker and made plans to put the machine into production. He built a pull-model picker as an "economy model" intended for small farmers, but it was necessary to go over each row twice. After receiving Ayres's endorsement of their work, the Rust brothers went on to other demonstrations at Stoneville. Their 1936 demonstration made national news and elicited fears about the impact of the machine on the South's sharecroppers. In 1937 they built a self-propelled tandem picker that broke all records by picking thirteen bales in a single day at Gilliam, Louisiana. This machine could be operated either with picking units mounted one behind the other for double picking a row in one operation, or side by side for two-row picking.[59]

Despite the publicity the Rust brothers received, the Rust Cotton Picker Company fell into bankruptcy. While Rust could produce prototypes, he did not have the resources to put a machine into commercial production. There was still another problem. Rust was aware of the need for longer life in components subject to friction and wear. The problem was not just a need to find tougher materials, but in the design of the parts themselves. The Rust prototypes lacked the durability needed in a commercial machine. The relationship between John and Mack was also plagued by discord. The Rust brothers and their wives lived together, and arguments were common. While Mack left the partnership and moved to California in 1942, John stayed in Memphis and went back to his drawing board. Out of this work came his postwar machines.

As these events played out, the Cotton South seemed as far away as ever from mechanization. The Great Depression forced down labor prices and dried up the potential market for labor-saving machines. International Harvester and John Deere put their marketing plans on hold, although they continued to do experimental work. Only Rust believed that he could put a cotton picker into production during the depression. Meanwhile, new forces of change began gathering like a distant storm.

The Agricultural Adjustment Administration and Structural Change in the Cotton South

In the early 1930s the Great Depression plunged the Cotton South into the worst economic crisis in its history. Cotton had always oscillated in a cycle of booms and busts. In 1894 cotton prices fell to four and a half cents a pound and caused widespread suffering, but the system recovered on its own. The boll weevil invasion, the roller-coaster market of World War I and the postwar period, and then the Great Depression created havoc in the cotton market. This time the cotton industry could not survive without federal intervention, but survival meant the structural transformation of the entire cotton economy. The Cotton South would have to face the consequences of mechanization.

In the 1920s cotton prices declined almost every year. When the stock market crashed in 1929, cotton was bringing almost seventeen cents a pound, but in 1930 it slipped to nine and a half cents, then hit bottom at five and a half cents in 1931, the lowest price since 1894 (table 4.1).[1] As a result farm income plunged, and farm foreclosures soared to record levels. On a single day a quarter of the entire state of Mississippi went on sale at auction for nonpayment of taxes.[2] Overall farm income fell by half between 1929 and 1933, and in order to compensate, farmers produced more cotton. The production gains during the 1920s paralleled an unstable, mostly declining cotton market. American cotton producers raised a record crop in 1926, but saw the price fall to twelve and a half cents.[3]

As low as prices were, price was only one problem that cotton growers faced. After World War I, the American cotton industry faced new pressures from foreign competition, synthetic fabrics, and women's fashions that used fewer yards of material.[4] As Egypt, China, India, and other countries increased their production of cotton, the United States' share of the international cotton market declined dramatically.[5] Production costs kept the price of American cotton too high to compete with cheap foreign cotton. At the same time, growers were unable to reduce production to levels that equaled demand. As a result cotton stocks, the annual carryover of cotton stored in warehouses, rose inexorably. By the 1930s cotton stocks amounted to over half of the nation's annual

TABLE 4.1. U.S. Cotton Production, 1920–1940

	Production in Bales (1,000s)	Cotton Price (cents)	Carryover in Bales (1,000s)	Carryover as Percentage of Annual Production
1920	13,429	15.89	3,824	28.5
1921	7,943	17.00	6,896	86.8
1922	9,755	22.88	3,322	34.1
1923	10,140	28.69	2,325	22.9
1924	13,630	22.91	1,556	11.4
1925	16,105	19.62	1,610	10.0
1926	17,978	12.49	3,543	19.7
1927	12,956	20.20	3,762	29.0
1928	14,477	17.98	2,536	17.5
1929	14,825	16.78	2,312	15.6
1930	13,932	9.46	4,530	32.5
1931	17,097	5.66	6,370	37.3
1932	13,003	6.52	9,678	74.4
1933	13,047	10.17	8,165	62.6
1934	9,636	12.36	7,744	80.4
1935	10,638	11.09	7,208	67.8
1936	12,399	12.36	5,409	43.6
1937	18,946	8.41	4,499	23.7
1938	11,943	8.60	11,533	96.6
1939	11,817	9.09	13,033	110.3
1940	12,566	9.89	10,564	84.1

Source: U.S. Bureau of the Census, *Historical Statistics of the United States: Colonial Times to 1970* (Washington, D.C.: GPO, 1975), series K 554–56, p. 517.

production. As an imperishable crop, cotton stocks mounted in warehouses from year to year, maintaining a glutted market and keeping prices low. In 1938 cotton stocks neared the point that the carryover exceeded the annual production (table 4.1). The following year cotton reserves did exceed production.

For the Cotton South overproduction emerged as an intractable problem. According to the law of supply and demand, prices would remain high or would rise if production were limited. But an industry with hundreds of thousands of independent producers seemed powerless to limit production. The outbreak of war in 1914 caused a "cotton panic"; and as the price of cotton plunged, farmers hoped to gain relief in a "buy-a-bale" campaign. The war, however, pushed cotton prices to record levels, reaching 35⅓ cents in 1919. During the 1920s the acreage planted in cotton soared, especially in Texas and Oklahoma, as cotton farming moved westward.[6] Some farmers turned to a "burn-a-bale" plan in a desperate effort at production control. The next cotton crisis occurred in 1926, when record production again forced prices down. While some farmers favored compulsory acreage restriction, those who advocated voluntary methods won out with a demand for reducing acreage by 25 percent and organized an unprecedented campaign to balance production and demand through voluntary acreage curtailment. The movement did succeed in Oklahoma and Louisiana, where farmers decreased their planting by 18 percent. As a result twenty-cent cotton returned, but only briefly as production again pushed upward.[7]

In the early depression years the Cotton Belt faced the same combination —overproduction, falling prices, and low demand. By 1931, as cotton hit a new low of five and a half cents (table 4.1), growers again cried for help. Borrowing an idea from a group of planters in north Louisiana, Gov. Huey P. Long proposed a simple but bold plan: Louisiana and other cotton-producing states should legally ban the planting of cotton in 1932, imposing an extraordinary "Cotton Holiday." When Long proposed a conference in New Orleans to discuss the plan, however, only Arkansas and South Carolina's governors accepted his invitation. In conference sessions, participants proposed limiting the implementation of the plan until joined by states producing three-fourths of the nation's total cotton crop. Texas Gov. Ross Sterling strongly opposed Long's plan, the Texas legislature refused to enact it, and the cotton-holiday plan collapsed since Texas was the nation's largest cotton producer. The debate on cotton control quickly aligned growers who advocated a mandatory holiday against others who favored voluntary reduction.[8]

The mandatory no-crop, or "drop-a-crop" plan, as it was called, was wildly popular in Louisiana, and the legislature enacted it into law, prohibiting the planting, gathering, and ginning of cotton during 1932.[9] The Texas legislature, however, passed a law mandating that farmers reduce the acreage by 30 percent for both 1932 and 1933 in order to achieve an overall 50 percent reduction. The Texas plan attracted strong support because of the state's dominant position in American cotton production.

In Arkansas, Gov. Harvey Parnell called the state's legislature into special session to pass a cotton control bill. He favored the mandatory Long plan, but it lacked support. With the South facing the second largest crop on record, the Arkansas legislature enacted the Texas scheme providing for a 30 percent reduction and a crop rotation provision in the name of soil conservation.[10]

The cotton reduction movement also captured the imagination of beleaguered cotton growers in Mississippi despite the opposition of Gov. Theodore G. Bilbo. Mississippi enacted a law identical to the Texas bill, as did South Carolina, but all such laws were contingent on three-fourths of the cotton states joining the reduction movement.[11] That criteria was an impossible goal. The desperate movement to curtail production fell apart because a lack of central coordination doomed it to failure. Though cotton reduction was unsuccessful, the resulting controversy laid the groundwork for the federal cotton reduction program a year later.[12]

It seemed that even nature itself had turned against long-suffering farmers. With cotton prices already at near-record lows, Arkansas suffered a severe drought in the summer of 1930 that reduced the state's annual cotton production by 39 percent. But the drought also reduced the value of the 1930 crop by $81 million, or 67 percent below the 1929 crop.[13] In Washington, Congress debated various plans to supply farmers with drought relief, but no plan won a consensus.[14]

When Franklin D. Roosevelt took office in March 1933, he promised not merely action against the depression, but also "bold, persistent experimentation." In its so-called three R's, the New Deal embodied a series of programs to bring immediate relief to those in distress, recovery from the economic collapse, and reform of financial institutions so that a major depression could not happen again. The Federal Emergency Relief Administration (FERA) loaned money to farmers who were drought stricken and offered a few of them a chance to buy small farms.[15] In 1935 the Works Progress Administration (WPA) assumed the major responsibility of providing relief for farmers who were out of work.

The New Deal's recovery program for agriculture was embodied in the

Agricultural Adjustment Administration (AAA), popularly known as the Triple-A. The AAA operated programs for cotton, as well as for wheat, corn, hogs, rice, tobacco, and milk. The cotton program was intended to reduce cotton acreage under the assumption that fewer acres growing cotton would raise cotton prices.

In 1933 cotton reserves were so high that the cotton stored in warehouses could have met the entire world demand. In other words farmers did not need to plant any cotton that year, but when spring arrived they had to plant or starve. All efforts at voluntary acreage reduction had come to nothing, and the South faced the prospect of another bumper crop with cotton already under six cents a pound. The entire region was prepared at last to accept mandatory cotton acreage controls.

Enter the AAA

When the AAA became law on May 12, 1933, cotton had been planted and the seedlings were already pushing above the soil surface. An emergency program had to be undertaken if cotton farmers were going to have higher prices that year. The AAA launched a dramatic plow-up campaign to destroy 10 million acres, cutting production by one-fourth.[16] As an incentive to sign up, cotton farmers received a benefit payment of seven to twenty dollars per acre they released from production, based on yield. They could also choose smaller cash payments along with an option on an amount of cotton equal to what they plowed up at six cents a pound. The intent was that farmers would receive checks from the government as well as higher cotton prices.[17]

The AAA plow-up was a whirlwind effort that sent the Cotton Belt reeling. The concept of more from less flew in the face of common sense; people were "ill-housed, ill-clothed, and ill-fed," yet the government was destroying supplies of basic commodities, including food. The plow-up also violated farmers' instincts against the destruction of a standing crop, and even for mules government compliance was hard. Mules were forced to walk on the cotton plants they had been trained not to trample. The plow-up removed 10,497,866 acres of cotton, reducing the yield by an estimated 3,983,125 bales with the AAA mailing out $179,105,577 in benefit payments.[18] In subsequent years, the government limited cotton acreage in a less heroic fashion.

In the spring of 1933 Arkansas cotton farmers planted almost 2,800,000 acres, and that summer 99,808 farmers signed contracts with the AAA agreeing to plow up 927,185 acres, saving an estimated 395,480 bales that would

TABLE 4.2. AAA Cotton Plow-Up Results for Arkansas, Mississippi, and Louisiana, 1933

	Contracts	Acres rented	Estimated Yield per Acre	Estimated Bales saved	Acres planted in 1933 on All Farms	Acres planted in 1933 on Contracted Farms	Percentage Planted on Contracted Farms	Percentage of Cotton Acreage on Contracted Farms Rented	Percentage of Total Cotton Acres Rented
Arkansas	99,808	927,812	213	395,480	3,548,000	2,796,399	78.8	33.2	26.1
Louisiana	108,533	454,230	198	179,616	1,767,000	1,407,480	79.7	32.3	25.7
Mississippi	62,130	931,813	200	372,670	3,820,000	2,894,449	76.0	32.2	24.4
Delta States	270,471	2,313,855	204	947,766	9,135,000	7,098,323	77.7	32.6	25.3
United States	1,031,549	10,487,991	190	3,985,437	40,852,000	29,885,725	73.2	35.1	25.7

Source: Payments Made under the Agricultural Adjustment Program, 74th Cong., 2d sess., S. Doc. 274, 1936, pp. 26, 28; Henry I. Richards, Cotton under the Agricultural Adjustment Act: Developments up to July 1934, Brookings Institution Pamphlet Series No. 15 (Washington: Brookings Institution, 1934), 36–37.

have been grown on those acres (table 4.2).[19] In Mississippi and Louisiana, the results were similar. Across the Delta, the AAA plow-up took 2,313,855 acres out of production and saved an estimated 947,766 bales. In the three states combined, 270,471 farmers signed contracts and in payment received $43,883,090, or an average of $162.25 each.

A smaller crop with government price supports drove up the price of cotton from five and a half cents per pound to more than ten cents in the fall of 1933. The AAA was a popular success with large Delta cotton farmers, who enthusiastically endorsed its continuation.[20]

Unfortunately the AAA was unsuccessful in reducing the cotton surplus. The 1933 season produced one of the highest yields on record, totaling some 13,047,000 bales, as compared with the 14,660,000 bale average for the years 1928 to 1932 (table 4.1). Whether this outcome was due to favorable weather or to more intensive cultivation of the acres still in production cannot be determined. Whatever the cause, it showed the limits of voluntary acreage controls. With the annual carryover already running at almost 10 million bales, the 1933 crop resulted in a reduction of only about 1.5 million bales in cotton stocks. The 1933 plow-up did dramatically increase the income of cotton growers, more than doubling their income from the 1932 crop.

While the Cotton South breathed a sigh of relief at the short-term increase in cotton prices, the AAA cotton program produced repercussions that were as far-reaching as they were unexpected. When the Census Bureau took the 1935 census of agriculture, officials found an extraordinary change that apparently stemmed from the reduction in cotton acreage. For the first time since the Civil War, the percentage of farm tenants in the Cotton South had declined. Between 1930 and 1935, tenants as a percentage of farm operators dropped from 55.5 percent to 53.3 percent. The absolute number of tenants had actually increased by 40,692, but the number of farm operators had increased over four times as fast, dropping the percentage. Sharecroppers experienced an absolute decline of 60,022, or 7.7 percent (table 4.3).[21]

Similar changes extended to the Mississippi River Delta states. The most significant decline for tenants occurred in Mississippi, where their numbers dropped by 8,053, or 3.6 percent. But in Arkansas and Louisiana the change in the number of tenants was negligible. In Arkansas, the absolute number of tenants fell less than 1,000 in this five-year period, while in Louisiana the number increased slightly. Only in Arkansas among these states did the number of sharecroppers decline, dropping 9,791, or 13 percent.[22]

The decrease in the number of sharecroppers resulted in part from the

TABLE 4.3. Tenants and Sharecroppers in Cotton South and Arkansas, Louisiana, and Mississippi, 1930–1935

	1930	1935	Increase or Decrease	Percentage Change
Cotton South				
All Tenants	1,790,783	1,831,475	40,692	2.3
Sharecroppers	776,278	716,256	-60,022	-7.7
All Tenants				
Arkansas	152,691	151,759	-932	-0.6
Louisiana	107,551	108,377	826	0.8
Mississippi	225,617	217,564	-8,053	-3.6
Sharecroppers				
Arkansas	75,214	65,423	-9,791	-13.0
Louisiana	49,428	50,219	791	1.6
Mississippi	135,293	136,913	1,620	1.2

Source: Farm Tenancy: Report of the President's Committee (Washington, D.C.: GPO, 1937), 96–99.

AAA cotton program. When planters reduced cotton acreage, they obviously needed fewer sharecroppers. The exact number of families displaced by cotton acreage reductions can never be known. There is no way to make a comparison of the AAA's impact on labor between 1933 and 1934. But contemporary observers reported that displacements were relatively modest. In 1935 Fred C. Frey and T. Lynn Smith, two rural sociologists, used data from a sample of southern counties to estimate the AAA's impact on poor farmers. They found that sharecroppers decreased by 11.6 percent over this five-year period. The absolute number of sharecroppers within their sample counties declined by 36,217.[23] According to their data, Arkansas lost 4,806 sharecroppers, or 11 percent, near the regional average. The change in the number of tenants as opposed to the number of sharecroppers was relatively insignificant. Louisiana and Mississippi reversed this pattern with the loss of tenants larger than the change in the number of sharecroppers.[24]

Another contemporary scholar, Henry I. Richards, an economist with the Brookings Institution, failed to "substantiate the alarmist statements which have been widely circulated that a great number of tenants and croppers have been displaced or their tenure status reduced" as a result of the AAA cotton program. While some displacement had occurred, it was not substantial. He found, as expected, that landlords did receive most of the increase in income from government payments for taking land out of production.[25]

Whatever the precise impact of cotton reduction on labor, the AAA cannot be blamed for all changes in tenure statuses between 1930 and 1935. Economist Gavin Wright observed that considerable displacement occurred during the crisis period between 1930 and 1932.[26] Contemporary studies pointed to 1932 as the peak year for tenant displacement.[27] In other words the turmoil of the early depression as well as the free-fall in the cotton market as it plunged to five and a half cents per pound very likely had a larger impact on southern tenants than did the AAA. The New Deal's early relief agency, the Federal Emergency Relief Administration (FERA), may have even contributed to the loss of tenants by offering them jobs outside of agriculture.[28]

The most controversial aspect of the AAA quickly became its impact on the South's tenants and sharecroppers.[29] As critics of the AAA have tirelessly pointed out from the 1930s until the 1960s, the New Deal cotton program was devised by large plantation interests without regard for the region's poorest farmers, many of whom were black.[30] The AAA director of finance was Oscar Johnston, head of the Delta and Pine Land Company at Scott, Mississippi, reputedly the world's largest cotton plantation.[31] Yet these critics typically failed to mention that in the formulation of its program, the AAA had to face the fact that landlords controlled the land. Indeed, a contract favorable to them was the price paid for their cooperation, which was needed for a large sign-up. Landlords claimed they had been hurt by the depression, since their taxes and interest rates remained high in relation to current income. In addition, they argued, they had "carried" their tenants when the tenants' share of the crop was less than the "furnish" advanced to them.[32]

The AAA dealt with landlords, not tenants. Payments for taking land out of production went to landowners, and they withheld their tenants' share, applying the amount to their debts. Moreover, reduced cotton acreage meant reduced labor requirements. As a result many planters evicted tenants whom they no longer needed because they had fewer acres growing cotton. In addition they planted substitute crops—usually corn or legumes—that required minimal labor, still further reducing labor needs.

As the AAA focused the nation's concern on the displacement of sharecroppers, it was unexpectedly sharecroppers themselves who took steps to draw attention to their plight. In the summer of 1934 a group of sharecroppers, black and white, met near Tyronza, Poinsett County, Arkansas, to form a union in protest against evictions and in hope of getting their share of benefit payments. Under the leadership of H. L. Mitchell and Henry Clay East, two local businessmen, the Southern Tenant Farmers Union (STFU) emitted a "cry from the cotton."[33] From across the nation sympathizers joined the union's cause, assisting it with money and other resources. While union leaders argued that poor farmers should receive their part of government checks, their strongest protest was against evictions in a time when jobs were scarce. Landlords, the union argued, should keep not only the same number of tenants but also the same individual tenants despite acreage reductions; and the union marshaled an attack on the AAA both in the national press and in filing individual complaints with the AAA.

AAA officials denied that the cotton program had caused massive displacement of tenant families. For their part, they argued that southern tenancy had always featured high turnover rates as well as poverty. To require landlords to keep the same tenants would be an extraordinary requirement not demanded of any other employer. Indeed, the South should have applauded any reduction in the number of poor sharecroppers.

As the controversy shook his administration, President Roosevelt advised patience and sought to calm critics of the AAA; he needed the votes of southern congressmen to enact New Deal legislation.[34] Senate Majority Leader Joseph T. Robinson of Arkansas and Sen. Pat Harrison of Mississippi were both supporters of the AAA. Some New Dealers believed, though they did not express the view publicly, that agriculture was oversupplied with labor, and surplus labor should be forced out of farming in order to improve the living standard of those families who remained.[35]

In its first two years the AAA investigated more than three thousand complaints between tenants and landlords, finding that most disputes were due to misunderstandings, but adjusted almost one thousand contracts and canceled thirty-eight.[36] From all over the Cotton Belt, tenants claimed that they had been displaced, that their tenure status had been reduced, or that landlords were withholding benefit payments. Many share tenants complained that they had not been allowed to sign a contract along with their landlord. On average the agency received only three or four complaints per county, but about 25 percent of the total complaints came from the northeast corner of Arkansas, where the STFU was strongest.

Curiously the 1935 agricultural census reported that the number of farms in this area had actually grown more than 10 percent since 1930. But the fertile bottomland of the region, which was late in opening to cultivation, had lured large numbers of new migrants, including numerous white families from the highland areas of Arkansas and from nearby states. Thus the supply of tenants had increased, and the STFU derived in part from this unique situation.[37]

The evictees were unfortunate victims of social and economic change. They fell a rung down the agricultural ladder, often becoming wage laborers for the same landlord. Many presumably went on relief rolls but still remained in the area and were available for work at chopping and picking time. This pattern was consistent with economist Richard Day's view that migration was a two-stage process, with migrants leaving the farm but not the area. In the second stage, they joined the migration from farm to city, leaving their home state to compete with the urban unemployed for jobs.[38]

As a result of the AAA and the STFU, the public discovered sharecropping as a social problem in newspaper and magazine reports from the rural South and in the works of writers like Erskine Caldwell, John Steinbeck, James Agee, and Walker Evans.[39] The Farm Security Administration's documentary photographs preserved the stark images of southern poverty—images of broken-down men, gaunt women, and pitiful barefoot children staring hauntingly into government cameras.[40]

This body of work brought together the themes of rural poverty, mechanization, and migration. The popular fear of technological monsters that displaced families and cast them adrift from their cultural heritage had a powerful appeal. From the Luddites of early-nineteenth-century Britain to modern Luddites like Kirkpatrick Sale, who once used a sledgehammer to smash a computer before an admiring audience, technology has been a scapegoat for unemployment.[41] In the early depression *technocracy* was a term that encapsulated the fear of technology and the unemployment it was assumed to create.

For depression America, the southern sharecropper emerged as a sympathetic figure who was widely depicted as the victim of the increasing use of tractors. Across the South, it was presumed, migration occurred as people were evicted from the land and replaced by tractors. In *Land of the Free* (1938), Archibald MacLeish first used the phrase "tractored off." In the late 1930s, Dorothea Lange and Paul Taylor traveled throughout Texas and California and photographed scenes of abandoned houses with cotton rows plowed right up to the front door. They recorded the words of a black farmworker in Greenville, Mississippi: "Tractors are against the black man. Every time you kill a mule you kill a black man. You've heard about the machine picker? That's against the black man too."[42] The image of evil tractors was also found in John Steinbeck's *The Grapes of Wrath,* which chronicled the story of the Joads and their trek west after they lost their Oklahoma farm. The story hit on all the themes of the era: drought, tenancy, migration, and agricultural mechanization. Steinbeck depicted drought and the tractor as the twin forces that were pushing people from the land. In a well-known passage, he wrote:

> And at last the owner men came to the point. The tenant system won't work any more. One man on a tractor can take the place of twelve or fourteen families. Pay him a wage and take all the crop. We have to do it. . . .
> The tenant men looked up alarmed. But what'll happen to us? How'll we eat? You'll have to get off the land. The plow'll go through the dooryard. . . .
> The tractors came over the roads and into the fields, great crawlers moving like insects. . . . Snub-nosed monsters, raising the dust . . . across the country, through fences, through dooryards, in and out of gullies in straight lines. . . .[43]

As sharecroppers became a cause célèbre, the movement followed the usual steps that sociologists identify in the development of social movements. First, sharecroppers found themselves in the agitation stage as they sought to make their case against the AAA in national publications. With the help of speakers like Norman Thomas, the socialist presidential candidate, croppers influenced northern opinion and garnered financial backers. They even enjoyed the support of a cadre of officials within the AAA itself. This group consisted of lawyers with urban, not rural, backgrounds who sought to protect the rights of landless farmers. When Congress passed and President Roosevelt signed the Bankhead-Jones Farm Tenant Act of 1937, the movement had clearly reached the legitimization stage as federal authorities tacitly acknowledged the union's cause.[44] Yet the STFU never successfully operated as a union; and as government programs co-opted its role as spokesman for the rural poor, the union's influence waned.

The AAA created a storm of controversy with its cotton program, and both tenants and landlords had a right to expect the government to compensate them fairly for property that was destroyed. Yet the agency faced no easy task in throwing together a vast organization in a few weeks and persuading over a million cotton farmers to sign contracts agreeing to limit their production of cotton—something that had never before been accomplished. The legal morass was an awesome challenge in itself since the legal status of tenants varied from state to state, with many states viewing tenants not as persons with a vested interest in the land and the crop, but merely as workers who were paid a share of the crop.[45] As a result the agency's greatest challenge was to solve the problem of how to distribute benefits among landlords, tenants, and possibly creditors who may have had an interest in the cotton growing on land taken out of production.

The 1933 contract left the landlord with the task of dividing the benefit payment among the interested parties in proportion to their interest in the crop. In reality, however, the contract contained no provision that tenants must receive any part of benefit checks. For local enforcement or monitoring, the AAA relied on county agents, an existing network of officials associated with the state extension services, and on local committees that were dominated by landlords.[46] The government initially mailed benefit checks to landlords, who decided how to distribute the money to their tenants. Whether to give them cash, to credit their tenants' account, or to give them nothing was the landlord's call. Most tenants received only whatever the landlord chose to give them.[47]

The 1934–35 contract, drafted without the emergency of the previous agreement, was if anything more biased in favor of landlords than the original contract. During these two years the secretary of agriculture agreed to make two kinds of benefit payments, rental payments and parity payments; but in both, according to a contemporary observer, "the landlord has everything to gain and the cropper everything to lose."[48] The administration of the program again relied on committees of local farmers.

Since complaints about cheating and evictions by landlords were widespread, the "discovery" of the southern sharecroppers and rural poverty as social problems continued to make news, and several government investigations were conducted. Exposés made good reading and enforced the image of the benighted South. Though sharecropping existed across the Cotton South from the Carolinas to Texas, the Southern Tenant Farmers Union attracted enough attention to make it appear that the problem focused on Arkansas. In Washington, the debate over the AAA and sharecropping reached a crisis point. In early 1935 Jerome Frank and other liberal lawyers within the AAA who had opposed the evictions of tenants lost their jobs in a "purge" ordered by Chester Davis, head of the agency.[49]

The 1934 and 1935 program, however, included an effort to deal with landlords who had dismissed a portion of their tenants. The contract contained a clause providing that producers shall

endeavor in good faith to bring about the reduction of acreage contemplated in this contract in such manner as to cause the least possible amount of labor, economic, and social disturbance, and to this end, insofar as possible, he shall effect the acreage reduction as nearly ratably as practicable among tenants on his farm; shall, insofar as possible, maintain on this farm the normal number of tenants and other employees. . . . [50]

This section was a study in hedging, qualification, and weasel words: "endeavor in good faith," "insofar as possible," "as ratably as practicable among his tenants." These provisions, though ridiculed by historians, represented a change in policy with important repercussions.

While the AAA must accept a degree of culpability in dealing with southern tenants, the agency's critics have not acknowledged that for the rest of the decade federal regulations enlarged the rights of tenants under acreage reduction contracts and increased their share of benefit payments. Under the Soil Conservation and Domestic Allotment Act of 1938, tenants received not only a larger share of benefits, but also their checks were mailed directly to them, while the landlord's share fell steadily.[51] What made this pro-tenant policy important was that it gave landlords an economic incentive to use more wage labor.

The Brave New World of Wage Labor

While the question of labor displacement has attracted the attention of most historians, the most important question concerning the AAA cotton program was how it created structural changes in the South's plantation economy. The cotton program was not intended to solve the social problems of the South, much less to revolutionize its social relations. Yet it did unleash unintended forces for social change, which produced revolutionary effects. The AAA did more than reduce the number of tenant farmers, which was positive in itself. It also initiated a redistribution among labor statuses, particularly sharecroppers and wage laborers, the lowest rungs on the agricultural ladder. The reduction in the number of sharecroppers offered farmers greater flexibility that they used to mechanize their operations.

The AAA assumed that acreage reductions would be shared proportionately by landlords and tenants alike. But an equitable distribution was never remotely possible. Landlords saw that their best option was to reduce their tenant acreage but to report it (or "reassign" it to be tactful) as coming from their own land, which they typically operated with wage labor. They reduced their tenant acres because the program's incentives gave them smaller benefit payments if they assigned acreage to tenants and croppers.[52]

Landlords would have been foolish not to switch to wage labor. For

TABLE 4.4. AAA Benefit Payments per Acre, by Labor Status, 1933–1939 (in Dollars)

| Landlord's Amount from | ON AN ACRE YIELDING 200 POUNDS LINT IN A YEAR | | | | | | |
	1933	1934	1935	1936	1937	1938	1939
Cash tenant	$0.00	$0.00	$0.00	$0.00	$0.00	$0.00	$0.00
Managing tenant	3.00	6.50	4.13	5.25	5.75	3.80	3.65
Share tenant	3.00	12.50	7.63	5.25	5.75	3.80	3.65
Sharecropper	6.00	13.00	8.25	8.00	8.75	7.60	7.30
Wage worker	12.00	14.00	9.50	11.00	12.00	15.20	14.60

| Landlord's Amount from | ON AN ACRE YIELDING 350 POUNDS LINT IN A YEAR | | | | | | |
	1933	1934	1935	1936	1937	1938	1939
Cash tenant	$0.00	$0.00	$0.00	$0.00	$0.00	$0.00	$0.00
Managing tenant	5.25	11.38	6.22	9.00	9.87	6.46	6.39
Share tenant	5.25	21.88	13.34	9.00	9.87	6.46	6.39
Sharecropper	10.50	22.75	14.44	13.63	14.94	12.92	9.77
Wage worker	21.00	24.50	16.63	16.63	20.25	25.85	25.55

Source: Warren C. Whatley, "Labor for the Picking: The New Deal in the South," *Journal of Economic History* 43 (December 1983): 915.

example, on land yielding 200 pounds per acre, a landlord received twelve dollars in benefit payments if he used a wage worker, but only half that amount per acre on land that he rented to a sharecropper (table 4.4). The amount varied from year to year, but from 1933 to 1939 it was clear to landlords that their advantage lay in using more wage labor than sharecropped labor. For land yielding 350 pounds per acre, the advantage was ever greater in most years.

The AAA provided a powerful, if not irresistible, incentive for landowners to reduce their tenant acreage and expand their use of wage labor, since they had to share benefit payments with tenants but not with wage labor. Indeed, if they operated acres using wage labor, they pocketed the entire payment. The switch to wage labor had other benefits as well. The price of labor fell to a low level during the depression and remained low, a fact that amounted to another wage labor incentive for planters. Many of the tenants who were displaced remained in the region and performed farmwork as wage laborers at times of peak-labor demand.[53] Besides taking the full government payment for acreage reduction, planters had no obligation to "furnish" wage labor, who presumably relied on federal agencies for relief when not working. Finally, they found that land farmed by wage labor produced more cotton than land worked by share-croppers.[54]

During the 1930s the average wage rates for picking 100 pounds of seed cotton ranged from 40 cents to 75 cents in Arkansas (table 4.5). A rate of 75 cents per hundredweight meant a cost of $11.25 in total picking cost per bale (assuming 1,500 pounds of seed cotton equaled one 500-pound bale of lint cotton). With the price of cotton at 12.36 cents (table 4.1), a bale was worth only $61.80. Farmers often argued that picking costs should be no more than 25 percent of the value of the cotton. In this case, however, it was only 18.2 percent of the value of a bale.

The transition from tenancy to wage labor was the most important cotton development of the 1930s. By favoring tenants the AAA inadvertently magnified the trend toward wage labor that it had initiated in 1933. During the late

TABLE 4.5. Average Wage Rates for Handpicking 100 Pounds of Seed Cotton, 1929–1950

	Arkansas	Louisiana	Mississippi
1929	$1.06	$1.01	$1.08
1930	.56	.61	.56
1931	.40	.41	.39
1932	.44	.39	.40
1933	.52	.48	.49
1934	.60	.55	.55
1935	.55	.55	.55
1936	.75	.65	.75
1937	.70	.70	.80
1938	.60	.55	.55
1939	.60	.55	.60
1940	.65	.55	.57

Source: U.S. Department of Agriculture, Economic Research Service, *Statistics on Cotton and Related Data, 1920–1973,* Statistical Bulletin No. 535 (Washington, D.C.: GPO, 1974), table 70, p. 86.

1930s the Cotton South witnessed a decline in tenancy and the expansion of wage labor. This trend was expected to reverse when the economy improved, but it did not reverse at all until World War II, when labor shortages motivated farms to return to sharecropping as planters sought to ensure their labor supply.[55]

As a result of New Deal agricultural policies plantations took the first steps away from decentralized tenant farms and toward large-scale, consolidated, mechanized, and wage labor–dependent operations. Planters took advantage of federal programs to increase their income, and at the same time these programs enabled them to cut costs, particularly labor costs.

The decline of tenancy and the expansion of day labor was reported in many contemporary studies. J. A. Baker and J. G. McNeely studied Arkansas cotton farms between 1930 and 1935 and found a decline overall in tenancy. In the Delta the number of sharecroppers decreased by 12 percent. "The reduction in cotton acreage probably decreased the number of families needed for cotton production," they noted. "The burden of furnishing food, clothing, and supplies to a large number of families, during the economic depression, was too great for many landlords who were unable to obtain credit. Under these conditions, it was easier to operate plantations with wage hands, who when not employed on the farm, might go on relief."[56]

In a follow-up study McNeely and Glenn T. Barton found that between 1932 and 1938 the trend was away from both sharecroppers and share renters to wage laborers. The increase in wage hands paralleled both a drop in total labor requirements—since the crop most often substituted for cotton was corn, requiring substantially less labor than cotton—and an increase in the use of tractors. Sharecroppers who remained saw their cotton allotment decline from fifteen to ten acres per family, and share-renters from twenty-five to twelve acres. To make up the difference, planters relied increasingly on wage labor.[57]

In the 1930s and 1940s planters used sharecroppers when the labor supply was tight or uncertain, while favoring wage laborers when labor was oversupplied and cheap. If labor were a buyers' market, sharecropping agreements committed people to work on a farm all year, while wage workers offered landowners maximum options in a sellers' market.[58]

On the STFU's home ground in northeast Arkansas, planters and workers fought over the status of labor. As many plantations moved to wage labor and released their tenant families, union members protested. They wanted independent land ownership; but since that was unattainable, they preferred sharecropping to wage labor. Sharecroppers earned more money than did laborers, and sharecropping did provide for some independence, at least symbolically, that wage laborers did not have. Sharecroppers did not work in gangs and they lived in plantation houses rent free, possibly with their own gardens. The move to wage labor had the curious effect of emphasizing the positive points of sharecropping, a development usually overlooked by urban reformers. In northeast Arkansas, when planters began to switch to wage labor it was former sharecroppers who voiced the loudest complaints.[59]

Mississippi experienced a similar transition.[60] In the Yazoo-Mississippi Delta plantation owners struggled with low prices and attempted to reduce production costs. Wage laborers and tractors became increasingly common. As the amount of land operated by wage labor increased, the proportion of land that was sharecropped declined. But the risk of not having an adequate supply of labor unavailable during hoeing and picking seasons limited the widespread use of wage labor and large-scale machinery. Owners anticipated that the perfection of mechanical cotton harvesters would remove this obstacle. The move to wage labor and tractors encountered resistance from workers who still preferred working on shares.[61]

While the plight of sharecroppers was emotionally appealing for reform-ers, the AAA cotton program that reduced their numbers, intentionally or not, was the most effective approach to the problem of poverty in southern agri-culture. Since the South was already overpopulated, it needed fewer farmers, not more. The displacement of tenants may have been cruel, even tragic, but the South had to take population reductions any way it could get them. Clearly, agencies like the Farm Security Administration (FSA) were on the wrong track with their effort to nurture the efforts of small farmers. Even on the most successful FSA projects, the farm units were too small to be eco-nomically viable. With the advent of tractors in the 1930s, leading agricultural experts realized that future cotton farms would be mechanized and therefore larger.

The most important consequence of the AAA was the unexpected struc-tural changes its program created in southern agriculture. Lifting the dead hand of the region's past, the shift away from sharecropping paved the way for mechanization by eliminating small, inefficient farm units which restricted the amount of land suitable for mechanization. The increase in wage labor implied the consolidation of small units and the adoption of tractors, the first step toward the mechanization of southern cotton farming.

Though tractors were already widely used in the Midwest, the South as usual trailed in mechanization. Between 1930 and 1940, southern farmers rushed to catch up (table 4.6). The number of tractors per thousand acres increased an average of 113 percent in plantation counties and even 65 percent in non-plantation counties. In the Mississippi River Delta, tractors increased by 204 percent, rising from 0.51 per thousand to 1.55 per thousand during the decade. Few southern states showed a decrease even in their non-plantation counties.

In summary, the AAA provided the cotton farmer with a strong incentive to move his operation from tenancy to wage labor. This reorganization was possible only through the use of tractors. The forces of social and economic change began to converge. As Gavin Wright put it, "mechanization in the South was *induced* by economic incentives, and in the 1930s, these incentives were largely created by government programs."[62] Wright, however, questioned the notion of southern planters using AAA benefit checks as down payments on tractors. The lack of cash or credit was not the problem, Wright argued. The technology for mechanizing the preharvest operations had been available

TABLE 4.6. Tractors per 1,000 Acres Harvested, 1930–1940

| | NON-PLANTATION COUNTIES | | | PLANTATION COUNTIES | | |
	1930	1940	Percentage Change	1930	1940	Percentage Change
South	.52	.86	65	.40	.85	113
Southeast[a]	.79	.88	11	.39	.69	77
Delta[b]	.36	.51	42	.51	1.55	204
Alabama	.70	.60	-14	.27	.45	67
Arkansas	.28	.40	43	.46	1.30	183
Georgia	.43	1.02	137	.35	.87	149
Louisiana	.39	.94	141	.43	2.09	386
Mississippi	.54	.46	-15	.55	1.39	153
North Carolina	1.40	.96	-31	1.27	1.11	-13
South Carolina	.74	1.02	38	.58	.86	48
Tennessee	.70	1.34	91	.53	1.90	258
Texas	.88	2.54	189	1.16	1.36	17

[a] Counties in North Carolina, South Carolina, Georgia, and Alabama.

[b] Counties in Arkansas, Louisiana, and Mississippi.

Source: Gavin Wright, *Old South, New South: Revolutions in the Southern Economy since the Civil War* (New York: Basic Books, 1986), 234.

since 1930, but a cheap, plentiful supply of labor as a result of the depression meant that machines were not needed. Hand labor was just cheaper than machine labor. As long as the harvest remained unmechanizable, planters relied on sharecroppers as their guarantee of sufficient harvest labor. But they moved away from tenancy in the 1930s because AAA programs offered incentives to consolidate their operations and operate with tractors and wage labor. Growers found that wage laborers produced more cotton than did sharecroppers. By the mid-1930s planters used more off-plantation labor to pick cotton, and they often assigned their croppers too few acres to ensure a minimal livelihood, forcing them also to supplement their income as wage laborers.

At the end of the 1930s many observers still did not sense that fundamental changes had occurred in southern agriculture. They could not see that the STFU was unjustly criticized as a radical organization; indeed, it was the AAA and southern planters who were sponsoring revolution in the South.

The 1930s ended without solving cotton's basic problems, and cotton farmers continued to puzzle over their situation. The annual carryover was higher than ever. Cotton prices rose to more than twelve cents but fell to less than ten cents by 1937, and the price of labor showed signs of increasing. American cotton was steadily losing market share to foreign cotton. What cotton farmers needed was a dramatic increase in their efficiency. This meant larger operating units and more machinery, which would reduce their man-hour requirement per acre and enable them to produce cotton more cheaply while still making a profit in a low market. Fortunately, the key piece of the puzzle seemed ready to fall into place—the mechanical cotton picker.

Chapter 5

Impending Revolution: John Rust and Reactions to His Machine

As early as 1932 the mechanical cotton picker evoked the worry that continued throughout the decade: The United States was in a major depression with thousands of people unemployed. The invention of a mechanical picker would have the effect of putting additional hundreds of thousands of people out of work. Additionally, the South was a poor and backward region; and its poorest people—those at the bottom of the agricultural ladder in the cotton fields, the lowly sharecroppers and tenant farmers—were the ones most vulnerable to the impact of cotton mechanization. Dispossessed of their pathetic livelihoods, these jobless masses would then pour into northern cities in a vain search for jobs.[1]

By 1935 the widespread use of mechanical cotton pickers seemed both inevitable and imminent, as did the further collapse of the South's economy. Another worry, sometimes unstated, was not only that a whole new class of unemployed people would be released to invade northern cities, but that they were unemployed blacks.

The fear of social upheaval was a specific reaction to the Rust cotton picker. In May 1935 John and Mack Rust happily showed off their machine at the National Cotton Show in Memphis and announced that it was ready for production. They predicted drastic and sudden readjustments in cotton farming. "The sharecropper system of the Old South," John Rust said flatly, "will have to be abandoned. The wheat industry could not have progressed to its present proportions with the use of the hand sickle." Operating at the rate of an acre each hour, the Rust picker did the work of between fifty to one hundred men, reducing labor needs by 75 percent. John and Mack Rust expected to put the machine on the market within a year.[2]

When the Rust brothers moved to Memphis in 1935, they entered an exciting period in which their work appeared to enter its final and most successful stage. In 1934 tests in Arkansas, the Rust machine gathered in seven and a half hours as much cotton as a diligent handpicker gathered in an eleven-week season. The Rust brothers built a new model called the Universal Pull-Model, which they demonstrated in late 1935. They estimated its operating cost at ninety-eight cents per acre of cotton. According to *Time* magazine, planters believed they could grow cotton at a profit with such a machine even if the price of cotton dropped below five cents per pound.[3]

In February 1936 the Rust brothers secured a Tennessee charter for the Rust Cotton Picker Company, successor to the Southern Harvester Company. For the next several months, they worked feverishly in a small shop on the south side of Memphis to prepare a demonstration model for a new series of tests.[4] They intended to put the Rust cotton picker on display as the latest debutante in the Cotton South. That fall, they arranged for the toughest kind of audience—a crowd of skeptical cotton men in Mississippi.

On Monday, August 31, 1936, at the start of the picking season, a crowd of planters, ginners, and reporters gathered on the Delta Experiment Station at Stoneville, Mississippi, to see the Rust brothers' machine in action. Their white shirts and straw hats shimmered under the bright, hot sun. The attention focused on this event underscored both the fear and hope that the Rust machine represented.[5]

All day Mack Rust drove a tractor pulling the picker up and down the dusty cotton rows as a steady stream of white staple spewed into a hopper. The picker straddled row after row and drew the plants into an inverted trough, where 1,300 moistened spindles rotated on a drum, extracting the cotton fiber from its bolls when it adhered to the spindles. A set of steel teeth pulled the staple off the spindles in the rear of the machine and a fan sucked it through a funnel-shaped pipe into the hopper.[6] Observers crowded around and fingered the mechanically picked cotton and wondered why so simple an idea had not been discovered long ago. Proud of his work, Mack Rust claimed that their machine would pick a bale of cotton in about an hour at a cost of about one dollar per acre.[7]

The reactions to the demonstration were mixed. Critics of the machine's operation said it knocked too much cotton to the ground and accumulated too much trash (bits of leaves and stems) in the staple it picked. The trash lowered the grade and, of course, the price. Some observers estimated the amount of cotton that was left on the ground as high as 33 percent, but opinion varied widely. White cotton lying on the ground stood out so vividly that the amount was easily overestimated, as other observers pointed out. But some bolls were missed, and a second pass was required to do a thorough job of picking.

W. H. Hutchins, who owned a 1,400-acre plantation near Greenville, Mississippi, saw the machine as "the salvation of the farmers." "It is a greater success than I had expected," he said. "We won't have to beg for labor to help pick cotton. No man can pick all the cotton he grows, and with the machine he won't have to hire day labor."

The experts agreed that the Rust machine was not perfected, but its implications were clear. Oscar Johnston, the manager of the huge Delta and Pine Land Company at Scott, Mississippi, predicted: "It is the death knell for family size farms and for tenants, if successful. The machine presents a genuine, serious economic problem greater than any labor saving device I have seen. It will develop large holdings and eliminate the small farmer." Small farmers who grew only four or five bales each season had too little acreage to afford the picker.[8]

A. F. Toler, Johnston's business manager, said frankly, "I hope it won't work, because it would upset our present system and Southern agriculture would be in a turmoil in the future." He noted the cotton picker still could not chop cotton in the summer. "We've got to keep labor to do that work." W. E. Ayres, superintendent of the Delta Experiment Station, commented that the Rusts "have the right idea—it isn't a finished machine, but they are on the right track."[9]

Wallace A. Clemmons was vice president of the Rust Cotton Picker Company. He claimed the company would "possibly build 500 machines this year" and have them ready for operation in fall of 1937. He planned to lease the machine on a no-cost basis of about $2,000, to be paid over three years. The picker would pay for itself in two seasons, he claimed.

However imperfectly the Rust machine functioned, it sent a shock wave through the country. The reality of a practical machine that would actually pick cotton loomed over the South. The reactions were extreme in some cases. In Mississippi, the *Jackson Daily News* editorialized:

> The machine is said to be quite practical, works well, and will do the work of at least a dozen hand pickers.
>
> That being true, it should be driven right out of the cotton fields and *sunk into the Mississippi river,* together with its plans and specifications.
>
> Nothing could be more devastating to labor conditions in the South than a cotton-picking machine. Imagine, if you can, 500,000 negroes in Mississippi

just now lolling around on cabin galleries or loafing on the streets of the cities and towns while machines are picking cotton.[10]

The racial implications of the demise of tenancy always lurked in the background of all fears of the mechanical picker's impact.

Congressman E. H. Crump, Democratic National Committeeman and the political boss of Memphis, urged legislation to ban the cotton-picking machine from Tennessee.[11] But more typical was Arkansas Gov. Carl E. Bailey, who told a visiting reporter in 1937:

> I don't know what the mechanical cotton pickers are going to do. But they have already been built. They function now, it is true, with indifferent efficiency. But that they function at all is a warning that they will be perfected. And when that is done, they will displace thousands of individuals in the cotton belt, thus creating suddenly the most perplexing social and economic problem. I'm afraid of the meaning of the picker; but we might as well face it. . . . I'm scared of the human consequences.[12]

Everyone was scared of the human consequences of mechanized cotton farming.

As the popular press explored the implications of the Rust machine, two distinct views emerged. The first embodied an alarmist view of a future featuring a range of evils from social and economic upheaval to simple catastrophe. The entire political and social structure of the South—the world of hand labor and sharecropping—faced imminent upheaval.[13] With unemployment already running high in the depression, the commercial use of the Rust machine would immediately throw additional millions of people out of work.[14]

The whole Cotton South shuddered at the Rust machine. Using the popular term *technocracy,* many people already blamed technology for the depression itself.[15] As everyone who saw the 1931 classic movie knew, Frankenstein's monster turned on his creator and destroyed him. The lesson for many people was that unemployment was the result of labor-saving machinery.[16]

The second view, most often found in scientific journals and agricultural publications, played down the prospect for drastic change by arguing that mechanization would be a long, slow process.[17] Some experts initially voiced alarm, but in time the sense of crisis passed. Even if the picker did work, according to many professionals it would not eliminate all need for hand labor. Chopping weeds still had to be done by hand. In a wild overestimate one writer claimed that farmers would need 10,000 machines to pick a mere 10 percent of South's cotton crop.[18] Still another argued that the South really did not need a cotton picker, because farmers needed labor on their farms for a multitude of tasks; and even if they purchased a cotton picker, it still would not be possible to reduce the amount of hand labor needed. Small farmers could not afford such a machine, nor did they need it because the family picked its own cotton.[19]

Upheaval, Revolution, and Chaos

The alarmist view was the first to appear. In 1932 the U.S. Labor Department announced that the Texas A & M Agricultural Experiment Station had developed a cotton stripper that could accomplish in three hours what it normally took a man seventy-seven hours to do.[20] In response the *Christian Century* warned that "the displacement of hand labor is going to mean doing away with the means of livelihood of multiplied thousands, perhaps millions, of Negroes." They will have nowhere to turn. "The prospect," the magazine predicted, "is that with a general introduction of a cotton picking machine, the South will be overrun with a shifting, irresponsible army of Negro drifters, who will gradually find their way into the north in far greater numbers than at any time in the past. There they are likely to disrupt entirely the market for common labor." Readers were reminded that the cotton industry's previous invention, Eli Whitney's cotton gin, had laid the foundation for the Civil War.[21]

In 1935, Charles Johnson, Edwin Embree, and W. W. Alexander attacked the AAA in a little book called *The Collapse of Cotton Tenancy*. While they were critical of the AAA for displacing southern tenants and sharecroppers, the mechanical cotton picker loomed as a more ominous threat. They issued this warning:

> There is impending a violent revolution in cotton production as a result of the development of the mechanical cotton picker. Cotton has awaited this event with the eagerness that it awaited the development of the gin. When it comes it will automatically release hundreds of thousands of cotton workers particularly in the Southeast, creating a new range of social problems. Within the past two years . . . there has been tried out, at the Delta Experiment Station in Mississippi, a mechanical cotton picker capable of doing in seven and a half hours, the work of three and a half months of a good hand picker. It is not expected that sentiment or public policy can prevent its use on the grounds that it will displace workers. This is the course of machinery in every field.[22]

The Rust demonstration in 1936 alarmed economist Broadus Mitchell about the revolutionizing potential of the cotton picker. "It is going to make unemployment on a scale unheard of before; it will render the millions of bales of stored cotton worth far less than even at present; it will break banks and batter insurance companies holding farm mortgages," he predicted. What was happening in Rust's little machine shop, Mitchell said, was as important as what happened in the "basement of the Nathaniel Greene plantation house where Eli Whitney worked with rollers and wires."[23]

By 1936 the *Reader's Guide to Periodical Literature,* an index to popular magazines, recorded an escalation of articles speculating about the "sociological" implications of cotton mechanization. While engineers at International Harvester were also working on their own picker, they avoided publicity; and Rust's name became primarily associated with the prospect, good and bad, of mechanizing cotton harvesting.[24]

In early 1935 John Rust received his first national publicity because, he believed, of an article published in the *American Mercury.*[25] In a foreboding essay entitled "The Revolution in Cotton," Oliver Carlson reviewed the changes in the Cotton South and announced that the South faced a "new era"—nothing less momentous than the end of the plantation system. He predicted that the mechanical cotton picker would dispense with the labor of four million tenant farmers and sharecroppers, make the mule and plow obsolete, and even cause the South's tumble-down shacks to disappear. Comparing the mechanical picker with the cotton gin invented 140 years earlier, Carlson stressed that cotton had changed little, while tractors, the gang-plows, and combines had become standard equipment in the grain-growing Midwest.[26]

Carlson presented a persuasive case for revolution. A good picker, he claimed, averaged not more than one hundred pounds per day. Allowing for sick days, weekends, and bad weather, he picked a bale a month or three bales per three-month season. For planters, picking was the problem. The main reason for contracting with tenants was to guarantee an ample supply of labor at picking time. Even if planters bought tractors and other implements, Carlson said, they had to keep as many tenants as before unless harvesting cotton was also mechanized.[27]

The Rust picker, Carlson predicted, marked the beginning of the end of the tenant farming mode of production. The great plantations will dispense with hundreds of thousands of hands. "The old mule and the primitive plow will have to take their place in the agricultural museum of the has-been," he said. "That tumble-down shack, which our tin-pan-alley boys sing so much about, and in which over 4,000,000 black and white tenants live today, can be torn down or burned up. Wage labor will replace tenantry, and from 75% to

85% of all labor now used in growing and gathering the cotton can be eliminated." In summary, the dispossessed would trek to cities on a scale unparalleled in American history. This new and frightening era would open for King Cotton, he predicted, within two years.[28]

Carlson's view was typical of early discussions of the Rust picker.[29] The Rust brothers were very much aware of the potential impact of a mechanical cotton picker on labor, and they agonized over the problem. In 1936 John Rust explained to *Time* magazine why he and Mack had become interested in inventing a cotton picker:

> We got down on our knees and picked cotton when we were boys. We decided then that we would try to invent a machine that would do this back-breaking toil. We have that machine. It will do the work of 50 to 100 men. Thrown on the market in the manner of past inventions, it would mean, in the share-cropped country, that 75% of the labor population would be thrown out of employment. We are not willing that this should happen. How can we prevent it?[30]

Rust's question was a plea. For *Time* the worry was "the plight of the great mass of black humanity in the South which makes its living picking cotton."[31]

In appealing for advice John Rust said,

> We want to enlist the aid of the state and federal governments to introduce this invention in a socialized manner through national co-operation. A part of the profits could be used to administer a social insurance scheme for the disabled and the aged, and a program of rural industrialization and diversification should be developed side by side with the use of the picker.
>
> We want the aid of the government and the international labor office of the League of Nations in controlling use of the invention abroad, as it is here, so that it will not be used for the national advantage of this or any other country.[32]

John Rust was never guilty of underestimating the potential impact of the mechanical picker.

He and Mack often faced questions about the social consequences of their invention. In their defense, they argued that since cotton workers were the poorest paid people in America, they would be doing them a favor when they freed them from "the back-breaking slavery of the cotton fields." They expected that the labor displacement would take place over a period of years, allowing workers time to find other jobs.

The Rusts explored noncommercial options: Could a cotton picker be distributed through cooperatives or unions of sharecroppers? They loaned one of their machines to the Sherwood Eddy cooperative farm at Hillhouse, Mississippi, and sold two machines to the Amtorg Trading Corporation for use in the Turkestan Republic of the Soviet Union.[33]

Their soul searching continued, however. They sought advice from labor union and cooperative leaders like Eddy as well as from the Department of Agriculture. Should they lease their invention instead of selling it? In so doing, lessees could be required to maintain a living wage and recognize collective bargaining. Should they release the machine under the auspices of the U.S. Department of Agriculture and allow the government to manage the resulting problems? Should they organize a foundation that would redistribute the profits for educational purposes and for the development of cooperative communities? Or should they simply throw their machine on the market like International Harvester would do?

In a statement entitled "The Cotton Picker and Unemployment," John and Mack Rust revealed their thinking. They believed they had solved the mystery of the mechanical cotton picker, and that the potential profit was immense. But they also believed that part of this profit should be used for rehabilitating the unemployed masses the picker created and for carrying on educational activities with a view to ending unemployment and poverty once and for all.

They continued in this idealistic vein:

> We will encourage the establishment of co-operative enterprises and such other organizations as tend to raise the economic and social status of the people as a whole. We are also considering the idea of leasing our machine only to those who will establish a system of fair wages and working conditions for their employees.

The influence of socialism stood out in their plans for an organization called the Rust Foundation:

> We believe that the final solution of these problems will come with the introduction of a planned economy of abundance, based on production for use, wherein at least our credit and basic industries are socialized. . . .
>
> It seems to us that some form of co-operative commonwealth is bound to supplant our decaying capitalist society, and it is our wish that this transition may take place with as little confusion and violence as possible. To this end we will co-operate with all progressive forces looking toward a new and better society, where new inventions will no longer take the workman's job but will shorten his hours of toil. In our country we already have the means for producing more than enough for all. We Americans have proved ourselves good mechanical engineers. Now let's turn our hands to social engineering and build a new soci-

ety that will give every man, woman and child a chance to enjoy life, liberty and the pursuit of happiness.[34]

After rejecting the leasing plan as unworkable, on August 24, 1938, John and Mack Rust announced the creation of the Rust Foundation as a Tennessee corporation. The purpose of the Rust Foundation was to "promote the well-being of mankind" and in particular to help rehabilitate the sharecroppers and farm laborers of the Cotton South.[35] Chartered as a nonprofit educational institution, the Rust Foundation pledged not to discriminate against any person because of race, creed, or color.

As a display of unselfish idealism, John and Mack Rust proposed an extraordinary plan to limit the income of foundation officers. The Rust Foundation would compensate no trustee, officer, or employee more than ten times that of the lowest paid employee. The Rust brothers meant this limitation to apply to themselves as well as to anyone else.

In limiting their own income they were giving away a potential fortune even before they made it. As John Rust stated, "We think the idea of limiting the spread in income to 10 to 1 would make an interesting experiment and we have decided to try it on ourselves."[36] The brothers acknowledged they wanted to enjoy a comfortable living as their reward, but not great personal fortunes. They considered imposing wage and hour requirements on users of the Rust machines, but in the end concentrated on administrating to themselves their view of social good.[37]

According to one analysis the Rusts could earn $8,320 a year and still pay the lowest-paid employee forty cents an hour, the minimum wage rate specified in the Fair Labor Standards Act of 1938. After World War II, when Rust's patents earned him large royalties and consulting fees, there was no more talk of limited income. Nonetheless, John Rust became a serious philanthropist, making large donations to colleges and universities to support the education of the sons and daughters of sharecroppers.

In 1938 the Rust brothers seemed satisfied that their picker was ready for quantity production. The Rust Cotton Picker Company, which was completely separate from the Rust Foundation, planned to manufacture and market the picker as soon as possible. Press reports indicated that six machines were being assembled for use in Arkansas, Louisiana, and Mississippi during the current season. Rust had developed two types of machines: The larger machine was a tandem picker mounted on a tractor. Having abandoned their leasing and cooperative plans, this machine would be offered for sale at $4,800. The other machine was a lower-priced single unit pull-model with a price of $995, including freight.[38] By 1939, the Rusts planned to build a manu-facturing plant in Memphis that was expected to produce fifty to one hundred pickers for the 1939 picking season. Rust hoped the factory would eventually have a capacity for one thousand machines a year. The immediate future seemed alive with cotton pickers.

In Rust's vision the Rust Cotton Picker Company would produce the machines that would revolutionize the cotton industry, and the Rust Foundation would help rehabilitate the displaced labor that resulted.[39] In this way they would abolish "'the last great field of hand labor and the greatest single source of child and woman labor in America,' and at the same time do no vio-lent harm to their friends and neighbors, the planters and the tenants."[40]

The press reaction to the Rust brothers' philanthropic plans was highly positive. Calling them "astonishing," the *Survey Graphic* said, "It may be that the Rusts will create a new South, as Eli Whitney created the old."[41] In the late 1930s the Rusts were increasingly compared with Whitney. Henry Goddard Leach, the editor of *Forum,* praised the Rust brothers for being "socially minded." He supported the idea that co-operatives could be formed to rent the Rust pickers and "offer the services of the machines to the cotton planters."[42] The *Christian Century* saw the Rust brothers in a modern dilemma, which "turns out to involve the question as to how they can exercise their own mag-nificent individual initiative without creating hell on earth among their fel-lows."[43] The magazine later noted that while the Rusts were members of no church, "Prominent clerics and religious workers seldom visit Memphis with-out asking to be shown the Rust headquarters."[44] The Rust brothers and their social consciousness only enhanced the press' fascination with them.

The 1936 Stoneville demonstration intensified the fears and hopes for the Rust machine. But as the initial panic over the Rust picker waned, the discus-sion became less strident and more balanced.

In a *Harper's* article that appeared just as the Stoneville test occurred, Robert Kenneth Straus—an official with the Resettlement Administration and heir of the Macy fortune[45]—offered a more positive view of the future than most other popular commentators.[46] Even if the introduction of the Rust machine put a million sharecroppers off the plantations and on the road, Straus predicted that it would also result in better conditions for those who remained in agriculture. "It certainly looks," he observed, "as if the Rust machine would do more for the ending of the chaotic conditions on the cotton plantations that have attracted so much attention in the past few years than any other agency of amelioration which is on the horizon."[47]

The secret behind the adoption of new technology, Straus emphasized, lay in comparative costs. In 1935, he reported, handpicking in the Mississippi Delta cost $9.00 per bale when using labor hired for $.60 per hundred pounds of seed cotton. In contrast, U.S. Department of Agriculture figures put the average cost of harvesting cotton at $4.84 per acre. Since a third of a bale of lint cotton was typically produced by each acre harvested, the total cost of harvesting a bale of cotton was $14.52 (3 × $4.84).

According to Straus, the Rust machine's operating cost was widely underestimated. John and Mack Rust usually claimed that their machine would cost one dollar per hour to operate the tractor and pay the tractor driver and the operator of the picker. But other expenses had to be included as well. As Straus realized, the full operating costs must include depreciation, repairs, and maintenance; and the final cost per bale would also depend on the yield per acre and number of pickings. Taking all of these considerations into account, Straus estimated the cost of machine picking at $13.50 per bale, more expensive than the cost of handpicking in the Delta but slightly less expensive than USDA's figures. Straus concluded that the Rust machine offered only marginal advantages over handpicking except under the most favorable conditions on large plantations.

While the defense of technology was not fashionable in the 1930s, machines still had their proponents. A 1936 editorial in *Collier's,* a weekly magazine that reached a popular audience, conceded the potential for labor displacement in a successful cotton-picking machine but criticized the central idea of technocrats who argued that machines eliminated jobs. *Collier's* maintained that in the long view, machines created, not eliminated jobs. "Cotton picking at best is tedious and ill-paid labor," the editorial said. "Few who can choose prefer cotton picking to other kinds of employment." Using the emancipation analogy, the editorial said, "In after years those displaced by the cotton picker and similar inventions may look back upon the machine as their emancipator from meagerly paid drudgery."[48]

In the months after the Stoneville demonstration, the pessimism associated with early discussions of the Rust picker gave way to more judicious assessments. While reporting that Rust would soon start construction on a factory in which to build cotton pickers, *Newsweek* predicted that no cotton picker, a Rust machine or any other, would affect more than a small fraction of human pickers for some time. The reasons for expecting a delay were practical, economic considerations:

- Mechanical pickers were practical in only the flat or gently rolling areas of the Cotton Belt like the Mississippi River Delta.
- The average cotton farm consisted of 15 acres with a 200 pound output per acre. Only plantations producing 100 bales or more a year would it find feasible to introduce a machine that replaced 50 to 100 workers.
- The cotton picked by the Rust machine was a grade lower than hand-picked, producing a 12 percent reduction in the value of the cotton.[49]

The obstacles to the imminent, widespread use of mechanical pickers had become clearer. The pessimists had wildly overstated the immediate threat.

Professional Judgment

Among agricultural professionals the Rust picker drew reactions ranging from the sanguine to outright skepticism. One of John Rust's strongest champions was W. E. Ayres of the Delta Experiment Station. Since the 1920s Ayres had followed the progress of several inventors, including Hiram N. Berry, who lived nearby at Greenville, Mississippi, and invited Rust to test his picker at the station in 1932.

After Ayres first saw the Berry picker in the 1920s, he became convinced that spindle-type machines would ultimately pick American cotton. He did not believe that hand-directed machines like pneumatic pickers would work effectively. By the mid-1930s, he saw possibilities in the work of Berry, International Harvester, and George R. Meyercord, and he encouraged them all. But he declared that "the eyes of the world are on Rust Brothers pickers. . . . The [Rust] machine is a better cotton picker, relatively, today than automobiles were road transportation units in 1915."[50]

Ayres took the view that the South's cotton farms were overpopulated. As a result, he was not worried about labor displacement. Indeed, he maintained that the farm labor population had to be reduced by 30 to 50 percent if farmers were going to raise their income. Modern farm machines were just as essential to farmers who wanted to enjoy high living standards as was modern equipment in any industry.[51]

Ayres also believed that worry over the unemployment created by mechanical picking was exaggerated. Such changes will be evolutionary rather than revolutionary. Skeptics, he predicted, would be slow to try new machines until they first saw their neighbors successfully using them.

Ayres wrote Rust in 1934 and repeated his views on mechanization:

Notwithstanding the objections that some have raised to such a machine because of present unemployment, I have maintained for ten years that it isn't up to agriculture or to cotton producers, as a class of agricultural people, to absorb at starvation wages machine-replaced industrial labor. Printers, ginners, textile manufacturers and other industrialists are just as much obligated to throw their labor-saving devices into the back alley in behalf of unemployment as is the cotton producer. . . .

Your machine is much simpler and can be produced much more cheaply than other mechanical cotton pickers in the process of development. There is no question but that it works and works well. . . .

We sincerely hope that you can arrange to build and market your machine shortly. Lincoln emancipated the Southern Negro. It remains for cotton-harvesting machinery to emancipate the Southern cotton planter. The sooner this be done, the better for the entire South.[52]

Rust treasured Ayres's letter and often showed it to visiting reporters.

Government studies also fretted over the impact of the mechanical cotton picker. In 1937 the National Resources Committee issued a study entitled *Technological Trends and National Policy.* In the section on agriculture, economist Roman L. Horne offered guarded predictions about the impact of mechanical pickers on labor. This machine, said Horne, was the leading invention with the high probability of upsetting present economic and social conditions. With the use of mechanical pickers, he believed, one-fourth to three-fourths of sharecroppers and tenant farmers across the ten cotton states would no longer be needed to pick cotton, not to mention eliminating the need for 10 million horses and mules since greater tractor use would accompany mechanical pickers.[53]

As the decade wound down, agricultural professionals gained increasing confidence that the South faced no immediate upheaval because of the Rust picker. In a series of professional meetings held in the late 1930s, experts commented on the potential impact of cotton pickers. While none of the experts were guilty of over-optimism, the consensus was that the use of cotton pickers was still years in the future.

Rural sociologist B. O. Williams expected machines to reshape the character of the region's farm population, but he predicted the gradual mechanization of agriculture. While mechanization had already advanced much further than was recognized, he said, the changes were not noticeable because industry in the cities had absorbed the labor surplus. "The cheap price of farm labor in the South has retarded mechanization in the past. It is not economical to substitute machines for labor until labor becomes dear, and this fact will without doubt be an active factor in retarding rapid mechanization of farms in the South for some time to come." Another possibility, he noted, was the migration of large numbers of surplus and displaced laborers to other areas.[54]

Though Williams expected change to be gradual, the prospects for the future were grim. He foresaw the permanent loss of jobs for poor farmers and laborers and a resulting labor surplus for which he could imagine no solution. Indeed, he believed in early 1939 that the only prospect for a solution to rural labor surplus was an "international crisis"—in other words, a world war. In response, one commentator found consolation in Williams's view that our "descent into social disintegration" was "in the nature of a downward spiral rather than a sheer downward plunge." Another observer envisioned the current dilemma as one in which "we cannot continue farm mechanization without great social cost nor can we stop it without great social cost."[55]

C. Horace Hamilton of the Texas A & M Experiment Station concurred in the pessimistic tone. He expected that mechanical cotton picking could become a reality within the next ten or fifteen years. "When that time comes," he said, "the southern part of the country may present the nation with its social and economic problem number two!"[56] This was a reference to Roosevelt's declaration of the South as "the nation's No. 1 economic problem."[57]

Unlike many of his colleagues Clarence A. Wiley of the University of Texas found amusement in the popular fears of the Rust machine. "At one time 'The Stars Fell on Alabama,'" he said, "but now hell is soon to reign in the whole Cotton South because of the inventive genius of the Rust brothers—so say the prophets of doom." The widespread fear of disaster was real, he said, but the hysteria was premature. He refused to be perturbed, not because the machine did not work; it worked well. The cost of operation, however, was high, although the costs had been represented as comparatively low. "The demonstration at Stoneville indicates that the mechanical picker can pick 10 bales per day, or approximately a bale per hour, where the yield is one bale [1,500 pounds of seed cotton] per acre. But all the cotton the machine will be called upon to pick will not be in Stoneville." "The limiting factor to larger production per family in that region," he added, "lies in obsolete production methods and not in the rate of picking."[58]

Wiley also criticized the comparisons often heard between the relative picking abilities of the machine and of the so-called average hand picker. These comparisons were invalid, he argued. The estimates of how many hand pickers the machine will replace were grossly exaggerated. The performance of the machine under favorable conditions was typically and unfairly compared to that of the worst hand picker under most unfavorable conditions. That is, the machine will probably pick less on the average, and hand pickers can pick more than they were credited with.[59]

In 1938 F. D. McHugh published an assessment of the current development of mechanical cotton pickers in the highly regarded journal *Scientific American*. McHugh mentioned four machines: Rust, International Harvester, Hanauer-Berry-Gamble, and A. R. Nisbet and H. G. Wendland's Wind-Roll.[60] The first three were variations of the spindle idea, while the Wind-Roll machine used rollers instead of spindles. McHugh argued that while they worked well, so many problems remained to be solved that no one could say that mechanical pickers in their present form would cause a social upheaval or economic revolution. He predicted that they would cause neither. "In fact," McHugh said, "it is not wholly a question of cotton-picking machines displacing human pickers; rather a lack of sufficient hand labor caused the adoption of the sledding and stripping method in Texas and has given great impetus to the perfection of mechanical pickers." In any event, widespread use of mechanical pickers lay "in the distant future," and the necessary adjustments will be scarcely noticeable. The general use of the machines, he estimated, would occur between twenty-five and fifty years—that is, between 1963 and 1988.[61] The low estimate turned out to be correct.

Many cotton men professed not to be impressed with the Rust machine, but everyone kept a close watch on its development.[62] Rust had always welcomed visitors representing large implement companies and individual inventors, inviting them to watch his demonstrations. In October 1936, H. B. McKahin, a Deere executive, visited Stoneville and Clarksdale, Mississippi, to look at the Rust picker.

McKahin observed the operation of four Rust machines, noting their features in great detail, and compared them with the Berry machine, which he felt was inferior to the Rust picker. The Rust picker he observed had a characteristic shared by other Rust machines: "in every round or two some mechanical attention [was] necessary, and on the day the writer saw one of the machines in operation there were three mechanics on the job. These mechanics seemed to be watching particularly for bent needles and also gummed needles to which cotton was sticking that the doffer had not scraped off."[63]

In McKahin's view the Rust machine still did not have all the bugs worked out. "The general feeling around Clarksdale," McKahin reported, "seemed to be that while the machine might find some use under certain conditions, yet there was no feeling that the machine would come into general use or that it would revolutionize the raising of cotton." McKahin left reassured about the immediate future of the Cotton South and Deere's competitive position in the cotton picker market. Rust had taken the lead in developing a picker, but he still had not built a marketable machine.[64] At the same time, McKahin complained about the "large amount of free publicity these [Rust] people have obtained."

In 1936 the *Kiplinger Agricultural Letter,* a source of insider information, acknowledged that the Rust machine picked cotton and picked it fast. But, it said, "its main weakness is that of other mechanical cotton pickers—the cotton it picks contains green leaf and trash." Referring to the recent Stoneville test, the Kiplinger report added that "[t]he demonstration shows that the mechanical cotton picker's effect on the economic and social order of the Old South will not be felt for several years—and then gradually." This was the view of "practical cotton men and competent agricultural engineers who witnessed the demonstration." But the engineers did agree that mechanical picking was only a matter of time.[65]

So the 1930s ended with fears unrealized: no mechanical cotton picker went into commercial production. Rust failed to secure sufficient financing to carry his machine to the necessary finished design. But the Rust machine also contained inherent flaws that made it mechanically unsound. No one, not even International Harvester, was quite ready with a marketable machine. Beyond that, the low cost of hand labor during the depression consistently undercut the projected expense of machine picking.

Though Deere discontinued its experimentation on spindle pickers early in the 1930s, International Harvester continued its development work but maintained a low profile. Inventors who appealed to implement companies as potential purchasers of their patents were all politely turned down. The big companies closely followed Rust's progress and that of other inventors.[66] Corporate players watched him for ideas, worried about his progress, and complained about his press attention. They also let him run interference for them so they would not have to take responsibility for evicting millions of sharecroppers.

Yet John Rust had inadvertently—or shrewdly—made himself into a celebrity. What made Rust appealing was his personification of the underdog individual inventor who was beating the huge corporations at their own game. Individuals still had the innovative ideas in many cases, but only large corporations possessed the resources for years of development work and the production facilities to produce a commercial product for a mass market. They also possess the national marketing organization necessary to reach potential buyers. Edison's cliché, "Genius is 1 percent inspiration and 99 percent perspiration," can be read to favor large corporations.[67]

Rust compared himself to Eli Whitney and believed that he endured the same skepticism and criticism as other famous inventors. Rust attracted attention wherever he traveled with his machine. The press sought him out, and he was very much aware of his celebrity status. He gave interviews freely to anyone, from reporters for national magazines to high school students. Memphis visitors wanted to see his Florida Street headquarters, making his modest shop a popular attraction.

When Robert Kenneth Straus visited Rust's shop in 1935, he felt a sense of excitement. "If you are in Memphis and take a trolley out Florida Street until you reach the outskirts of the city proper," he advised, "you will come to a small made-over garage, across the exterior of which is draped a cloth sign lettered "Home of the Rust Cotton Picker." Here in these humble surroundings a visitor sensed "the web of drama," a feeling that he could look around and see where history was being made. While Mack assembled pickers in the back of the shop, John talked with visitors about social problems.

John Rust carried both the hopes and fears of the Cotton South—the hope for change and improvement and the fear of utter economic disaster.[68] He was the lone inventor pioneering a technological frontier. He was also one of those contradictory characters like Charles Lindbergh. While, like Lindbergh, he was a throwback to a simpler time, he was simultaneously riding the cutting edge of twentieth-century technology. Yet the basic principle of his picker was so simple that spectators wondered why it had not already been done. Rust possessed an empathic personality; he seemed genuinely not to want his invention to hurt anyone but instead to relieve poor people of an onerous task. People could relate to him better than they could identify with large corporate bureaucracies like International Harvester or Deere.

The moral implications of the Rust machine were frightening and brought Americans face to face with one of the central problem of the 1930s. A single cotton picker would displace dozens of hand pickers, creating a class of people with no livelihood and nowhere to go. Since many of the southern sharecroppers who would be replaced by mechanical pickers were black people, the potential impact of Rust's invention invoked visions of racial turmoil.

As the depression waned and the nation turned its attention to the outbreak of World War II in September 1939, the threat of technological catastrophe passed unnoticed. But technological change had only been delayed, not averted. In the meantime Americans confronted the challenge of winning a world war. As they prepared for new dangers in Europe and the Pacific, they did not realize how much the war would change American life at home and serve as a springboard for the next stage of cotton mechanization. In a form of social redress, the changes induced by the war would ease the transition from hand labor to machine labor.

Cotton Harvester Sweepstakes: The Race for the Cotton Picker Market in the 1940s

On July 13, 1942, an International Harvester (IH) cotton picker caravan left Hinsdale Farms, near Chicago, Illinois, heading for cotton fields in the lower Rio Grande Valley. During the 1940s this trek became an annual fall ritual. Harvester engineers had worked for the past year making adjustments on their experimental picker in preparation for three months of testing in the late summer and fall. The development of the mechanical cotton picker was always handicapped by the limited time available for testing during each harvest, and south Texas cotton offered an early start. In October the caravan moved on to northeast Arkansas, where later varieties of cotton were ready for picking.

During each cotton season from 1941 to 1949, International Harvester sent its caravan southward—often more than one. In some years the company prepared ten pickers for testing and usually sold eight of them to interested planters, keeping two for further testing purposes. The caravans carried sufficient tools to make repairs and modifications in the field as needed. In 1942, for example, engineers were prepared to test several types of spindles and other variations. The company built a machine shop on the Ohlendorf plantation near Osceola, Arkansas. Harold F. Ohlendorf, like Richard and Howell Hopson Jr., was a pioneer in supporting the development of the mechanical cotton picker.[1]

The 1942 caravan was one of the most successful. The cotton picker was hauled on a semitrailer, followed by a pickup truck loaded with equipment, tools, and harvester parts that were removed to ensure clearance on public highways. Though the first production models of IH pickers were one-row machines, this picker was a two-row single drum model designed to pick from one side of the plants. The machine included an air conveyor system and a basket to receive the seed cotton—all of which was attached to a model H Farmall tractor. What made this picker innovative was that it was mounted on the tractor backward, so the tractor was driven in reverse during the picking operation. In 1940, for the first time, engineer Clarence R. Hagen suggested reversing the direction of the tractor.[2]

The caravan reached Raymondville, Texas, on July 22, and three days later the picker made its first run on the R. D. Smith farm east of Lyford. Over the next three weeks, it harvested fourteen bales. On August 21 the caravan arrived in Plano, Texas, where a public demonstration was scheduled for cotton gin and cleaner equipment representatives.

The cotton picker caravan arrived at Osceola, Arkansas, on September 25 for an extended stay on the Ohlendorf plantation, where the harvester picked ninety-seven bales during October and November. This cotton was used in drying and cleaning tests with equipment that International Harvester had installed on the plantation. Once the season ended, the 1942 caravan trucked the picker back to Chicago, arriving on November 23.[3]

Meanwhile, at the end of August, Harvester engineers completed a second 1942 model cotton harvester and shipped it by rail to the Hopson plantation at Clarksdale, Mississippi. Harvester also sent a reconditioned 1941 harvester to the Delta Experiment Station at Stoneville. In late September this machine was used for picking tests in both defoliated and undefoliated cotton. During the next few weeks, it was moved to several locations for additional tests in Arkansas and Mississippi. By late October it too operated on the Hopson plantation, where it picked eighty-five bales. This small fleet of mechanical cotton pickers enabled Harvester engineers to test fully their latest prototypes under real conditions.

From the late 1930s and into the 1940s International Harvester engineers relied heavily on field support at the Ohlendorf and Hopson plantations. The owners of these two plantations were unusually supportive of technological developments in agriculture, and their cooperation gave Harvester shop facilities in the South, eliminating a problem that hampered Angus Campbell and other early inventors.

On October 21, 1942, Harvester put on a demonstration of three pickers at the Hopson plantation for local planters and a delegation from the Delta Experiment Station. After the machines made several rounds, the spectators examined them closely. As they began to discuss the problems of the cotton industry and their relationship to mechanical cotton harvesters, the sky turned dark when a thunderstorm moved into the area, and the group sought shelter in a seed storage building. The animated discussion continued. Was there a need for a mechanical harvester now? Would it be economically advantageous? And in its present state of development, was the International Harvester picker ready for release to the commercial market? The group agreed that the answers to all three questions were yes. D. L. Edson, the county agent at Greenwood, Mississippi, mentioned the problem of labor shortages during the war and the possibility that "the southern farmer may never again have the benefits of cheap hand labor." Howell Hopson Jr., who had seen tests of various models of mechanical pickers over the past several years, amused and impressed everyone with his instant offer to purchase five or six machines for the 1943 season if they could be made available. The rain stopped before the fields became too wet for further picking, and the demonstration continued.

With low labor prices in the depression, International Harvester had delayed plans for commercial production. Just as Rust and other individual inventors continued to experiment and hope for breakthroughs, Harvester engineers also continued testing. With the outbreak of World War II, Harvester launched a final push to perfect its picker.[4] At the close of the 1942 season Hagen and his engineers believed that they had at last created a production-ready mechanical cotton picker.

Fowler McCormick—chairman of the board of International Harvester and the grandson of two of the world's richest men, Cyrus H. McCormick and John D. Rockefeller—formally announced in December 1942 that his company had a commercial cotton picker ready for production. "Refinements will come," McCormick said, "but we are certain that it is a commercial machine right now."[5] International Harvester had spent $4.5 million over two decades on experiments with mechanical pickers.[6] In his statement McCormick said, "The International Harvester Company has been experimenting with mechanical cotton pickers for approximately 40 years.[7] It has proved to be the most difficult designing and engineering job in the modern history of agricultural machinery. Up to now we have never said that we had a successful cotton picker."

"We are now ready to state that our picker has been tested exhaustively," McCormick added, "and we know it will pick cotton profitably under conditions prevailing in the principal cotton growing areas of the country."[8]

International Harvester engineers had developed a spindle-type picker, but unlike Rust they used a barbed spindle, which improved its ability to snag cotton fibers. Rust mistakenly believed that barbed spindles would never work and gave up on them. For him, cotton fibers were too difficult to doff from barbed spindles. In addition Harvester executives saw their picker as the solution to labor shortages caused by the war. Harvester pickers would have appeared on the commercial market during the war if it had not been for the scarcity of steel. The War Production Board allocated only enough materials for building a few models for continued experimentation.[9] International Harvester continued the caravans hoping to make further refinements to their picker as well as to conduct other demonstrations.[10]

World War II

When McCormick made his announcement in 1942, the nation's farmers faced a dramatically altered labor market that in time would enhance the marketability of mechanical cotton pickers. The war produced a labor shortage that in time would impel cotton growers to turn to machines. World War II accelerated the forces of urbanization, industrialization, and economic diversification, all trends that continued in the postwar period.

The war's greatest domestic impact, especially in the Cotton South, was that it set people in motion. During the 1940s the South lost 2,447,000 people (866,000 white and 1,581,000 black) to areas with better economic opportunities.[11] By 1945 the South's farm population had declined by 3,660,000, or 22.3 percent. In a great surge from the farm most of the region's metropolitan areas gained population. During the 1940s, the South's urban population increased by 50 percent, while its rural population declined by 8 percent.[12]

The Mississippi River Delta states reflected this dramatic population shift. During the war years, Arkansas and Louisiana's farm populations each fell by 28 percent, with Mississippi losing 20 percent of its farm people (table 6.1).[13] While the region lost 25 percent of its farm population, it also saw 14 percent of its farm disappear.[14] Over the decade from 1940 to 1950 Arkansas and Mississippi recorded the largest population losses in the nation, losing 11.6 and 8.3 percent of their populations respectively.[15] Out-migration from the three states of the Mississippi River Delta totaled one million people, or 40.9 percent of the South's total migration loss during the 1940s.

Arkansas and Mississippi—along with Texas—also led the South in a redistribution of people from rural to urban residence. Arkansas's rural population fell 15 percent, with Mississippi losing 10 percent during the 1940–49 decade.[16]

The Mississippi River Delta's population changes translated into a major labor shortage with significant impacts on cotton production and labor costs. During the war the number of acres harvested declined along with the number of bales produced (table 6.2). The war saw the price of cotton climb from less than ten cents per pound to more than twenty-two cents, or more than

TABLE 6.1. Population of Farms in Arkansas, Louisiana, Mississippi, and the South, 1940–1945 (in 1,000s)

	FARM POPULATION			NUMBER OF FARMS		
	1940	1945	Percentage Change	1940	1945	Percentage Change
Arkansas	1,113	798	-28.3	217	199	-8.3
Louisiana	854	608	-28.8	180	129	-28.3
Mississippi	1,403	1,119	-20.2	291	264	-9.3
Regional Totals	3,370	2,525	-25.1	688	592	-14.0
South	16,400	12,740	-22.3	3,007	2,881	-4.2

Source: U.S. Bureau of the Census, *Historical Statistics of the United States: Colonial Times to 1970* (Washington, D.C.: GPO, 1975), series K 45, 60, 62, 63, pp. 458–59.

TABLE 6.2. U.S. Cotton Production, 1940–1945 (in 1,000s)

	Acres Harvested	Production in Bales	Price per Pound*	Stocks Carried Over in Bales	Average Wage**
1940	23,861	12,566	9.89	10,564	$.62
1941	22,236	10,744	17.03	12,166	1.09
1942	22,602	12,817	19.05	10,640	1.41
1943	21,610	11,427	19.90	10,657	1.66
1944	19,617	12,230	20.73	10,744	1.92
1945	17,029	9,015	22.52	11,164	2.50

*Cents.

**Wage for picking a hundred pounds of seed cotton.

Source: U.S. Bureau of the Census, *Historical Statistics of the United States: Colonial Times to 1970* (Washington, D.C.: GPO, 1975), series K 553–56, p. 517; U.S. Department of Agriculture, Economic Research Service, *Statistics on Cotton and Related Data, 1920–1973,* Statistical Bulletin No. 535 (Washington, D.C.: USDA, 1974), 86.

double, but during the same period the cost of handpicking increased four times. Picking costs doubled by 1942, tripled by 1944, and quadrupled by the end of the war in 1945. The carryover of warehoused cotton was still as high as it had been for the past decade.

Between the fall of 1942 and early 1943 southern agriculture shifted abruptly from labor surplus to labor deficit. Migration and military manpower needs took an increasing toll on the region's labor pool. With wages rising around the country, no one wanted to work for pathetically low wages anymore, and no one had to do so.

The South experienced the worst labor shortages of the war during the 1944 cotton season. By early October newspapers reported that much of Delta cotton was going unpicked. Planters complained that the labor supply was 20 to 25 percent below that of the previous year with a larger crop.[17] According to reports from Mississippi, the labor supply was 15 percent below 1943 and 34 percent below available manpower in 1942.[18] Across the Cotton Belt that fall, the lack of labor endangered the harvest. Ginning fell far behind schedule.[19] In Arkansas, according to estimates, less than two-thirds of the number of needed pickers were at work. Out of 35,000 pickers needed, only 22,000 had been supplied. Pickers earned from $2.00 to $2.50 per hundred pounds.[20] Cotton farmers knew they needed to find workers soon and pick their cotton, which was open and ready, because bad weather lowered the value between $5.00 and $20.00 a bale. The Delta needed at least 10,000 more hand pickers, according to newspaper reports, and hoped to get them from hill areas.[21] Arkansas pulled out all stops to secure the needed workers. The state Agricultural Extension Service furnished free transportation to critical labor shortage areas, bringing in workers from north Arkansas counties.[22]

Domestic workers, however, were not enough. Besides using German prisoners of war, planters at a meeting in Little Rock asked for Japanese-American labor from the War Relocation Authority's camps at Jerome and Rohwer. They were wanted for work in the areas near McGehee, Dumas, Portland, Eudora, and Pine Bluff.[23]

For the first time since the Civil War, the Cotton South faced a double crisis of soaring labor costs and dwindling labor control. Plantation interests fought to keep cotton prices high and wages low; but they had lost control of their cheap, dependent labor supply, and they knew it. In a seller's market, workers gained real bargaining power, which destroyed the deference that the plantation system required.[24]

From the planter's perspective the problem was labor scarcity; for workers, the issues were higher wages, better living conditions, and freedom from planter control. Since workers could be more selective about employment, planters could no longer resort to force in dealing with recalcitrant laborers. If they did so, the word spread fast, and they could not hire anyone to pick their cotton. Historian Jay Mandle has argued that "[t]he plantation economy rested not merely on coercion, but also upon deference. It was dependency as well as control which characterized the organization of production on the estates."[25] The farm labor shortage of World War II suddenly swept away both dependency and control.

While cotton farmers justly complained about labor shortages, they also received special treatment in dealing with their labor needs. In November 1942, when the problem of labor shortages first became acute, Congress enacted the Tydings Amendment that provided a draft deferment classification for farmworkers, and more than 1.6 million farm deferments were granted. Farm deferments, however, only slowed the drift of farm boys to the city.[26]

World War II also placed the Cotton South under the regulation of more federal agencies than ever, even more than during the New Deal. The Selective Service drafted men into the armed forces. The Office of Price Administration (OPA) ran rationing programs to keep consumer prices low. The War Manpower Commission (WMC) sought to balance the supply of labor with war production needs. The U.S. Employment Service (USES) operated a farm labor program to balance labor demand with supply. Working with the Employment Service, the WMC transferred labor from one region to another according to their view of war production priorities. The Farm Security Administration (FSA), a New Deal agency and an old irritant of Delta planters,[27] assisted migrant workers with housing and transportation. Planters opposed the removal of workers from the hill areas adjacent to the Delta and from Memphis for work in distant regions.[28]

At the end of the war planters looked to the federal government as an ally in helping them keep wages down. In the fall of 1945 and 1946 the Department of Agriculture held hearings on a proposed wage ceiling for picking cotton in the Mississippi River Delta. By 1944 wages for picking cotton in Mississippi had increased to three dollars, tripling the cost of the cotton harvest since 1940. In a series of meetings with USDA representatives held in Delta towns, most planters favored wage ceilings. They realized that their competition for workers was in part driving up the price of labor.[29]

The worries of planters came out clearly at these hearings. They were already seeing too many cars with Michigan and Illinois license plates parked at their tenant cabins. They wanted to believe that labor would soon return to the farm, but no one really believed workers would exchange high-paying factory jobs for low-paying work in cotton fields. The war had given everyone a taste for the good life, and no one was going back. Many former Delta residents had an aversion for returning home. "The negro who said he had rather be on relief in California than on the best job in Mississippi," according to a popular saying, "expressed the views of 90 percent of the negroes in the Delta."[30]

On the other hand, the Southern Tenant Farmers Union opposed the imposition of a wage ceiling for workers they contended were the most underpaid agricultural workers in the nation. Union representatives contended that it was low wage rates that pushed workers out of the region. In 1945 H. L. Mitchell, STFU president, submitted a statement to the Secretary of Agriculture Clinton P. Anderson in which he advocated five dollars for a ten-hour day as a minimum wage for farm labor.[31]

In September 1945 the wage ceiling was established at $2.05 in Arkansas and at $2.10 in Mississippi per hundredweight of cotton picked. The conflict over wages demonstrated that planters could no longer command labor on their own terms as they once had. Long hours and low wages were difficult conditions to sell workers after the war.[32]

The Agricultural Adjustment Administration (AAA) had forced the South to shift partially from sharecropping to wage labor, but wartime labor problems caused a temporary move back to sharecropping. For planters, croppers represented a more reliable, dependable labor supply. Fewer people were willing to work as day laborers when high-paying industrial jobs were available, and sharecropping represented a more secure status as well as more money than wage labor. These changes were temporary, however, and ultimately World War II accelerated the decline of tenancy. The draft took away many men who would have worked as tenants, the rise in farm income enabled some tenants to buy land, and the increased mechanization created fewer but larger farms.[33]

What had happened during the war was momentous: the plantation system entered its death throes. Labor control, the sine qua non of plantation agriculture, had been lost, and as a result the plantation system fell apart. By 1945 the plantation system as it existed since the Civil War had disappeared.

The war brought about other changes in cotton farming as farmers struggled to produce more with less labor. In 1944 Otis Osgood and John White, two rural sociologists, published a study of how wartime changes in cotton farming affected Arkansas share renters, sharecroppers, and wage laborers. In Chicot, Mississippi, and Pulaski Counties, they found a decline in the numbers of resident families and single wage hands. This decline paralleled a redistribution of families by tenure. Starting about 1941, there was a shift from wage families to sharecroppers. Wage families tended to move off the farm to urban employment. Many farmers preferred sharecroppers to wage hands as they believed that croppers were more likely to continue throughout the crop season. This was a reversal of the trend since the New Deal, which had increased the cotton acreage worked by wage labor. Farmers were growing less cotton because of labor shortages. In 1944 the number of resident families per acre of cotton was only 81 percent as high as in 1938, but yields were about 25 percent higher. Osgood and White predicted that the most common type of laborer in the near future would be a combination of cropper and wage laborer.

Another significant development was an increase in the number of tractors. As farm labor decreased, many farmers operated four-row cultivators and planters. Curiously, the increase in tractors was not followed by a decline in the number of horses and mules, as would be expected, and operators indicated that they had more work stock than they needed. They were skittish about leaving behind the old system entirely.[34]

While the Mississippi River Delta experienced increasing mechanization, western cotton areas saw the most dramatic changes. In 1946 Harris P. Smith, who had played a pioneering role in developing cotton strippers at Texas A & M, wrote, "Heretofore in referring to developments in the mechanical harvesting of cotton we have been prone to say that it was just around the corner, *now we can say that mechanical harvesting of cotton is here.*"[35]

Because labor had been plentiful in the past, Smith said, farmers had been uninterested in mechanical harvesting, but they showed increasing interest as labor left the farm during the war. "Much of this labor is not returning to the farm," Smith stated. "Therefore, the cotton farmer is forced to mechanize, especially harvesting the crop." In addition, machines were previously not economical investments because handpicked cotton commanded higher prices. By the end of the war, farmers trimmed costs wherever they could.

The war's lesson was that agriculture faced labor shortages and high wages in the postwar South. The world had changed. The plantation mentality would not be part of the future. If planters were going to continue to grow cotton, the only answer to the cotton industry's labor problem was complete mechanization.

World War II not only ended the plantation system, but also cushioned the transition to capital-intensive agriculture by drawing massive numbers of people from the South, where they could not make a living. The more people attracted to industrial jobs, the fewer people machines would displace.

In October 1944, as the war moved into its final months, attention turned to dramatic announcement. The Hopson plantation, where so many mechanical cotton pickers had been tested, produced a cotton crop entirely by machine. The Hopson brothers had set aside an eighty-acre field to experiment with mechanical farming, using mechanical planters, cultivators, and pickers, which replaced mules, hoes, and field hands. These tools substituted for thirty to forty men working with the old methods. "On that block," a spokesman said, "there has never been a hoe-hand employed. It was planted with traction power, cyanamid dusted by airplane, cultivated by 'flame throwers' and cultivators, cross plowed and machine picked." The Hopsons operated a fleet of harvesters that picked a bale to the acre and picked faster than a four-stand gin with an eight-bale capacity could gin it. The Hopson brothers used International Harvester pickers. The Coahoma County Agent, Harris Barnes, predicted, "We are going to bring about radical changes in this section. When sufficient machinery can be obtained the major portion of our labor problems will be solved." Only farms with mechanical pickers will be able to survive in the cotton farming business, he predicted, and mechanized cotton farming will spell the end of the small cotton farmer. Machine-produced cotton would be cheap enough to meet the competition of synthetic fabrics and low-cost foreign-grown cotton.[36]

Covering four thousand acres, the Hopson plantation had been owned by the same family since 1852. In the early 1930s it was a conventional operation of mules and sharecroppers. When the brothers Richard and Howell Hopson Jr. assumed management of the plantation in the mid-1930s, they began to modernize every aspect of the operation from tractor repair to cost accounting. From the start the Hopsons operated twenty-two tractors and phased out 140 or so mules, and they began converting to four-row planters and cultivators. By 1944 only five of the old mules remained, largely as pets. Because of AAA cotton controls, they experimented with new crops including oats, barley, soybeans, hay, and clover; but cotton remained the principal crop in acreage, value, and profit. They also shifted from sharecropping to wage labor. By 1944 almost 80 percent of the acreage was worked with wage labor paid on an hourly basis.[37]

The Hopson plantation utilized all of the latest ancillary developments and technology, not just mechanical. To eliminate weeds and grasses, they tried check-row planting and cross-plowing, but favored "flame weeders" as show-ing greater promise (see chapter 7). New cotton varieties produced a lower plant that was more suitable for machine picking, since large plants would not enter the machine's picking area without excessive crowding. They also saw merit in defoliation, which was still in the experimental stage.[38] Improvements at Hopson gins also tackled the problem of trash in machine-picked cotton.

Over the years the Hopsons hired floating labor from nearby towns, transient labor from other sections of Mississippi, migratory labor from the West, Mexican labor, and, late in the war, prisoners of war. "They were secured wherever, whenever, and however they could be had," Howell Hopson Jr. said.[39] In his view handpicking was costly and the labor supply highly uncertain. At an early point, the Hopsons' attention turned to mechanical harvesters, and they opened their plantation to International Harvester for testing and experimentation. When the first production models rolled off IH's assembly line, the Hopsons snapped them up. By 1944 the plantation owned eight cotton harvesters and wanted more. They believed that when hand labor was available, it was still cheaper than machine picking, but Hopson declared that "in the absence of hand labor the comparative merits of handpicking and machine harvesting ceases to be a subject for debate."[40] In 1943, almost six hundred bales were harvested on the Hopson plantation with four machines at less than $2.50 per bale. After adding in repair costs and depreciation amounting to $5.00 per bale, the total cost of mechanically harvesting each bale was reportedly $7.50. (In comparison, at the cost of $3.00 per hundred, handpicking a bale costs $45.00; at $2.00, $30.00.)[41]

The Hopson plantation had a marvelous story to tell reporters who came to see it firsthand. In the fall of 1944, 2,500 visitors swarmed over the plantation to watch an event that they saw as a historic milestone, a preview of an agricultural revolution. "Eight big machines, painted fire-engine red, lumbered through the fields. They were the first production models of International Harvester's cotton picker," a reporter said. "Each was picking cotton sixty times as fast as a man could pick it. Together, they were doing the work of 480 pairs of hands."[42]

These machines worked continuously without breakdown. They picked all day, and at dark the headlights were switched on and they kept on picking.

The Hopson plantation ran like "a Detroit assembly line," according to one reporter.[43] The workforce consisted of about forty workers, instead of the 130 tenant families previously employed. For those who watched the pickers operate, the worry remained that the mechanical picker would displace labor, resulting in a surge of migration to northern cities. Howell Hopson Jr. asked, "Is it better to take steps to improve the lot of people who remain on Southern cotton farms, or to tolerate a stagnant arrangement which holds no hope?"[44]

The Hopson brothers saw themselves occupying the cutting edge of agricultural change. "While Whitney's gin is given credit for creating the tremendous cotton industry of our nation," Howell Hopson said, "the emergence of International Harvester's mechanical cotton picker as a practical machine may prove to be the savior of that industry."[45]

With the Hopson achievement coinciding with the wartime labor shortage, excitement over the prospects of mechanical cotton pickers surged through the Mississippi River Delta. From all over the region men came to Clarksdale to stand in the field and stare in awe at the red machines. In early November some three hundred representatives from the cotton industry assembled in a spontaneous meeting at the Coahoma County courthouse to demand that the government increase materials allocated for the manufacture of mechanical cotton pickers, the only farm machine with production specifically limited. Anxious to shift from hand labor to machines, Mississippi planters predicted that if one thousand machines were made available for the 1945 harvest, the Yazoo-Mississippi area could absorb all of them even though none were sold in Arkansas or elsewhere. A Tunica County planter boasted, "I'd buy six of them myself—and pay cash for them."[46]

International Harvester

The race to produce the first commercial model of a mechanical cotton picker was won by International Harvester. In 1943 Harvester sought approval from the War Production Board to build a new factory near Memphis, Tennessee, in the hope that pickers could be ready for the 1944 picking season, but the application was rejected.[47] The nation faced critical shortages of steel in the midpoint of the war. As a result the production of mechanical cotton pickers was delayed for five years. In 1949 Harvester began full production at Memphis Works, a factory built in a 262-acre cotton field on the north side of the city.

Memphis offered numerous advantages as the site for an International Harvester cotton picker plant. The city's central location in the Cotton Belt was an obvious advantage, as was its location on the Mississippi River together with rail and highway transportation. The selection of Memphis also symbolized the postwar movement of industry from the North to the South. The plant represented an investment of $9 million and at full production employed three thousand workers with a $3 million annual payroll. Memphis Works formally opened in April 1948 with an initial production schedule calling for the delivery of 1,000 mechanical cotton pickers in time for the 1948 crop, along with mobile hay balers and other farm equipment. From 1943 to 1948 Harvester built and sold 325 pre-production pickers. After Memphis Works went into full-scale production in 1949, Harvester produced 4,111 pickers in the next three years, or an average of 114 per month.[48]

International Harvester's first production picker, the McCormick-Deering M-12-H, was a one-row machine. It picked an acre of cotton in an hour and fifteen minutes, gathering 95 percent or more of the cotton lint. Mounted on a Farmall M tractor, the picker was driven in reverse gear and equipped with fifteen vertical picker bars, each one containing twenty horizontally mounted, chromium-plated spindles. Each spindle had small projecting barbs that caught and extracted the lint from the open bolls. Traveling in an oval path to eliminate raking action and revolving at 2,000 rpm, the moistened spindles picked from both sides of the row. The picker had a hydraulic basket that held 750 pounds of cotton, with the machine's overall weight at 10,250 pounds.[49]

Deere and Company

In the "cotton harvester sweepstakes," as *Business Week* called it, Deere and Company of Moline, Illinois, became the second entrant among the large farm equipment makers with the announcement in 1944 that it had purchased the patents developed by Hiram N. Berry and his son Charles R. Berry. The elder Berry had died and his son continued his father's work.[50]

Deere's interest in cotton harvesters, however, went back to 1928. While marketing a cotton stripper, Deere conducted experiment work on spindle pickers. The first experimental Deere picker was a two-row machine mounted on a tractor. These early Deere machines departed dramatically from most picker configurations by using an "overhead reel" that rolled over the plants and probed them with long, straight spindles. The results of tests were unsatisfactory, but Deere continued to test the reel design from 1929 until 1931.

Faced with a series of disappointments, Deere decided in 1931 to discontinue work on spindle machines. Deere did not build any more spindle pickers or conduct any more experimental work until 1944. Deere engineers, however, continued to work on cotton strippers.

After purchasing the Berry patents, Deere returned to the spindle idea with a program to develop a spindle picker at its Spreader Works in East Moline, Illinois. From 1944 through 1946, Deere tested machines that embodied the principles of the Berry design using V-belts to drive the spindles, but test results were unsatisfactory. As a consequence Deere's engineers adopted the approach used in the Price-Campbell patents—that is, the use of revolving barbed spindles mounted on a picker bar, which in turn were mounted in a drum that moved with the same speed as the machine. International Harvester, as Deere acknowledged, had adopted this approach in the 1920s.[51]

In field testing under the leadership of Fred Thomann and L. N. Paradise just after World War II, Deere tried several variations: engineers first tested a tractor-pulled picker with a separate power source, then mounted the machine on a reversed tractor using the power take-off to operate the unit. Deere settled on a two-row, self-propelled unit, designated as the No. 8, and placed it in production at the John Deere Des Moines Works at Ankeny, Iowa. Like Harvester, Deere relied on its existing national network of dealers, the basis of its strength in the picker market.

Though building on the work of others, Deere also made its own innovations in picker design. The first doffers were metal strippers that brushed against the spindles. Engineers eventually adopted a rotary doffer with a solid rubber pad. The greatest challenge, however, was the spindle itself. Deere's first spindles were long, slender, and not very rigid, then straight, short, and rigid, with many different barbed and fluted designs in various combinations. Eventually, the short, rigid, tapered spindle appeared and became the basis of Deere production designs.

A year after International Harvester began commercial production of pickers, Deere and Company emerged as IH's strongest competitor in the picker sweepstakes. The Ankeny plant began production of the No. 8 in 1950. Rather than mounted on a tractor, the No. 8 was a completely self-propelled unit carrying two picker heads for harvesting two rows at once, the first machine to do so. It used sixteen picking bars in the front drum and twelve in the rear, with a total of 1,120 chrome-plated spindles. Deere claimed it was a "phenomenal advance" in cotton harvesting, able to pick as much as eighty field hands in one day. With its two-row capacity and larger basket, this picker could do almost twice the harvesting job as one-row machines.[52] It was five years later that International Harvester brought out a two-row self-propelled picker.

As a complement to the larger model, Deere also developed a smaller picker mounted on a tractor. Unlike the No. 8, the picking unit could be dismounted and the tractor used for other purposes. Like International Harvester, Deere pickers also took advantage of the reversed-tractor design.

In 1958 the Model 99 Picker, Deere's second two-row picker, went on the market. Farmers had continued to complain about trash in machine-picked cotton, which was the result of the picking unit itself sucking trash as well as lint into the basket. This machine eliminated the trash problem by using suction from above the conveyor ducts that lifted the lightweight lint and allowed the heavier trash to fall out through the bottom of the machine. Deere called this feature Air-Trol, and claimed it produced cotton as clean as handpicked. The Deere 99 also used a deeper-barbed spindle, which pulled out more lint than previously possible. These spindles were breakable if bent one-eighth of an inch, making replacement easy and cheaper, since a broken spindle was simpler to replace than a bent spindle. Like International Harvester, Deere built low-cost models of its pickers targeting small farmers with low-yielding cotton (forty bales or fewer).

In 1961, to dramatize the shift from hand to machine picking, Deere staged a promotional event billed as the "World's First Trainload of Cotton Pickers." The company shipped 441 cotton pickers, worth nearly $7 million, from John Deere Des Moines Works on a 108-car freight train. The average price of these pickers was $15,873. The trainload of pickers headed for Atlanta, where the shipment was broken up for delivery in Georgia, Alabama, and South Carolina. Those states, still under 50 percent machine picked, had been slow in adopting mechanical harvesting. The mile-long train was said to be the largest single shipment of farm machinery ever made by rail. According to Deere officials, the train represented less than half of the pickers being shipped to southern cotton fields that year.[53]

Allis-Chalmers

The Allis-Chalmers Manufacturing Company (A-C) of Milwaukee, Wisconsin, represented the ultimate in diversification, with products ranging from flour mills to electrical equipment to farm machinery. The company originated in a series of mergers in 1901, taking the names of Edward P. Allis, who was best known as a manufacturer of steam engines, and William J. Chalmers. Allis-Chalmers entered the farm machinery business at the time of World War I with a specialization in tractors. In 1932 Allis-Chalmers pioneered the first rubber-tired tractor.[54]

As the Rust Cotton Picker Company slipped into bankruptcy, Allis-Chalmers saw an opportunity to diversify into a new and potentially large market for cotton pickers. Though financial reverses reduced Rust to nothing but his drafting board, he set out in 1943 to redesign his picker from scratch. He retained the basic principles of his original idea, but improved the spindle by roughing its surface to make it more aggressive. While he was in Washington in 1944 to file patents on his improvements, representatives of Allis-Chalmers approached him with an offer to manufacture machines using his patents. He agreed to grant them a license to manufacture and sell Rust pickers. In 1944, the Allis-Chalmers plant at La Porte, Indiana, produced two experimental models under Rust's supervision and shipped them southward for testing. Four more machines were built in 1945. With the Rust agreement, Allis-Chalmers gained an important role in the picker sweepstakes. Rust used these machines for testing purposes and lived on the fees he received from custom picking and from Allis-Chalmers as a consulting engineer.[55] At last he enjoyed some modest financial success.

In 1947 Allis-Chalmers leased an ordnance plant at Gadsden, Alabama, for the production of cotton pickers.[56] By 1948 Rust had designed a tractor-mounted picker that operated with a minimum of repairs. After new tests with experimental models, Rust believed he had conquered the durability problem. Unfortunately, a protracted labor strike and a shortage of materials prevented Allis-Chalmers from fulfilling its contract. By 1949 the company lost its exclusive right to the Rust patents but continued to manufacture Rust pickers in various configurations.[57]

Ben Pearson

In early 1949 unpicked cotton still remained in the fields of Jefferson County, Arkansas. Planters had been unable to hire enough labor during the past fall to finish picking the crop. Since Rust's name was nationally known, they turned to him for a solution to their labor problem. Frank Fletcher of Tamo and G. D. Long of Moscow, both located in Jefferson County, organized a group of planters to go to Clarksdale, Mississippi, where one of the Rust machines was located. They saw it in operation and invited Rust to bring it to Arkansas.[58]

In February and March 1949 Rust conducted several demonstrations of his machine in Jefferson County. The first demonstration occurred on the Long plantation near Moscow during the week of February 14. He conducted a public demonstration near Frank Fletcher's gin at Tamo on March 3, and the next day went to the Hall farm south of Grady in Lincoln County. About two hundred farmers saw the picker in operation. Rust called this model the New Universal Rust Cotton Picker. Mounted on a Ford tractor, the machine was a lightweight model, stripped of unnecessary parts to reduce its weight as well as its price.

The Rust machine performed well under less than ideal conditions; the cotton standing in the fields should have been picked five months earlier, and it was badly beaten down by the weather. But the machine drew rave reviews. "The picker is the best mechanical picker I've seen so far," Fletcher said. "Under any conditions even approaching satisfactory, it does a nearly perfect job of picking."[59]

As excitement mounted over the Rust picker, the Implement Truck and Supply Company, an International Harvester dealer in Pine Bluff, ran an ad in the Pine Bluff *Commercial* promoting International Harvester's pickers.[60] According to the ad, Jefferson County farmers already owned nine International Harvester pickers. In addition, Allis-Chalmers was almost ready to begin manufacturing Rust pickers. But implement companies were far short of being able to satisfy the market demand, which was on the verge of exploding.

The Rust demonstration inspired local leaders to launch an effort to establish a "cotton picker factory" in Pine Bluff. A group of businessmen in the Pine Bluff Industrial Foundation approached Rust with the idea of licensing a local company to manufacture Rust pickers. The Farm Bureau also contributed to the effort. The *Commercial* and its farm editor Victor K. Ray devoted their pages to securing the local plant.

By mid-March Rust had agreed to bring cotton picker manufacturing to Pine Bluff. Ben Pearson Manufacturing Company Inc., a company best known for archery equipment, had been looking for a new area of expansion.[61] Nothing was hotter than cotton pickers after the war. On April 2, 1949, less than two months after Rust first came to Pine Bluff, the *Commercial* announced in a front-page headline "Very Important Chapter in South's Agricultural History Opened Here." Ben Pearson agreed to build one hundred machines if farmers would place orders for them and if they each put up $1,000 in advance. The machines were to be delivered by October 1, 1949, at a unit cost of $3,750. Farmers could have their pickers made to fit either a Ford-Ferguson or a John Deere tractor. The first machines were sold directly from the factory, but Rust hoped that future machines would be sold through co-ops. Ben Pearson's future plans were grandiose. The company believed it could turn out five thousand machines per year.[62]

In 1949 Rust moved to Pine Bluff and worked as a consultant with Ben Pearson engineers in building mechanical pickers. By the end of the year, Pearson had manufactured one hundred Rust pickers and sold ninety-nine of them.[63] The first Pearson model was a one-row picker mounted on a tractor, but it suffered from Pearson's lack of the experience in building farm machinery. In 1950, after a reengineering effort, the Pearson picker became a self-propelled unit in a design that was more reliable.

Painted blue with yellow trim, the machines manufactured by Ben Pearson were equipped with two picking units, which could be rigged one behind the other for double picking on a single row or side by side for two-row operation. They used Rust's latest innovations. Though he still favored smooth, spring wire spindles, his postwar machines contained a device to roughen the spindles and make them more aggressive for use under adverse conditions. He also added a fluffer. When bolls were small and knotty, they were difficult to pick. Rust's fluffer—a whirling rubber paddle wheel—struck each boll just as it entered the spindles, exploding the cotton into a fluffy mass. The fluffer made cotton easier to pick, and, according to Rust, eliminated the need for double harvesting. Rust called his machine the "universal cotton harvester" because he claimed it would operate well under all conditions. He still maintained that "plain spring wire spindles" were just as aggressive and superior to machines equipped with "more costly barb type spindles."[64] Based on a design from the late 1930s, Rust developed for the 1951 season a machine called the Universal Pull Model designed for small farms.

After the first run of Rust pickers, Ben Pearson produced and sold four hundred Rust pickers in 1950 and 1951.[65] Pearson went on to produce variations of the Rust picker, including units that could be mounted on Case and Massey-Ferguson tractors. The company continued to manufacture its own Rust pickers until the mid-1960s. The Ben Pearson Rust Cotton Picker proved most popular in the western cotton areas and in foreign markets. In the Mississippi River Delta, most cotton farmers went red and green—the colors of International Harvester and Deere, respectively.

Allis-Chalmers and Ben Pearson competed in the shadow of the giant implement companies. They both were able to sell their machines by associating their products with the Rust name. By mid-1953, according to Rust, Allis-Chalmers had produced 2,000 pickers using his patents, and Ben Pearson had manufactured 1,500.[66]

The Cotton Picker Market

As farm implement companies, large and small, began commercial production of mechanical pickers, they faced a series of crucial questions: How large was the market for mechanical cotton pickers? Considering the small size of most cotton farms and the relatively high cost of the machines, what farmers could afford to purchase and profitably use a mechanical picker? In what geographical areas should sales efforts be concentrated?

In a 1946 market study International Harvester divided the nation's 1,589,706 cotton farms, as reported in the 1940 census, into five groups based on their cotton acreage and production in bales, income, and other factors.[67] The company's market analysis identified farms that produced one hundred or more bales each year as the "top market" for potential cotton picker sales (table 6.3).

TABLE 6.3. Potential Market for Mechanical Pickers by Number of Bales Produced, 1946

Bale Group	No. of Farms in Group	Potential Customers	TOTAL POTENTIAL PICKERS	
			One-Row High Drum	Low-Cost
100 and over	5,608	5,608	7,200	None
50–100	10,884	10,884	5,600	11,000
25–50	35,651	22,318	*	22,000
10–25	193,584	*	*	*
1–10	1,343,979	*	*	*
Totals	1,589,706	38,810	12,800	33,000

*Undetermined.

Source: J. A. Hamilton, "A Study of the Market for Cotton Pickers," January 31, 1946, McCormick International Harvester Collection, 1881–1985, IHC Documented Series, box 468, vol. 1, item 18.

These "top market" farms embodied a series of characteristics that indicated their ability to purchase and use mechanical pickers:

- Average net income from $4,400 to $36,000
- One or more tractors
- High yield—average of a bale to the acre
- In areas best adapted topographically to mechanical production
- Annual outlay for handpicking approximating or exceeding the cost of a picker (the cost of handpicking at $2.25 per hundredweight for seed cotton amounted to $33.75 per bale, or $3,375 on each one hundred acres)

Assuming an average annual capacity of two hundred acres per picker, this group of 5,608 farms would require 7,200 harvesters. Additionally it was assumed that IH's one-row, high-drum picker was designed specifically for the "extreme conditions" where most of the farms in the group were located—that is, in the Mississippi River Delta and the irrigated cotton areas of the far West.

International Harvester believed that farms in the next group, producing between fifty and one hundred bales, represented an ideal market for a low-cost picker (table 6.3). These farms were expected to need either 5,600 high-drum pickers or, if available, 11,000 low-cost pickers. Farms in this classification were already highly mechanized, with 76 percent having tractors and sufficient income, from $2,000 to $3,000, to purchase a low-cost machine. Harvester even believed that the next lowest group, producing twenty-five to fifty bales, might be able to afford a low-cost picker since 62.7 percent of these farms, too, already had tractors.

Taking into account income, tractor ownership, and acreage in cotton, this market study predicted 38,810 potential customers for mechanical cotton pickers. In its initial sales efforts, however, International Harvester focused on the top market—that is, farms producing one hundred or more bales per year.

Harvester's marketing studies apportioned the picker market among its dealer network. Using slightly revised figures, the marketing department envisioned 5,476 cotton farmers harvesting one hundred bales or more as potential customers (table 6.4). At two hundred acres per machine, the market for cotton pickers consisted of 7,113 pickers.[68] The Memphis district, where Harvester manufactured its pickers, was the largest potential market. Here International projected the sale of 1,444 units. California and Texas districts also represented large markets, but most districts were very conservative in estimating their potential sales. Memphis, for example, estimated sales at only

55 percent of what IH's estimates said their sales should be. Overall, however, IH dealers in the Memphis district projected sales of 2,843 pickers, or only 40 percent of the 7,113 estimated as being in the top market. Most dealerships were apparently not eager to build up heavy inventories of cotton pickers without knowing more about how farmers might assess the labor situation.

International Harvester's initial sales were indeed sluggish, especially in the South, where the company expected to see the largest response. With the entrance of Deere as a major competitor—along with Allis-Chalmers and Ben Pearson—the market for cotton harvesting machines became intensely competitive. The market was also highly changeable, with both pickers and strippers being sold in areas where they were initially not assumed to have general use. Some farmers shifted between pickers and strippers as new cotton varieties were introduced. Still another factor in the volatile market was the introduction of lower-priced machines, thus expanding the potential market by making it possible for smaller farmers to justify such a purchase.

In response International Harvester's marketing department lowered its primary cotton picker market from farms with one hundred bales to cotton farms with fifty or more acres of cotton. Harvester believed that as little as fifty acres of bale-to-the-acre cotton could be harvested with a mechanical picker at no more than the cost of hand labor. This revision increased the number of potential farms from 7,113, which IH initially believed could purchase 5,476 pickers, to 58,541 farms with the potential for purchasing 44,480 pickers (table 6.4).

The reason for this action was clear. By January 1952 there were already 7,855 mechanical cotton pickers in use across the country; in other words, the initial IH estimate of the top market had already been exceeded. The market had to expand if Harvester along with its competitors were to continue manufacturing pickers. In the Memphis district, for example, 1,250 pickers were already in service by 1952; these machines covered 87 percent of the original estimated market, leaving only 194 prospective sales. The region's new estimated potential, however, increased the market from 1,444 machines to 8,095. As a result IH could operate on the assumption that only 17.8 percent of the market had been covered; the region still had the potential for absorbing 6,651 additional machines.

The revised market strategy proved highly successful. Between 1949 and 1954 Harvester had sold only 2,699 pickers in the southern region, less than

TABLE 6. 4.   Potential Cotton Picker Market by District and Number of Bales Produced, 1947–1953

	1947 STUDY		1953 STUDY	
	Farms Reporting 100 Bales of Cotton	Pickers Required at 200 Bales Per Picker	Farms Reporting 50 Acres of Cotton	Estimated Cotton Picker Market
Amarillo	240	433	0	0
Atlanta	216	212	3,341	1,517
Birmingham	76	109	3,107	1,650
Charlotte	168	204	2,308	1,389
Dallas	291	350	9,563	3,281
Houston	153	345	4,932	2,131
Little Rock	354	469	6,620	3,281
Los Angeles	744	995	2,005	6,519
Memphis	1,287	1,444	9,774	8,095
Nashville	0	0	0	0
New Orleans	4	4	469	221
Oklahoma City	24	38	152	55
Richmond	0	0	0	0
San Antonio	448	735	7,220	4,709
San Francisco	665	790	2,426	6,324
Shreveport	216	255	2,053	1,062
St. Louis	179	200	1,643	1,073
Sweetwater	411	530	2,738	3,055
Other districts	0	0	190	118
Totals	5,476	7,113	58,541	44,480

Note: Computed on a county basis and accumulated for the district total, which varied from a simple division of acres by two hundred acres per picker.

*IH stated that these figures probably included dealer estimate covering adjacent territory.

Source: J. A. Hamilton, Comparison of Cotton Picker Potential Market with Branch Sale Estimates, March 10, 1947, McCormick International Harvester Collection, 1881–1985, IHC Documented Series, box 468, vol. 2, item 35; M. J. Steitz to C. M. Albright, January 30, 1953, box 468, "Farm Machinery Reports," vol. 4, item 90, ibid.

half of their annual production. Between 1949 and 1964, however, the company sold 24,003 cotton pickers, reaching 61.8 percent of what its marketing department had considered to be the potential market in 1946 (table 6.5). Over the fifteen years between 1949 and 1963, IH produced an average of 133 pickers a month. By going after smaller farmers, the company increased its potential sales in the southern region to over 80 percent. Western sales remained weak because Harvester had aimed its effort at the market for spindle pickers in the old Cotton Belt.

In estimating the potential picker market, International Harvester's marketing department also kept close watch on the labor situation. The following statement appeared in a 1946 internal assessment:

TABLE 6.5. International Harvester Cotton Picker Sales, 1949–1963

	U.S.	SOUTHERN REGION	Percentage	WESTERN REGION	Percentage
1949	1,178	743	63.1	406	34.5
1950	742	175	23.6	557	75.1
1951	2,191	767	35.0	1,394	63.6
1952	2,338	1,014	43.4	1,295	55.4
1953	2,408	1,930	80.1	369	15.3
1954	1,143	973	85.1	36	3.1
1955	1,377	1,121	81.4	70	5.1
1956	1,720	1,474	85.7	123	7.2
1957	702	417	59.4	234	0.9
1958	337	135	40.1	202	33.3
1959	1,155	908	78.6	186	16.1
1960	2,391	2,024	84.7	233	9.8
1961	2,457	2,151	87.5	172	7.0
1962	1,977	1,697	85.8	185	9.4
1963	1,887	1,539	81.6	236	12.5
Totals	24,003	17,068	71.1	5,698	23.7

Source: M. J. Steitz, 1965 Farm Equipment Sales Data, January 22, 1965, box 470, vol. 10, tab 215,

The return of any large amount of labor to the cotton harvest after cessation of hostilities in Europe and Japan did not materialize as planters anticipated. For that reason it was fortunate that the 1945 cotton crop (9,000,000 bales) was the smallest in this century excepting for 1921. As it was, labor shortages were so great that had it not been for the Prisoner of War labor much of the cotton would not have been harvested.

All Prisoners of War are expected to be repatriated by the early part of 1946, so that this type of labor will not [again] be available for the cotton harvest. Nor do planters now feel that pre-war harvest labor will return for several years, at least not while there are opportunities for employment in the industrial areas.

In the [Mississippi River] Delta Area, for instance, the few families that returned in 1945 demanded a better type of tenant house than had been afforded them before. The planters' reaction to this is to invest their money in mechanical harvesting equipment rather than in housing facilities. In that way they can reduce the number of cropper families from one for every 25 acres to one family for every 100 acres. The remaining families would be required for the hoeing and chopping.

It can be concluded that if mechanical cotton pickers are available in the next year or two, planters (who are now very much in the frame of mind to mechanize) will do so without any qualms about their so-called obligation to labor. However, if production of mechanical pickers is delayed any length of time, and labor filters back into the cotton fields, planters will be forced to invest in the costly maintenance of families that has contributed so greatly to the high production cost of cotton. In such an event the acceptance of the mechanical cotton picker will be retarded seriously.[69]

Given postwar labor conditions, the company saw a window of opportunity to take control of the market for cotton pickers. Still struggling with a labor shortage, Delta farmers retained German POW labor to ensure sufficient labor for picking cotton in the fall of 1945, six months after the war in Europe ended.

In its assessment of labor conditions IH echoed the widespread view that, first, labor was gone from the cotton fields; second, that labor would not return to cotton picking at prewar wage rates; and, third, cotton farmers did not want labor to return if they could mechanize their cotton harvest. In other words, farmers had come to see machines as a viable alternative to labor hassles and an expected postwar labor shortage.

International Harvester's sales strategy performed adequately in the overall cotton picker market. Combined production data for pickers and strippers are readily available, but production figures for pickers alone are sporadic.

Between 1948 and 1963, a period with relatively complete sales data, 80,688 pickers and strippers were produced and sold. Over this period, Harvester sold 24,003 units, a market share of 29.7 percent (table 6.6). This performance, however, confirmed the market's volatility. No single company could dominate the early cotton picker market.

By 1950 the development of a commercially successful mechanical cotton

TABLE 6.6. Production of Cotton Pickers and Strippers, 1948–1963

Year	Pickers	Pickers and Strippers	International Harvester	IH's Production Percentage
1948	—	2,552	—	—
1949	—	2,063	1,178	—
1950	—	2,213	742	—
1951	—	9,051	2,191	—
1952	4,771	8,282	2,338	49.0
1953	3,757	7,103	2,408	64.0
1954	3,123	4,150	1,143	36.6
1955	2,423	4,067	1,377	56.8
1956	—	11,066*	1,720	—
1957	—	1,038*	702	—
1958	1,107	3,256	337	30.4
1959	—	5,625	1,155	—
1960	—	10,830	2,391	—
1961	—	—	2,457	—
1962	—	—	1,977	—
1963	5,012	9,392	1,887	37.6
Totals	20,193	80,688	24,003	

*Shipments
—Data unavailable

Source: Table 6.5; *Implement and Tractor* 75 (November 12, 1960): 52–53; idem, 76 (November 15, 1961): 75. See also U.S. Bureau of the Census, *Current Industrial Reports,* Farm Machines and Equipment, Series M35A; and Tractors (Except Garden Tractors), Series M35S (Washington, D.C: GPO, 1948–1964).

picker had been accomplished, the culmination of a concerted effort over the past twenty years and an investment of millions of dollars. The mystery of how to build a machine that would actually pick cotton, so daunting at first, had been solved. For more than a decade the Cotton South lived with the fear that the cotton picker would cause turmoil and chaos in the region's economy and social structure. With the dreaded machine ready at last for production in large quantities, that time had arrived.

Handpicking cotton in Arkansas, 1947. Picking was often a family affair. National Archives, 16-G-116–1–11/16-S-14962.

International Harvester experimental one-row, pull-type picker, 1927. State Historical Society of Wisconsin, Whi(X3)51734.

John Rust operating an experimental cotton picker at Stoneville, Mississippi, 1934.
National Archives, 16-G-116–1–5067.

Rust portrait by Pietro Lazzari. Pine
Bluff/Jefferson County Historical
Museum, Pine Bluff, Arkansas.

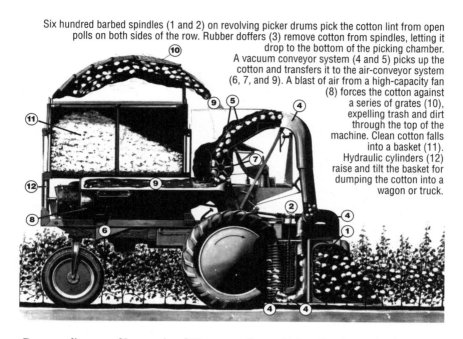

Six hundred barbed spindles (1 and 2) on revolving picker drums pick the cotton lint from open polls on both sides of the row. Rubber doffers (3) remove cotton from spindles, letting it drop to the bottom of the picking chamber. A vacuum conveyor system (4 and 5) picks up the cotton and transfers it to the air-conveyor system (6, 7, and 9). A blast of air from a high-capacity fan (8) forces the cotton against a series of grates (10), expelling trash and dirt through the top of the machine. Clean cotton falls into a basket (11). Hydraulic cylinders (12) raise and tilt the basket for dumping the cotton into a wagon or truck.

Cutaway diagram of International Harvester Cotton Picker showing path of cotton from picking unit to basket. State Historical Society of Wisconsin, Whi(X3)51733/I-2283-HH.

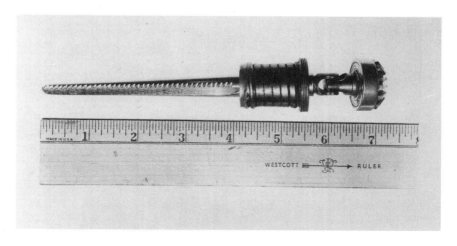

Spindle showing tapered body and serrations, International Harvester. State Historical Society of Wisconsin, Whi(X3)51731.

Fowler McCormick, president of International Harvester, operating a cotton picker on the Hopson plantation near Clarksdale, Mississippi, 1942. State Historical Society of Wisconsin, Whi(X3)51732.

Harvesting with a fleet of cotton pickers at Stoneville, Mississippi, October 1946. National Archives, 16-N-11980.

International Harvester picker in use near Stoneville, Mississippi, October 1946.
National Archives, 16-N-8690.

A 1936 experimental
Rust picker on the side
of a road south of Pine
Bluff, Arkansas, 1991.

"Ef'n It Doose Mah Wuk—Whose Wuk I Gwine Do?"

Cartoon published at the time of the Rust demonstration at Stoneville, Mississippi. *Memphis Commercial Appeal*, September 2, 1936. Copyright, 1936, The Commercial Appeal, Memphis, Tennessee. Used with permission.

A model M-120 International Harvester picker manufactured in 1954 on the James Santucci farm near Leland, Mississippi. This picker is still in running condition, 1999.

Close-up of spindles and doffers on M-120 picker.

A deteriorating International Harvester picker on display in front of the Hopson plantation commissary, 1999.

Chapter 7

The Cotton South's Gradual Revolution, 1950–1970

At last, after a century of testing and hundreds of patents, the mechanical cotton picker was a reality. Four corporations had cotton pickers in commercial production by 1950, and they were eager to sell and service them. The full use of the mechanical cotton picker in the South, however, was still a generation away. More than twenty years passed between 1948, when the earliest production models rolled off the assembly lines, and 1970, when the region's cotton was 100 percent machine picked. The South experienced a revolution, but a gradual revolution.

After the dramatic upheavals of the depression and World War II, the postwar South was on the verge of vast social and economic change. The outmigration of the previous decade had reduced the region's oversupply of cheap labor and improved the lives of most of the migrants. The Agricultural Adjustment Administration enabled cotton growers to eliminate many sharecroppers, to consolidate their landholdings, and to purchase tractors. These changes were definitely in the right direction.

At the end of the war, cotton farmers enjoyed the highest prices they had seen since 1918—more than thirty-two cents per pound.[1] But along with high prices came labor shortages and consequent higher labor costs. The wartime migration to defense industries and military service had given people, black and white, the taste for a life that they could not afford as sharecroppers and day laborers. They refused to return to the living standard they experienced before the war. As Gavin Wright argued, the low-wage southern labor market had merged into the high-wage national labor market.[2] Government wage ceilings imposed in 1945 and 1946 were only temporarily successful in holding down farm labor costs. But even with higher pay, labor was not only more recalcitrant, but also the quality of hand labor declined.[3]

If the future of the cotton industry appeared as problematic as ever, many popular writers expressed a positive view of the South's postwar prospects. World War II had lifted the region into unprecedented prosperity, purged it of its flaws, and, according to many observers, poised it for a new era of agricultural diversification and industrial progress. But this was a Pollyanna view of the South's future.[4] There was real worry among social commentators about the impact of mechanical pickers on the South's traditional structure of tenant farming and sharecropping, but even more alarming were the prospects of cotton itself in the world economy. The fundamental problem was the high cost of producing American cotton because its inefficient, archaic methods priced it out of world markets. The postwar South seemed to stand on the brink of fundamental change that would lead either to a better future—or to a future as bleak as that of the depression South.

The South's Future

In 1946 economist Peter Drucker published an article in *Harper's* announcing: "The Deep South is entering upon a process of change as dramatic, as rapid, and as profound as any of the major waves of the Industrial Revolution." He agreed that the South would eventually become prosperous, but the mechanization of cotton farming and the shift from cotton to other crops would drive millions of people off the land. This was no longer a promise or threat, he said, it was reality. Engineers had solved the problems of mechanical cotton picking, and assembly lines were ready to launch mass production of these machines. He predicted that five to eight million people would lose out. In his words, "The economic and social structure that was founded on one machine —Eli Whitney's cotton gin—is being razed by another—the cotton picker."[5]

Drucker believed that the world cotton market demanded that American cotton sell for much less than the current price or lose its market share. As a result American cotton growers had to lower their production costs. "Technologically," he emphasized, "cotton farming as it has been practiced in the South is two hundred years behind the times." Efficient production could only be achieved on large farms; thus, Drucker predicted, the nature of postwar agriculture would allow no room for the majority of the present farm population. Complicating this situation was the fact that the majority of these superfluous people were black.

In the *New Republic,* freelance writer J. Mitchell Morse asserted, "The mechanical cotton-picker has started an industrial revolution that is going to change the whole economic structure of the South." He predicted the loss of almost a million families. According to Morse, "Whole families will be not only unemployed but uprooted, stranded in the country without a house to live in or a place to go or a dollar in their pockets." Low southern wages—called the "southern differential"—had always been a threat to the living standards in other parts of the country; now the threat would take a new form: migration. "These problems are not new," he said. "The mechanical cotton picker did not cause them, but it will surely aggravate them."[6]

According to another liberal magazine, the *Nation,* cotton and the South were poised to strike a blow against the whole country. A one-row machine picker can do the work of fifty people, and a double-row picker can do the work of a hundred. As these machines come into general use, the *Nation* predicted, millions of southerners would become "displaced persons." The new mechanical cotton picker would push from five to eight million people off the land. "Illiterate or semi-literate, warped by poverty and ignorance," the *Nation* warned, "they will drag down the level of citizenship wherever they go."[7]

After the war, David L. Cohn, the Mississippi writer-lawyer-businessman, felt a deep sense of pessimism about the future. In his view:

> The coming problem of agricultural displacement in the [Mississippi] Delta and the whole South is of huge proportions and must concern the entire nation. The time to prepare for it is now, but since we as a nation rarely act until catastrophe is upon us, it is likely we shall muddle along until it is too late. The country is upon the brink of a process of change as great as any that has occurred since the Industrial Revolution. . . . Five million people will be removed from the land within the next few years. They must go somewhere. But where? They must do something. But what? They must be housed. But where is the housing?
>
> Most of this group are farm Negroes totally unprepared for urban, industrial life. How will they be industrially absorbed? What will be the effect of throwing them upon the labor market? What will be their reception at the hands of white and Negro workers whose jobs and wages they threaten?
>
> There are other issues involved here of an even greater gravity. If tens of thousands of Southern Negroes descend upon communities totally unprepared for them psychologically and industrially, what will the effect be upon race relations in the United States? Will the Negro problem be transferred from the South to other parts of the nation who have hitherto been concerned with it only as carping critics of the South? Will the victims of farm mechanization become the victims of race conflict?[8]

Cohn had more questions than answers, but he believed that the effect of black migration would be greater in the North than in the South.

Despite such dire warnings agricultural professionals were more balanced in their view of the South's postwar future. While their opinions varied, they expected mechanization to occur slowly enough to avoid major problems. Most of these professionals even welcomed the impact of capital-intensive agriculture.

In 1946 Arthur Raper, a sociologist working with the Bureau of Agricultural Economics, predicted that mechanization would solve some of the South's economic and social problems as well as create new ones. He foresaw an increase in the size of farms, a decrease in the number of farm operators, and a sharp decrease in the number of tenants, particularly black tenants. Raper estimated that each tractor put into use would displace at least one and possibly more families.[9]

For Raper, the South's problems derived from a complex assortment of causes, including a lack of mechanization, a labor shortage and a corresponding rise in farm wages, and the shrinking position of cotton in world markets.

> It's no mystery . . . [he said] why most cotton farmers have had small incomes and big debts. They have been using the money earned in a hand economy to buy consumer goods in a machine economy, and enough has not been earned to satisfy increasing wants. Work as hard as he may, a man with a mule can't win when he's living in an economy where most other men use machines.[10]

The only way to produce cheaper cotton, Raper declared flatly, was to mechanize cotton production. He also addressed the concern of those who argued that it was wrong for mechanization to proceed if it pushed people off the land. For Raper,

> [T]here was no more reason to put restraints on the mechanization of cotton production than there was to have stopped the use of machinery in factories, or of steam locomotives on the railroads, years ago. No one, I think, would argue that shoes should be produced by hand, that wheat should be cut with a cradle, or that automobiles should be made in a blacksmith's shop by one or two mechanics. Cotton is simply one of the last great enterprises to be mechanized.[11]

Indeed, while the mechanization of cotton would cause hardships, the lack of mechanization had also produced great human problems—small farms, low incomes, irregular school attendance, poor housing, debt and credit problems, soil depletion, and inadequate medical care for low-income families.

In a 1947 speech entitled "The Cotton Industry's Responsibility in Mechanization," Oscar Johnston, president of the National Cotton Council and head of Delta and Pine Land Company at Scott, Mississippi, cautioned against any sense of panic. He predicted that mechanization would emerge gradually since farmers still needed hand labor. At Scott he continued to employ hand labor because of the disadvantage of trash in machine-picked cotton, making it a practice to handpick cotton at least once before putting a mechanical harvester in the field. As for labor displacement, Johnston asserted that mechanization was replacing labor that had already left the South, not pushing workers off the farm.[12]

While mechanization caused foreboding among some commentators, Johnston's vision of the region's future was highly positive. He offered this reassurance: "I contend now as always that mechanization of cotton production means progress—not economic and social chaos—to the people of the Cotton Belt."[13]

Agricultural economists Frank J. Welch and D. Gray Miley saw the need for reform in southern agriculture, but they did not foresee a rapid shift to complete mechanization in the near future.[14] Despite the advantages of machine picking, popular opinion opposed it. Mechanization would destroy the mythology of the Old South plantation, which had its vested interests.[15] The "heavy hand of inertia" would delay, they predicted, the shift to mechanization even if comparative costs were favorable.

In 1950 rural economist John Leonard Fulmer argued that mechanical harvesting had not made as much progress as was generally believed, nor would it have serious repercussions in the near future. He suggested that the profitable use of mechanical cotton pickers depended on price and yield. If the price of cotton dropped under twenty cents, pickers would not be profitable compared to handpicking except for farmers whose land yielded a bale per acre.

Fulmer's lack of worry about mechanization emerged from several considerations, including the limited number of farms that had the necessary acreage together with the high yields necessary to afford full use of picking machines. Fulmer also estimated that the top limit of future labor displacement by the picker was about 518,000 workers, a large but not, in his view, an inordinate number. He noted that according to reports only 570 pickers were used in the Mississippi Delta in 1948—a number far too small to have an extreme impact on labor displacement.[16]

As it turned out, the cautious optimists were right about the South's future.

The process of mechanization seemed stalled on the verge of "take-off," not advancing as rapidly as some feared or as others hoped. At the end of World War II, the complete mechanization of the South's cotton industry was still far enough away to allow a gradual transition that would avoid panic and hardship.

Ancillary Developments

The reason for the postwar delay in cotton mechanization lay in the three distinct operations, or "labor peaks," as they were known, in the cotton production process itself: land breaking, planting, and cultivating; thinning and weeding; and harvesting.[17]

According to a 1939 study, the harvest alone consumed well over half of the man-hours required per acre (table 7.1). With the use of tractor cultivation, the total labor required only decreased from 150.3 to 135.8 man-hours. Tractor use made little impact as long as the hand-labor peaks of weeding and harvesting remained unchanged. Cotton production could not be fully mechanized until all three labor peaks were adapted to labor-saving techniques. This entire process covered a period of forty years. Until the 1960s cotton growers did not have a full set of technological tools to mechanize all labor peaks. Land breaking, planting, and cultivating with tractors were the first series of steps to be mechanized. Mechanical harvesting occurred next, but still left unmechanized one labor peak—weed control. The control of weeds with herbicides was the last to be conquered (figure 7.1).

Even after the development of tractors and cotton harvesters, the simple,

TABLE 7.1 Man-Hours per Acre in Cotton Production, Yazoo-Mississippi Delta, 1939

Activity	Hours	Percentage
Breaking, planting, and cultivating using one mule	9.3	6.2
Cultivating, thinning, and weeding	46.5	30.9
Harvesting	94.5	62.9
Total hours	150.3	100.0

Source: E. L. Langsford and B. H. Thibodeaux, *Plantation Organization and Operation in the Yazoo-Mississippi Delta Area,* Technical Bulletin No. 682 (Washington, D.C.: U.S. Department of Agriculture, May 1939), 58.

	1885	1910	1921	1924	1926	1928	1936	1942	1943	1949	1950	1950s	1955	1964	1970
Tractors (Land Breaking, Planting, and Cultivating)				IH began production of the general-purpose Farmall Tractor								Farmers widely adopt four-row equipment			
Mechanical Cotton Pickers (Harvesting)	Angus Campbell began work on a spindle-type picker	Campbell teamed with T. H. Price	IH experimented with a vacuum-type picker	IH began work on a spindle machine	West Texas farmers used homemade strippers	John D. Rust filed for his first patent for a picker with a moistened spindle	Rust demonstrated his machine at Delta Experiment Station, Stoneville, Mississippi	Fowler McCormick, president of IH, announced his company has a picker ready for production		IH picker went into full commercial production					100 percent of cotton in Mississippi River Delta was machine picked
Herbicides (Weeding)									Flame weeders tested at Stoneville, Mississippi		Herbicide oils appeared on the market		Diuron introduced by DuPont	The herbicide Treflan publicized in a television commercial and becomes household word	

FIGURE 7.1. Major developments in the mechanization of cotton production in the Mississippi River Delta, 1885–1970.

flat-bladed hoe still remained the most utilized instrument for grass and weed control. Even if harvesting were mechanized, cotton still had to be thinned and weeded in the summer and the labor required for these tasks was substantial.

The agricultural establishment—experiment stations and implement companies—tried a variety of techniques to solve the weed control problem. During the war many farmers cross-cultivated their cotton—that is, planting cotton spaced far enough apart in a checkerboard pattern so that they could cultivate not only up and down rows but also across rows. This technique eliminated much hand thinning as well as chopping. Cotton could easily be planted and then plowed "in checks." In addition, farmers experimented with a variety of mechanical cotton choppers, including "rotary hoes," but mechanical cotton choppers never achieved success. The weed problem was also closely tied to successful mechanical harvesting. Aside from the problem of choking out young cotton plants, mechanical harvesters could not operate in fields filled with grass and weeds.

The flame weeder, or "flame thrower" in World War II jargon, applied a flammable gas to kill weeds. The flame took advantage of the cotton stalk's reputation for toughness. The jets were adjusted so that the heat killed weeds, but the stalk remained unharmed. The flame cultivators were a sign, as geographer Charles Aiken noted, of "the desperate nature of the problem."[18]

These experimental techniques all had their drawbacks. Flame cultivation, for example, could not be used early in the cotton season before the cotton stalks had become tough enough to withstand unusual heat. Many farmers were understandably reluctant to risk killing their cotton plants by exposing them to flame. Cross plowing tended to produce rhythmic slugging of mechanical pickers as they crossed the rows, reducing their efficiency and their life span.[19]

The use of geese to weed cotton was a curious method tried on a limited basis in northeast Arkansas. In the 1950s the Lee Wilson plantation in Mississippi County experimented with "weeder geese," which ate weeds, especially johnsongrass, but left the cotton plants alone. One brace of geese could keep an acre weeded, and they were cheaper than hand hoeing or chemicals. Alas, geese too had their limitations. They grew fat and trampled young cotton plants, and insecticides could poison them. Cotton fields also had to be fenced. The unexpected sound of honking geese contrasted with the clatter of modern farm machinery. For motorists, geese always served to turn heads and they created astonishment as the birds honked their way across the fields.[20]

Chopping or thinning cotton was ultimately a problem of plant genetics.

As early as the 1920s new varieties of cotton with higher germination rates eliminated the practice of planting cotton in a solid drill. Eventually, a technique called "hill-dropping" ensured adequate spacing between plants, thus eliminating entirely the need for thinning.

The weed problem, however, was solved not by machines but by chemicals. The introduction of herbicides occurred in the 1950s, but reliable chemicals were not available until the 1960s. Preemergence herbicides were applied as cotton was planted but had a limited period of effectiveness, and hand weeding was necessary after four to six weeks. As the initial treatment lost its effectiveness, postemergence herbicides were applied to growing plants to continue weed control. The chemical Diuron became a successful herbicide in 1955; and a television commercial in 1964 made Treflan, a preemergent herbicide, a household word among the general public.

The use of chemicals required special care: preemergent chemicals could not be applied too early without the risk of killing the cotton plant; and they could wash away after a rain. As the process of experimentation proceeded, many farmers used a combination of flame control, cross plowing, and chemicals. By the 1960s farmers also had available better insecticides and fungicides.[21]

Thus the cotton picker alone, though a major development, was not enough to ensure the full mechanization of cotton production. The ancillary requirements seemed to go on and on. The cotton plant itself had to be changed. Mechanical pickers could not accommodate the rank plants that grew as high as six feet in the Mississippi River Delta. Instead, plant breeders created a shorter plant with bolls that remained high off the ground and opened more uniformly, eliminating extra passes through the fields. Since machine-picked cotton contained excessive trash, chemists developed defoliants that stripped cotton plants of their leaves before picking. Ginners installed dryers because machine-picked cotton had a high moisture content, as well as cleaners to reduce grade loss. There was unexpected good news, too. Despite the early fears that mechanical pickers might damage cotton fibers, it was found that machine-picked cotton was stronger than handpicked because machines picked the stronger fibers. "In other words," as Gilbert Fite observed, "before full mechanization of the cotton crop could be achieved the combined contributions of engineers, chemists and fertilizer specialists, plant breeders, entomologists, agronomists, and other scientists were necessary."[22]

In the various phases of technological development, public agencies stepped in to do research on mechanical pickers, plant breeding, and the application of chemicals. As early as 1927, the Texas A & M Experiment

Station carried on significant research with cotton strippers.[23] The Delta Experiment Station at Stoneville, Mississippi, emerged as a center of spindle picker research. In 1946 Congress enacted the Research and Marketing Act, which provided supplemental funding to agricultural experiment stations and encouraged them to cooperate to solve problems that affected agriculture in more than one state.[24] This legislation led to the establishment of the National Cotton Mechanization Project at Stoneville, since the station's location and its previous work on mechanization made it a natural choice. W. E. Ayres, superintendent of the Delta Experiment Station in the early 1930s, had an intense interest in early cotton pickers and encouraged many inventors, most notably John Rust, to demonstrate their machines at Stoneville. Under William E. Meek, an agricultural engineer, the Delta Station continued its research on various aspects of cotton mechanization across the Cotton Belt.[25]

The National Cotton Council, a trade organization formed in 1939, played a key role in pushing for full mechanization. As an advocate for the cotton industry, this organization worked to improve the competitive position of American cotton, arguing that mechanization was the only way to reduce production costs and make cotton profitable.[26] The organization's major goal was "to increase productivity and income among Cotton Belt farmers through mechanization." To bring together representatives of the farm machinery manufacturers, officials of the U.S. Department of Agriculture, agricultural experiment stations, and agricultural engineers, the council organized the first Beltwide Cotton Mechanization Conference at Stoneville, Mississippi, in 1947. In a hands-on session, Bill Meek demonstrated a flame cultivator, a stripper, a spindle-type picker, a rotary hoe, and other cutting-edge technologies.[27] At subsequent Beltwide meetings, held annually from Atlanta to Lubbock, spokesmen from the cotton industry kept their listeners up to date on the latest developments on flame weeders, herbicides, and other topics of interest.

Across the Cotton Belt from the Delta to the High Plains of Texas and Oklahoma, a select group of adventurous farmers eagerly tried whatever new equipment and methods were available. They worked closely with farm equipment manufacturers and experiment stations. They sometimes proceeded cautiously because new methods were not completely reliable. They all knew that machine-picked cotton was not as clean as handpicked, so they sent hand pickers into the fields first, only afterward using machines. One farmer purchased a mechanical cotton picker but withheld it from use. Since hand labor was plentiful, he kept his investment in reserve in case a labor shortage developed. Flame cultivators did not entirely eliminate the hoe, and farmers still hoed their cotton at least once, only partly reducing labor costs. And, chemicals did not work well without sufficient moisture.

The trepidation that some farmers felt about the use of new technology, often based on sound reasons as well as inertia, slowed the transition to full mechanization.[28] The design and operation of new machines were complicated, many farms were too small and hilly, early machines were expensive, and their useful life was short or uncertain. None of these reasons prevented or even slowed down producers who believed that the use of mechanical harvesters was profitable.[29]

Institutional versus Environmental Delay

In recent years economists have taken up the debate on the slow pace of southern agricultural mechanization. Two competing viewpoints have emerged. In one view the delay of mechanization was a problem in the institutional structure of the South, a reference to the "stultifying" influence of southern institutions like tenancy and sharecropping that were part of the region's historical legacy.[30] Economist Warren C. Whatley has argued that the southern practice of using annual contracts provided the key stumbling block.[31] In cotton production, farmers faced a highly seasonal labor market and used annual labor contracts to reduce variations in labor cost and supply. They had to cover two peak labor demands—weeding and thinning as well as the harvest. The timeliness of labor could make or break a crop. Cotton farmers, Whatley implied, really did not want tenants, but they tolerated them only because they found that annual contracts were the only means of guaranteeing sufficient labor for the periods of peak labor demands, especially picking. No one knew if sufficient labor would be available or at what price. In peak labor periods everyone was hiring labor, possibly forcing up labor costs. The production of cotton was not a full-time job since there were long periods of inactivity during the midsummer and winter. Tenants and sharecroppers contracted for the year, and they were not paid until after the harvest as an incentive to remain and work. For wage workers, employment in agriculture was uncertain and cyclical, but so were landlords' demands for labor. As a result, each side sought to force an annual obligation on the other.

The problem with the annual labor contract, according to Whatley, was not the share feature that so many critics have condemned. It was the annual nature of the contract itself. As Whatley put it, "Uncertain, and potentially costly, labor increased the profitability of adopting labor-saving tractors, but it also restricted the amount of land amenable for mechanization by driving land-lords to use annual share-tenant contracts."[32] So the course of least resistance for landlords was tenancy. As a result the scale of operations was kept small, and it was the small scale that impeded mechanization. If landlords purchased tractors and mechanized their preharvest operations, they still needed tenants to pick the cotton in the fall. Tractors, then, did not necessarily enable grow-ers to reduce the number of workers.

An alternative explanation, however, emphasized environmental factors. Economists Moses S. Musoke and Alan Olmstead compared California's experience in mechanizing cotton to that of the South.[33] While institutional structure partly explained the delay in mechanization, they believed that fac-tors like weather and soil quality associated with the environment were not fully appreciated. Soil quality, for example, related directly to crop yield since poor soil would reduce yields. Similarly, an environment that produced an abundance of weeds added to production costs for hoeing.

California—and the far West, generally—took the lead in cotton mecha-nization even before World War II. According to Musoke and Olmstead, farm mechanization in California was ten to fifteen years ahead of the South. For example, California machine picked over 50 percent of its cotton in 1951, ten years before Arkansas reached this proportion (fig. 7.2). The South fell behind because its agriculture lacked the far West's environmental advantages. California enjoyed exceptionally high yields that resulted from rich soils, ideal climate, irrigation, the best agricultural practices and fertilizer, the use of high-quality cottonseed, and relative freedom from pests. California cotton farms were three or four times as large as southern cotton farms. In California farms growing fewer than ten bales made up less than 20 percent of the state's grow-ers, while in Mississippi farms of that size produced 80 percent of the state's output. The existence of large operating units—not chopped up into small tenancies—created the scale of operations necessary for mechanization. While the Cotton South was taking tentative steps in the right direction, the institu-tional structure of the region was still not ready for mechanization. Specifically the effective size of farm units was still too small. In 1949 the average cotton acreage per cotton-producing farm was only 14.5 acres in Mississippi com-pared to California's 103.1 acres.[34]

In an effort to mechanize preharvest operations, California farmers adopted tractors earlier and in larger numbers than did southern farmers. Labor, too, was entirely different. In California farm labor was based on a piece-rate system with seasonal laborers under contracts. While strikes and

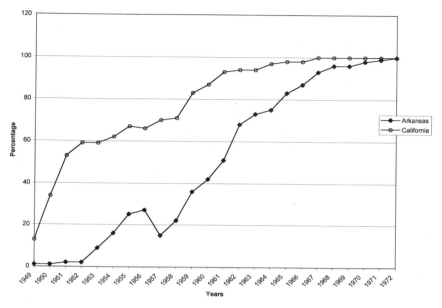

FIGURE 7.2   Percentage of machine-harvested cotton in Arkansas and California, 1949–1972.

Source: U.S. Department of Agriculture, Economic Research Service, *Statistics on Cotton and Related Data, 1920–1973*, Statistical Bulletin No. 535 (Washington, D.C.: USDA, 1974), 218.

even violent disputes marred its agricultural labor relations, California needed less labor than did the South. The seasonal pattern of labor needs was different largely because of the lack of weed problems, a fact that eliminated entirely one of the labor peaks associated with weedier southern fields. This advantage, a product of the California environment, was one reason why preharvest mechanization was easier. Finally, labor scarcity and, as a result, high labor costs provided an important impetus for mechanization.[35]

True, California-style agriculture was possible because of its environmental advantages, but its farms had also avoided the institutional disadvantages of the South. After years of stagnation, the structure of southern agriculture was just not ready for mechanization before World War II. Then several developments came together. The AAA inadvertently helped southern farmers reduce sharecropping with its annual contracts and permitted them to hire short-term wage labor. The out-migration during World War II lowered population stress on rural resources, and labor shortages during the war shattered the plantation economy.

From 1950 to 1970 southern agriculture experienced a series of dramatic changes. Many of its age-old characteristics rapidly broke down, signaling the end of the traditional system. The number of farms declined as the regional economy diversified, cotton acreage declined as southern farmers planted alternative crops like soybeans and rice, and the number of tenants plunged as people left the farm and took up other employment. While the number of farms declined, the size of farms increased. Farmers purchased tractors in greater numbers as they increasingly relied on machine power rather than on mules and hand labor. Tractor ownership was a sign that some or all of the preharvest operations were mechanized. In 1950 Arkansas farmers were the leading tractor users in the Mississippi River Delta, with Louisiana and Mississippi farms lagging behind. Over the next twenty years the ownership of tractors increased dramatically until three-fourths of the farms in the region used tractor power (fig. 7.3).

Mechanization on Large versus Small Farms

After the structure of the tenant economy crumbled and freed farmers from the constraints of annual contracts, it was small farmers rather than the largest operators who most eagerly purchased and used tractors in preharvest operations. Conventional wisdom correctly associates mechanization with large farms, but not in the initial stage of mechanization. Warren Whatley reported a technique that estimated a threshold for tractor use, identifying the smallest farm size that enabled farmers to mechanize.[36] Using county data on farm size in the Mississippi River Delta in 1930, he found that the tractor use was greatest on farms with as few as 260 acres. In other words, medium-sized farmers were most likely to have been the earliest to attempt mechanization. Though these farmers had fewer resources than large planters, they also had more flexibility, and as a result they were better able to accept the risks of mechanization.

When applied to later censuses, Whatley's technique provides additional support for the belief that medium-sized farms occupied the forefront of mechanization. In 1940 the threshold remained at 260 acres, but by 1950 it had fallen to fifty acres. Since the tractor threshold peaked at 260 acres and then declined, this trend implies that the largest farms were not the earliest mechanizers.

Farm size was the most important factor in determining total harvesting costs. Small farmers faced fewer labor problems than did large farmers with thousands of acres to harvest. For example, with the cost of handpicking at $2.75 per hundredweight, a farmer harvesting 50 acres of cotton paid $2,063 for handpicking, assuming a yield of a bale per acre. In contrast, a farmer with 500 acres paid $20,625 to have his cotton handpicked (table 7.2). At this price the small farmer could purchase an IH one-row picker for $4,738 in 1950 and use it for several seasons.[37] While a large farmer anticipated greater potential profit, he received no more for his cotton than did a small farmer. He had less flexibility and could not afford to switch immediately to full mechanization. For small farmers mechanization required less investment, and they could depreciate the cost of the picker over several seasons.

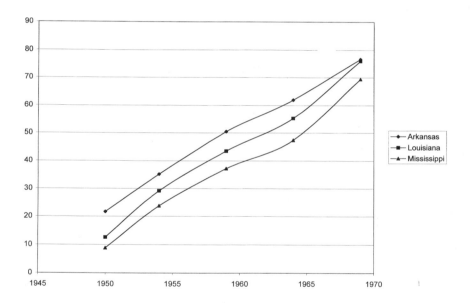

FIGURE 7.3 Tractor ownership as a percentage of farms, Arkansas, Louisiana, and Mississippi, 1950–1969.

*Tractors other than garden tractors.

Source: U.S. Bureau of the Census, *United States Census of Agriculture: 1950, Counties and State Economic Areas, Arkansas, Louisiana, and Mississippi* (Washington, D.C.: GPO, 1952), table 3; U.S. Bureau of the Census, *United States Census of Agriculture: 1954, Counties and State Economic Areas, Arkansas, Louisiana, and Mississippi* (Washington, D.C.: GPO, 1956), table 5; U.S. Bureau of the Census, *Census of Agriculture, 1959, Area Reports Series, Arkansas, Louisiana, and Mississippi* (Washington, D.C.: GPO, 1961), table 6; U.S. Bureau of the Census, *Census of Agriculture, 1964, Statistics for the States and Counties, Arkansas, Louisiana, and Mississippi* (Washington, D.C.: GPO, 1967), tables 5 and 8; U.S. Bureau of the Census, *Census of Agriculture, 1969, Area Reports Series, Mississippi, Arkansas, and Louisiana* (Washington, D.C.: GPO, 1972), table 6.

TABLE 7.2. Total Cost of Handpicking Cotton, by Selected Farm Sizes and Wage Rates per Hundredweight

Acres of Cotton	WAGE RATES PER HUNDREDWEIGHT					
	$1.00	$1.50	$2.00	$2.50	$2.75	$3.00
50	$750	$1,125	$1,500	$1,875	$2,063	$2,250
100	1,500	2,250	3,000	3,750	4,125	4,500
150	2,250	3,375	4,500	5,625	6,188	6,750
200	3,000	4,500	6,000	7,500	8,250	9,000
250	3,750	5,625	7,500	9,375	10,313	11,250
300	4,500	6,750	9,000	11,250	12,375	13,500
500	7,500	11,250	15,000	18,750	20,625	22,500

Note: These calculations are based on the assumption that 1,500 pounds of seed cotton are required to make a 500-pound bale.

Case Studies[38]

In the 1940s, the largest cotton plantation in the South—and presumably worldwide—was the Delta and Pine Land Company at Scott, Mississippi.[39] Delta and Pine Land was a British-owned concern that dated back to the late nineteenth century. Oscar Johnston, the plantation's manager, was also the best-known spokesman for the Cotton South.[40] Located near the Mississippi River in Washington County just north of Greenville, Delta Pine occupied 38,000 acres of rich alluvial land with 25,000 acres in cultivation (over thirty-nine sections of land). Before World War II the plantation was a sharecropper and mule operation that relied on a labor force of hundreds of tenant families.[41] Between 1935 and 1944 Johnston employed an average of 850 tenant families, each one living in their own house. By 1947, three hundred of those tenant houses were empty. The people who occupied them had left during the war, and no one was available to replace them. Johnston still employed 525 families but had to face the prospect that in the near future he was going to have to get along with even fewer tenant families.

Johnston worked hard to adjust Delta Pine to the requirements of mechanized agriculture. As early as 1930, with growing doubts about the tenant system, he had purchased four tractors for use on 3,000 experimental acres. In 1937, though some land preparation was done with tractors, Johnston still planted 11,700 acres of cotton using mules as the power source.[42] During the war, lack of labor and machines forced him to leave 6,000 acres idle. In 1947 he purchased five preproduction mechanical cotton pickers; he hoped by 1955 to have 150 such machines, along with the necessary tractors, plows, cultivators, and flame weeders in sufficient quantity to put the plantation on a "maximum machine basis." But he also planned not to reduce the number of farm families who worked as tenants. Nor did he expect those families to earn less income.

While these goals seemed contradictory, Johnston knew that the mechanization of cotton involved more than mechanical picking. Cotton choppers still had to thin the plants and keep them free from weeds to bring the crop to the picking stage. Mechanical picking obviously depended on how much cotton could be brought to maturity.

After the war, as more tractors, planters, and four-row cultivators became available for purchase, Johnston increased the plantation acreage worked by wage labor. He also increased the acreage allotted to tenants from 10.5 acres to 16 acres per family. The company "brought in the crop" on each tenant's land with mechanical methods, charging them a fee per acre. Many tenants with mechanical aptitude worked as tractor drivers. Tenants still had to do some hand chopping, including working for extra income by chopping some "wages cotton." In the fall they picked their own cotton to get the best, premium-priced fiber. Afterward, they picked the plantation crop at the prevailing daily wage.

Johnston's strategy was to use hand pickers to pick cotton as soon as the bolls burst open and white fluff dotted the fields. Hand pickers picked cleaner cotton than machines, as much as two grades better. Thus handpicked cotton brought a premium price. Later in the fall, when about 70 percent of the bolls were open, he dusted the cotton by airplane with calcium cyanamide, a defoliant. When the plants were bare of leaves, the sun reached the bolls and the late-maturing bolls opened. Only then did Johnston send in machines to harvest the remaining cotton.

Despite seeing the Rust machine demonstrated at Stoneville in 1936, Johnston was initially skeptical of the mechanical cotton picker.[43] But the need to reduce production costs provided a strong incentive for mechanization. Ten years later, his skepticism banished, he was "fully converted to the gospel of mechanized farming."[44]

At the end of the war, Johnston contemplated full mechanization. Under his direction during the 1940s, Delta and Pine Land Company routinely purchased 150 mule colts a year to replenish the supply of work stock; but in preparation to shift away from work stock to tractors he did not purchase a single mule in 1945.[45] Instead, he ordered two mechanical cotton pickers from International Harvester, planning to use them on an experimental tract of land, along with flame weeders and other new technology. The experiment was a success; as a result, Johnston no longer considered mechanized cotton operations in the developmental stage. He predicted that the next fifteen years "will produce a complete cotton crop untouched by hand."[46] At that point he launched a one-million-dollar mechanization program to convert his entire operation to mechanized farming. His plan was ambitious and expensive, but he believed the potential economies would be worth it. As mechanical equipment became available, he intended to operate the 8,700 acres they were allowed under AAA controls with 100 to 150 wage employees, replacing all of the plantation's tenant families.[47] He wanted to operate 75 to 100 cotton pickers along with the necessary complement of auxiliary equipment. But the project faltered. Johnston was unable to translate these grandiose plans into reality because International Harvester could not deliver all of the equipment he needed, and Johnston limited the scale of his mechanized operation.[48]

At Scott, then, full mechanization did not arrive early. Johnston retired in 1950 because of ill health. His successor, Charles R. Sayre, followed a gradual policy toward full mechanization.[49] Under Sayre's leadership, the 1950s was a decade of transformation. Making the transition from tenant labor slowly so as not to displace longtime resident families, he placed all labor on a wage basis by 1960.[50] But he had taken a decade to reach that point.

In 1959, aside from other crops, Delta Pine grew 9,382 acres of cotton averaging 832.6 pounds of lint cotton per acre. Machines picked 48 percent of the crop. An inventory of equipment in 1960 showed that the plantation owned 210 tractors and ancillary equipment and twenty-five cotton pickers. Across Mississippi, cotton farmers used machines to pick only about 40 percent of the cotton crop in 1960.[51]

In contrast to the vast acreage, workforce, and resources of Delta and Pine Land Company, the Frizzell farm in Lincoln County, Arkansas, was a small operation but an early farm to mechanize fully. The Frizzell operation was a model of postwar agricultural change in the Mississippi River Delta. In 1937 the Frizzells moved from Carlisle in Lonoke County to occupy a forty-acre farm unit on the Crigler resettlement project, which had been developed by the Farm Security Administration (FSA).[52] The Frizzell brothers—Burnice, the oldest; J. T.; Donald; and Nelson—grew up on the project and helped their father work the farm.[53] In 1939 Burnice married and moved to a farm of his own under FSA sponsorship. With his father he purchased his first tractor in 1940, borrowing the money privately since the FSA would not loan him money to buy a tractor.

When his younger brothers went off to war, Burnice stayed behind with a draft deferment. He and his father were anxious to mechanize their operation. They added a second tractor in 1943. Labor was scarce in Lincoln County during the war as many people left to work at the Pine Bluff Arsenal or entered the armed forces. After three years, Burnice bought the farm from the FSA but continued to rely on the agency and its successor, the Farmers Home Administration, for operating loans until 1945.

As his brothers returned home, they each bought a farm from the Farmers Home Administration and joined Burnice in his farming operation. The four Frizzell brothers owned their own land but pooled their equipment.[54] They formed a partnership so that they could have enough land to justify the purchase of machinery. Most of all the Frizzells believed in using the latest technology, and they were willing to take risks to make their operation efficient. When Burnice purchased their first mechanical cotton picker in 1950, he put the Frizzell farm on the cutting edge of change in his area.[55] The local county agent claimed the Frizzells did not have enough cotton to justify a mechanical picker. But they produced well over a bale of cotton per acre on 210 acres, and the size of their operation placed them in what International Harvester defined as the "top market" for a mechanical picker.[56]

Like other farmers the Frizzells faced a common problem: they could not hire enough labor, and they feared the labor costs would have been exorbitant if they had. Burnice observed, "Because of the shortage and high cost of farm labor we find it is better to get the necessary machinery to do the job fast and we are able to produce more."[57] Since their operation was small, they never had any tenant families, but they initially hired off-farm labor to help with chopping and picking cotton, though they found labor increasingly hard to find and especially unreliable. They complained that hand pickers, even when available, refused to accept direction and their work was of inconsistent quality. Hand pickers wanted to work only in unpicked, high yield fields rather than in picked-over fields that required more work.

The Frizzells knew that the secret to staying in cotton farming was mechanization. As soon as it became feasible they sought to mechanize cotton production completely—from land preparation through harvesting—with a goal of producing one and a half bales of cotton per acre. They already owned two tractors, which they used to prepare the seedbed and plant high-yielding varieties of seed. They also used fertilizer and relied on chemicals for weed control instead of hiring cotton choppers. They refused to worry about what cotton choppers would cost or even whether they would be available. Their weed control plan included both preemergence herbicides and flame control. In order to apply pesticides from the air, they bought an airplane and rented out a crop-dusting service to neighboring farmers. Finally, they installed an irrigation system, pumping water from nearby Bayou Bartholomew. With their first cotton picker, an International Harvester one-row spindle machine, they harvested 972 pounds of lint per acre.[58] The quality was not as clean as handpicked cotton, but the quality loss was offset by the lower picking cost. They purchased a second International Harvester picker in 1953. In the late 1950s they purchased two two-row John Deere pickers. Over the period they operated their farm, they owned eleven mechanical cotton harvesters. They even did custom picking for larger farmers who had not fully mechanized.[59]

Burnice Frizzell knew that equipment was expensive, but he said, "It pays off in the long run. We try to keep up with the latest developments in farming and try to work closely with the county agent and other agricultural workers in carrying on our farming operations."[60]

The Frizzell brothers were quick to adopt new agricultural technologies, and they had to experiment to achieve the best results. They kept changing grass-control methods, used different irrigation systems, and tried various defoliants. They were among the first local farmers to try new technologies whose value was still unknown. "I call it 'keeping up.' . . . I don't know whether that's a good word for it," Burnice Frizzell said. "But you've seen folks sit down and let the world go off and leave them. I think you've got to try to keep informed on what other people are finding out. Then you've got to try new things—not to prove they won't work—but to try to prove they will work."[61] The Frizzells pioneered mechanized farming in Lincoln County. The Frizzell farm achieved full mechanization by 1950, a decade before the Delta and Pine Land Company. Over a span of thirty years, the Frizzell operation went from 40 acres to 1,800, including 1,000 in cotton, 300 in soybeans, and the balance in pasture. But they also faced financial problems and, like other farmers in the 1970s, lost out in the continuing consolidation of Delta agriculture.

The Frizzells were able to mechanize earlier than large plantations like Delta and Pine Land Company because small farmers had less investment in the traditional sharecropping system, and as a result they were freer to take risks. At the same time labor was more of a problem for small farmers since they lacked resident families and had to hire day labor for chopping and picking. The Frizzells were dissatisfied with the quality of day labor. Labor shortages and poor labor quality led to their interest in mechanization.

The delay in the adoption of the mechanical cotton picker, then, was the product of many forces. The contrasts between the experiences of California and the old Cotton South were clear. In California labor was expensive because of labor shortages, and machines were relatively cheap. Southern labor, however, was cheap and plentiful, and the cost of machines was high. This contrast alone explained why California cotton mechanized earlier than southern cotton. In the South the small size of operating units under the sharecropping system with its annual contracts blocked change. The South had to shake off that system before mechanization was even possible.

The Cotton South achieved a major milestone in 1970 when finally 100 percent of its cotton was machine picked. As it turned out, the pessimists were all wrong. The social and economic upheavals anticipated both in the late 1930s and after World War II never occurred. The South changed, but change occurred gradually over a twenty-year period. By 1970 the South had urbanized, industrialized, and diversified its economy, and its people were more tolerant of racial and ethnic diversity. By then, millions of southerners lived in Chicago, Detroit, Los Angeles, and other cities. The increasing use of mechanical pickers fortunately coincided with the climax of the Great Migration from the South.

Chapter 8

Mechanization, Black Migration, and the Labor Supply in the Cotton South

Within twenty-five years after the end of World War II, the Cotton South had changed so completely that it was scarcely recognizable. While change came slowly, it was nonetheless drastic: the loss of millions of people through the largest migration of the century; the full mechanization of cotton production, including the collapse of the sharecropping system that had dominated rural life since the Civil War; the transformation of the old plantation system into capital-intensive agribusiness; the decline of cotton as the region's cash crop in favor of soybeans, rice, and cattle; and the emergence of the federal government as a dominant factor in shaping the region's rural economy. Beyond agriculture, other changes included the breakdown of the Jim Crow system and the civil rights revolution, the movement of northern industry into the South, and the rapid growth of southern cities. These changes, which were all long overdue, were all the product of a complex set of interrelated forces—agricultural mechanization, migration, and federal agricultural programs.

Beginning in the 1930s the popular press depicted the mechanical cotton picker as a monster that robbed hard-working people of their jobs—a view that forced people who bought and sold farm machinery into a defensive position. As the pace of mechanization increased after World War II, cotton planters denied emphatically that mechanization replaced labor; instead, they insisted, labor shortages forced them to adopt machines to replace labor that was already gone.

The opposing view was that plenty of labor was still available, but that planters wanted only cheap labor.[1] If they had paid their workers a higher wage, the supply and demand for labor would have been in balance. The relationship between mechanization and migration begins with the question of labor shortage. A labor shortage implied that workers migrated because they were "pulled" away from farms by better opportunities elsewhere. If they were "pushed" out, they faced a labor surplus and high unemployment.

No one has questioned the existence of a labor shortage during World War II.[2] The wartime demands of industry and the armed services drew 2.4 million southerners out of the South during the 1940s. Under pressure to increase production for the war effort, farmers received draft exemptions, used foreign labor where available, and explored new technology. At the end of the war, service men returned home to look for jobs, and factories released workers as they converted from wartime to peacetime production. This transition was difficult, but domestic industry maintained high production levels, and the nation's economy remained prosperous. As a result industrial employment remained high.

Despite the return of servicemen and women, cotton farmers still believed they faced a labor shortage. In the immediate postwar years some workers did return to farming, creating a brief but anachronistic back-to-the-farm movement. Planters feared that workers who had spent the war working in northern industries and earning high wages were not coming back at all.

Across the Mississippi River Delta contemporary observers agreed that farmers faced labor shortages. In late 1944 the general manager of the Staple Cooperative Association of Greenwood, Mississippi, said, "Our Negroes have moved away, and I don't think they will come back unless forced to by necessity."[3] When Texas agricultural engineer Harris P. Smith was asked in 1946 how many persons had been displaced by mechanical cotton harvesters, he replied that "instead of the machines replacing labor they were used to replace the labor that had left the farm." The labor that had produced the materials of war in shipyards and factories was not returning to the farm. The consequence was that cotton farmers were forced to mechanize.[4]

In a 1949 study published by the Mississippi Agricultural Experiment Station, Dorothy Dickins wrote,

> At the present time there is no problem of a displaced labor supply; in fact, there is a scarcity of labor on some plantations. One reason is that general economic conditions are so good that the shift [to] mechanization is taking place painlessly. Instead of outright displacement there is migration to places where opportunities seem better.[5]

Oscar Johnston, the best-known spokesman for the Cotton South, spoke for most planters when he wrote in the *Saturday Evening Post:*

Mechanization is not the cause, but the result, of economic change in the [Cotton South]. Most if not all of the migration of farmers and farmworkers which has taken place during the past few years has resulted from factors other than mechanization itself. All over the South, tenant houses now stand vacant on farms where mechanization has not yet achieved considerable development.[6]

According to agricultural historian Gilbert C. Fite in 1950,

[N]o serious labor displacement has been caused by the use of modern cotton production equipment. In most cases labor had already deserted the cotton fields and was no longer available in customary quantity so, where possible, the growers turned to mechanization. . . . The movement away from the farms has been a major factor in stimulating mechanization of the cotton fields. Since the farm population of the South is declining and since mechanization is progressing in a slow evolutionary manner, labor displacement does not seem to be a serious problem at the present time.[7]

Through the 1950s and into the 1960s cotton experts in the Delta consistently argued that labor shortages had forced them to mechanize and that machines were not replacing labor.[8] As one report stated, "Planter after planter . . . feel[s] impelled to reiterate and reaffirm the defense which became the byword of the area in the late 30's: 'Not one family, not one person has been displaced by machines on this plantation.' "[9] Even at higher wage rates planters frequently complained that they were unable to obtain enough labor to perform the essential operations during the peak-demand periods. In their view they either had to reduce their acreage in cotton or to increase their labor efficiency through mechanization.

Early studies of mechanization pointed out that the labor situation was most critical in the Mississippi River Delta and in the High Plains in contrast to southeastern states, where manpower resources remained available.[10] The Bureau of Employment Security issued a 1962 report entitled *Cotton Harvest Mechanization: Effect on Seasonal Hired Labor,* which found that the decline in seasonal agricultural workers resulted not only from workers who were involuntarily replaced by machines, but also from workers who voluntarily withdrew from farmwork and sought employment in other industries. In the Mississippi Delta, the report said, "mechanization has been stimulated by a shortage of seasonal workers at the peak of the harvest period."[11] From the adoption of mechanical reapers in the nineteenth century to the use of strippers in the 1920s, labor shortages and high wage rates have driven farmers to adopt machinery.

Even a generation later, the prevailing view of the relationship between mechanization and labor remained unchanged. In 1977 Jere Nash Sr., founder of the Delta Implement Company, an International Harvester dealership at Greenville, Mississippi, asserted that "the mechanization of cotton and the cotton picker did not displace workers, but did replace them." Taking the long view, Nash recalled that farmers in the Mississippi Delta faced a steady decline of workers as a result of World War I, the Mississippi River flood of 1927, and World War II.[12]

In hindsight, however, some investigators have denied that the Cotton South faced a postwar labor shortage. Scholars as dissimilar as James H. Street, Charles S. Aiken, Nan Elizabeth Woodruff, and Gavin Wright have all maintained that planters could no longer employ labor as cheaply as they enjoyed in the past, but plenty of labor was still available.[13] Similarly, labor unions argued that the problem was not labor shortage, but that planters did not want to pay a wage high enough to secure the labor they needed to pick their cotton.[14]

For proof, geographer Charles Aiken argued that the cost of labor was "inelastic" between the 1930s and the 1960s. Since planters did not raise wages to retain labor that was being lost to urban migration, they did not face a true labor shortage.[15]

This argument, however, lacks empirical support. Wages for unskilled agricultural labor did increase, and they increased dramatically, nearly tripling during World War II; and by 1948 wages were three and a half times their prewar level. Across the Cotton Belt the average wage for picking one hundred pounds of seed cotton climbed from $.62 in 1940 to $1.93 in 1945, an increase of 211 percent. In the postwar period the average picking cost continued to climb until it reached a peak in 1948 at $2.90 per hundredweight, a total increase since 1940 of 368 percent. In 1948 Arkansas and Mississippi experienced record high picking costs, with the rate rising to 400 and 470 percent, respectively, above 1940 rates. While the price of cotton also rose, the cost of picking a bale of cotton for Mississippi planters amounted to 31.4 percent of its value.[16] Street conceded that "the Delta areas emerged as a relatively high-wage district, and this may have had special significance for the mechanization of cotton production, as it was in this district that some of the most active experiments with newer methods of agriculture were conducted."[17] Since wages remained high in the postwar period, employers could not simply regard the increase in labor costs as a temporary wartime phenomenon.

This dramatic increase in the cost of handpicking was the result of wartime labor shortages. But after the war picking rates remained high (fig. 8.1). During the 1950s, for example, Mississippi wage rates did stabilize between $2.50 and $2.95, with an average rate between 1950 and 1964 of $2.64.[18] Since wage rates failed to continue rising in this period, Aiken concluded there was no labor shortage.

If the stability of wage rates in the 1950s disproved the existence of a labor shortage, it also ruled out a labor surplus that machines supposedly created in forcing workers out of agriculture. Wages would have fallen if farmers had faced a labor surplus. The correct conclusion was that for this period hand labor and machines competed with each other, with both having advantages as well as disadvantages.

The wage rate for picking cotton stabilized after 1949 at about $2.50 per hundred. Why did wages rates stabilize if labor was in short supply? The answer was simple. It was the price of cotton, not merely the price of labor, that was "inelastic," giving farmers a narrow profit margin. From 1930 to 1964, the correlation between the average wage for picking one hundred pounds of seed cotton in Mississippi and the price of cotton per pound was an incredibly high .968. Fluctuations in wages and cotton prices, in others words, were virtually identical.

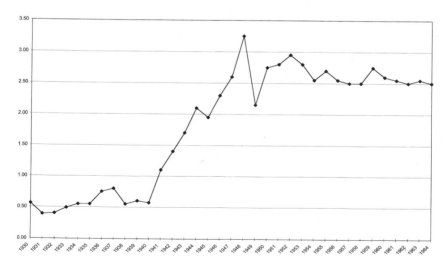

FIGURE 8.1 Average wage for picking cotton per hundredweight in Mississippi, 1930–1964.

Source: U.S. Department of Agriculture, Economic Research Service, *Statistics on Cotton and Related Data, 1920–1973,* Statistical Bulletin No. 535 (Washington, D.C.: USDA, 1974), 86.

After the Second World War cotton growers enjoyed for the first time a viable option to high labor costs. They did not have to pay higher wages or deal with recalcitrant labor; instead, they could mechanize. As a result, wage rates for handpicking cotton affected the pace of the adoption of mechanical harvesters.[19] "When cheap black labor became scarce," Aiken conceded, "even reluctant planters adopted machines and chemicals rather than raise wages."[20]

In his study of the adoption of mechanical cotton pickers, Frank H. Maier argued that producers embraced technology when they believed its use became profitable. The cost of hand labor determined where the point of profitability was located. Growers purchased and used mechanical pickers when the expected cost of machine picking dropped below the cost of handpicking, often a little earlier. Maier found that the Mississippi River Delta states all adopted pickers before they became hypothetically profitable.[21]

In Arkansas, for example, the crossover point occurred in 1958, when for the first time the cost of custom rates for machine picking cotton fell below piece rates for handpicking (fig. 8.2). The previous year, Arkansas farmers machine harvested only 15 percent of their cotton, but five years later the proportion reached almost 75 percent.[22] As the percentage of machine-picked cotton soared, the cost of mechanical harvesting fell, indicating that the use of machines occurred because of lower machine costs, not higher rates for handpicking.[23]

Contemporaries commented on the effect of mechanization in stabilizing wages. According to an observer in 1962:

> The increase in machine use had a tendency to stabilize wage rates according to some opinions. Many large cotton farms that were well mechanized operated on the assumption that it was profitable to hand pick cotton until wage rates reached a certain level. When rates reached this so-called "breaking point" the growers started using machines. Seasonal labor used on these farms was then released for employment on farms where mechanical pickers were not to be used or in fields where conditions such as heavy cotton foliage, excessive growth of weeds and grass, soft ground, etc., prevented the efficient operation of machines.[24]

The "breaking point" price was somewhere above $2.50. According to a U.S. Department of Labor study in 1962,

> Several factors determine the profitability of shifting from hand harvesting methods to machine use, but most important is the relationship of machine-harvesting costs to hand-labor costs. The hand harvesting wages rate at which

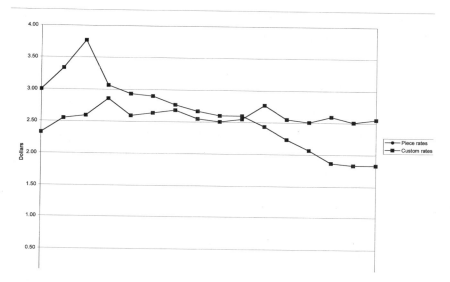

FIGURE 8.2. Piece rates for handpicking and custom rates for machine picking seed cotton per hundredweight in Arkansas, 1949–1964.

Source: U.S. Department of Agriculture, Economic Research Service, *Statistics on Cotton and Related Data, 1920–1973,* Statistical Bulletin No. 535 (Washington, D.C.: USDA, 1974), 86; Warren C. Whatley, "New Estimates of the Cost of Harvesting Cotton, 1949–1964," *Research in Economic History* 13 (1991): 220.

it becomes more profitable to harvest by machine varies with the amount of acreage to be harvested, the yield per acre, efficiency of machine and operator, and other factors. However, the break-even point is most likely to be at a hand-harvesting rate between $2.25 and $3.00 per hundredweight. This tends to stabilize wage rates at a point somewhere in that range.[25]

Not surprisingly, International Harvester's marketing department studied the relationship between hand-labor costs and machine-picking costs. Since the market for mechanical cotton pickers expanded and contracted with the cost of labor, IH factored labor costs into its estimates of market potential.

Harvester officials believed that a change of $.50 in wage rates for hand-picking costs had a large effect on the market for cotton pickers. Based on their estimates, an increase from $2.50 to $3.00 per hundredweight increased the size of the national market that could economically operate in competition with hand labor from 22,121 to 39,157 units. In the Mississippi River Delta, a $.50 increase more than doubled the market for mechanical pickers from 8,219 to 17,902 units. IH believed that the breaking point was located somewhere between $2.50 and $3.00.[26]

The reason, then, that wages for handpicking did not continue to rise was that farm operators were willing to switch from land labor to machines when hand labor costs rose somewhere above $2.50 per hundredweight. Every farmer had his price for labor, and that price varied according to the number of acres harvested and yield per acre. Farmers had many incentives to stay with hand labor, but they were willing to mechanize if labor costs exceeded their threshold.

When the cost of labor was $2.00 per hundredweight, hand pickers were in demand, but labor did not regard this wage as attractive. If the wage went to $3.00, the supply of labor was plentiful, but machine picking was cheaper and farmers were motivated to mechanize. As a result, the breaking point wage of $2.50 balanced labor costs with machine costs. Aside from labor costs, other considerations, including the weather and field conditions, played a large role. If wet weather kept machines out of the fields, growers turned to hand pickers even at a higher wage if they were available.

Cheap labor could drive out machines if wage rates were low enough, and that was just what happened in the 1930s, when low wages and labor surpluses kept the Cotton South unmechanized.[27] In the labor-short postwar period, it was unlikely that machines could drive out labor. The unavailability of labor was more likely the motivation for mechanization. Since the cost of machine picking continued to decline, it was the unavailability of labor that kept wages high.

The Great Migration

The Great Migration, the largest population movement in twentieth-century American history, formed the basis for the postwar labor shortage on southern farms. The South lost at least 1,000,000 inhabitants in each decade between 1910 and 1970 (table 8.1). However, during the 1940s, out-migration soared to a record 2,447,000 people; but migration did not cease once World War II was over. In the 1950s the region lost 2,578,000 people—another record; and during the 1960s out-migration continued at a rate just under the record levels. Thus between 1940 and 1970 the total loss for the region was 6,963,000 people.

TABLE 8.1. Net Migration from the South, 1870–1970 (in 1,000s)

Decade	Native White	Black	Total
1870–1880	91	-68	23
1880–1890	-271	88	-183
1890–1900	-30	-185	-215
1900–1910	-69	-194	-218
1910–1920	-663	-555	-1,218
1920–1930	-704	-903	-1,607
1930–1940	-558	-480	-1,038
1940–1950	-866	-1,581	-2,447
1950–1960*	-1,003*	-1,575*	-2,578
1960–1970*	-508*	-1,430*	-1,938
Totals for 1940–1970	-2,377	-4,586	-6,963

Source: Hope T. Eldridge and Dorothy S. Thomas, *Population Redistribution and Economic Growth* (Philadelphia, Pa.: American Philosophical Society, 1964), 3:90.

*U.S. Bureau of the Census, *Historical Statistics of the United States: Colonial Times to 1970* (Washington, D.C.: GPO, 1975), series C 55–62, pp. 93–95.

In the Mississippi River Delta states, out-migration increased strongly during the 1940s, with black migrants exceeding white migrants in Louisiana and Mississippi (table 8.2). White migrants made up over half of Arkansas's losses. In all three states, however, population losses for the 1950s were roughly the same as during the war decade.

Though the Great Migration involved people of all occupations, it was primarily a movement of people, black and white, from farms to cities in search for employment. After 1940 rural areas across the United States experienced a steady decline in the number of farmers. Before Pearl Harbor the nation's farm population was 30,547,000, or about the same number as in 1910. From 1940 to 1970 the farm population dropped to 10,307,000, a decline of two-thirds. During the same period, the South's farm population fell by three-fourths.[28]

During World War II the rural South produced the heaviest population losses in the nation. Between 1940 and 1945 the southern farm population decreased by 3,660,000 people, or 22.3 percent. The year with the heaviest

TABLE 8.2. Estimated Net Intercensal Migration of White and Black
Population, 1930–1970 (in 1,000s)

	1930–40*	1940–50	1950–60	1960–70
Arkansas				
Black	-33.3	-158	-150	-112
White	-95.5	-259	-283	38
Louisiana				
Black	-8.4	-147	-93	-163
White	15.3	-2	43	26
Mississippi				
Black	-58.2	-326	-323	-279
White	-32	-108	-110	10
Totals	-212.1	-1,000	-916	-480

*Survival-rate method; all other decades use components of change method.

Source: U.S. Bureau of the Census, Historical Statistics of the United States: Colonial Times to 1970
(Washington, D.C.: GPO, 1975), series C 58–60, pp. 93–95.

losses was 1943, when 1,473,000 people left southern farms. Within the
South, the largest losses occurred in the West South Central area, which
included Arkansas and Mississippi. These losses slowed after the war, but did
not stop. For the entire 1940–50 decade the South's farm population fell
4,504,000, or 27.5 percent.[29] Farmwork became increasingly unattractive compared to higher paying industrial jobs.

Confirming the notion of labor shortages, census figures reported a dwindling number of southern black people who were classified as "rural farm."[30] By
1950, after a decade of heavy migration, blacks who were defined by the census
as "rural farm" were already down to 21 percent of the total southern black
population.[31] The rural farm black population in the Mississippi River Delta
declined by more than a half million during the 1950s (table 8.3). By 1960 only
18.7 percent of Arkansas blacks were classified as "rural farm." Overall the proportion of the nation's black population living in the South fell from 90 percent
in 1900 to 68 percent in 1950, and the trend was still downward.

Many Arkansans, according to *Business Week*, dismissed population losses
"on the ground that it's made up mainly of undesirables, most of them Negro."

"We're just getting rid of our submarginal people who have been displaced by machines on the farm," shrugged one observer. But this impression was wrong. White population losses exceeded black losses from 1930 to 1960. Though the rural farm population showed the largest losses, most of the migrants came from the state's higher-income farmers rather than from the "restless pool of sharecroppers and farm laborers."[32]

In a 1960 study, economists Phillips H. Brown and John M. Peterson linked Arkansas losses to the business cycle, noting "that Arkansas tends to lose its people in greatest numbers when jobs are most plentiful elsewhere." As a predominately rural state Arkansas suffered population losses because farm employment and farm populations were declining all across the nation. Farmers produced the same or larger output with less and less labor. "In Arkansas," Brown and Peterson added, "tractors and cotton pickers have had something to do with this, but it is an exaggeration to attribute solely to farm mechanization the bulk of the increase in farm productivity." Migration was also a product of improved seeds, fertilizers, and more efficient farm methods generally. "It is the rapid growth of the rest of the economy," they added, "together with a lagging demand for farm products, and thus in farm income, that has created the 'pull' off farms." People were leaving their farms because they saw opportunities to earn a better living elsewhere. Arkansas, Brown and Peterson concluded, lacked sufficient manufacturing jobs to absorb its migrating farm population.[33]

In Arkansas out-migration created a labor shortage severe enough that cotton growers had to import labor. They sought labor from any available source

TABLE 8.3. **Black Population Classified as Rural Farm, Arkansas, Louisiana, and Mississippi, 1950–1960**

	1950	Percentage	1960	Percentage
Arkansas	197,339	46.1	73,076	18.7
Louisiana	234,847	25.5	91,399	8.7
Mississippi	595,003	60.1	299,102	32.5
Totals	1,027,189		463,577	

Source: U.S. Bureau of the Census, *Census of Population 1950*, vol. 2, *Characteristics of the Population*, pt. 1, *United States Summary* (Washington, D.C.: GPO, 1953), 1–108; U.S. Bureau of the Census, *Census of Population 1960*, vol. 1, *Characteristics of the Population*, pt. 1, *United States Summary* (Washington, D.C.: GPO, 1964), 1–250.

during the war. In some areas growers employed Japanese Americans in cotton production. German prisoners of war also worked in cotton fields; and despite the surrender of Germany in May 1945, POWs were not released until the 1945 crop was picked. The Bracero program, established as a wartime emergence measure to import Mexican labor into the Cotton South and the Southwest, became Public Law 78 in 1951. Between 1952 and 1964 Arkansas received some 251,298 Mexican nationals to chop and pick cotton (table 8.4).[34]

The existence of a labor shortage in the 1950s, then, was real, not imaginary. It was not the product of a desire to pay low wages despite the availability of sufficient labor. The nation's economy remained strong during the decade with only short-lived recessions, and migration out of the South continued unabated after the war.

In the 1950s and 1960s state employment security agencies operated farm

TABLE 8.4. Workers Employed in Picking Cotton, by Residence, Arkansas, 1953–1965

	Local	Non-local	Foreign*	Total
1953	80,650	10,225	23,125	114,000
1954	76,500	10,550	21,525	108,575
1955	77,396	6,468	28,956	112,820
1956	59,644	4,778	29,683	94,105
1957	58,749	5,445	25,757	89,951
1958	68,569	4,222	20,632	93,423
1959	67,285	3,814	39,001	110,100
1960	63,179	3,526	31,296	98,001
1961	62,742	3,137	20,924	86,803
1962	54,327	1,305	6,794	62,426
1963	44,066	750	2,200	47,016
1964	39,232	640	1,405	41,277
1965	32,710	500	—	33,210
Totals	843,224	55,460	251,298	

*Mexican Nationals employed under the auspices of the Bracero Program.
—Indicates the absence of this category of workers.

Source: Arkansas Department of Labor, Employment Security Division, *Arkansas Agricultural Report, 1954–1966* (Little Rock, 1955–67).

labor programs to assist unskilled agricultural workers in finding jobs and, conversely, to put employers in contact with the workers they needed. These programs grew out of wartime efforts to manage the changing labor situation from surplus to shortage.[35] The annual reports produced by farm labor officials recorded the transition from hand labor to machine labor. Officials followed closely the relationship between labor markets and the developing mechanization of cotton production.

As these annual reports suggested, the labor supply and labor demand—locked in a slow, dying spiral—were both falling rapidly. Employers worried about labor supply for peak periods and purchased machines as insurance against high labor costs and shortages. Anticipating less labor demand, workers looked for other opportunities. But farmwork was also less attractive than off-farmwork. Industrial jobs offered more pay, fringe benefits, and better working conditions. Young adult workers, the most productive segment of the labor force, were the most motivated to leave in search for new opportunities. The agricultural labor force increasingly consisted of the old, children, and women.

In 1954, when 20 percent of Arkansas cotton was machine picked, the *Arkansas Agricultural Report* noted that

> The full effect of the use of mechanical cotton pickers on the employment of farms workers is not shown clearly by available data. However, it is known that many . . . farm families are continuing to shift to urban areas and . . . former farm workers who secured jobs in industrial activities are reluctant to re-enter farm activities, even when unemployed. This situation is causing an ever-increasing unavailability of workers for seasonal farm jobs. The higher wages which farmers must pay because of the resultant labor shortages, and the need for adequate assistance at harvest time has stimulated the use of mechanical pickers.[36]

A year later, Arkansas farmers had 2,787 mechanical pickers available with 25 percent of the crop machine harvested. According to the 1955 report,

> The controlling factors limiting the use of mechanical cotton pickers have been the weather and field conditions, crop conditions and market prices. In most instances the market price of machine picked cotton has been lower than that of hand picked cotton but some of the price differential can be made up with the saving in harvesting expense when mechanical cotton pickers are used. . . . Since mechanical pickers operate most efficiently after the plants have been defoliated, many growers use seasonal workers for the first picking and then use mechanical pickers for second picking and scrapping operations.

The 1957 crop season posed a significant setback for mechanization. Across the Delta region, the weather was wet and cotton grew rank, limiting the use of mechanical pickers and causing farmers to fall back on hand labor. The portion of the crop harvested mechanically fell to 18.6 percent of the anticipated production compared to 33 percent in 1956.

Labor shortages occurred during the 1959 picking season. Without the use of mechanical pickers, farmers would have suffered losses because of the deterioration in the quality of cotton that would have remained in the fields over a prolonged period. By 1961 increased mechanization had reduced over-all labor requirements for the cotton harvest. Nonetheless, all domestic workers who sought work could still find employment in harvest activities.

By the early 1960s many Arkansas farmers contended that the switch to machines was a necessity rather than an option. They faced a steady decline each year in the agricultural labor market, producing a labor supply that was neither dependable nor adequate. They also took advantage of improved ginning equipment that narrowed the differential between handpicked and machine-picked cotton, and new seed varieties produced plants more suitable for machine picking and stripping.[37]

With more than 75 percent of Arkansas cotton harvested mechanically, farm labor experts still maintained that mechanization had not resulted in the displacement of domestic seasonal agricultural workers in great numbers. "During the past decade," the 1962 report stated, "there has been an almost continuous migration of agricultural workers to nonagricultural jobs where wages, working conditions, and fringe benefits were more attractive. This movement of domestic workers forced cotton growers to seek other sources of labor or resort to mechanization."

As late as the mid-1960s Arkansas officials still did not believe that all hand labor in the cotton field would ever be completely eliminated, at least not before laborers, through their own choosing, became unavailable. According to the 1964 report, "Many elements have combined to hasten the departure of labor from Arkansas farms. The wage, for example, has continually increased in industry while a fixed market price on agricultural products has prevented a proportionate increase on the farm. With the exception of working conditions, practically all farm labor problems revert back to the farm produce price structure. In order to stay within the price structure, the farmer has been forced to automate and to apply the most advanced technology available to him."[38] In other words, it was the price of cotton rather than the cost of labor that had stabilized.

Despite the growing use of mechanical pickers, handpicking had its advantages. Hand pickers could begin picking before it was economically feasible to operate machines because not enough bolls were open, and they could enter fields soon after rains, when heavy equipment would bog down. Hand pickers produced cleaner cotton with a better price. Arkansas officials believed the need for hand labor still existed and would continue to do so to some degree in the foreseeable future.

This judgment was wrong, however. The era of hand labor in agriculture was closing. By 1967, 93 percent of Arkansas cotton was mechanically harvested, and many cotton farmers handled their entire crop without the aid of any seasonal workers. In addition, machines were even being used to harvest vegetable crops.[39]

In Louisiana farm labor officials observed similar trends. Though acquiring mechanical harvesters, farmers still wanted to pick as much cotton as possible with hand labor. In the fall of 1959 the demand for hand pickers exceeded the immediate supply in some areas. Louisiana officials estimated that 4,500 openings were unfilled. At the same time many workers were becoming more fickle in accepting employment—an obvious sign of labor shortage. They refused to pick in grassy fields or under adverse conditions, and instead sought more favorable locations for work. They were also unwilling to migrate to other areas of demand. As a result, machines continued to supplement the diminishing number of hand pickers. The 1960 Louisiana report noted, "Although some farms are now replacing workers with machines, no local office has reported a lack of work for hand pickers because of machine use."[40]

In Mississippi the number of hand pickers also slowly dwindled. As in Arkansas and Louisiana, employers still preferred handpicking if sufficient labor was available at prices that could compete with machines. In 1957 Mississippi officials noted that workers had increased their mobility. The availability of plantation buses or trucks for transporting workers had declined, since employers had decreased their underwriting of transportation. Instead, small groups of workers traveled in personal automobiles, increasing their ability to bargain for work on a day-by-day basis, or to shift from one employer to another.

By the late 1950s loud-speaker systems saw use during peak chopping and harvesting seasons as a recruitment aid in the Delta area, along with handbills, posters, and the news media. In the early 1960s many growers still preferred hand pickers if they were available in the numbers needed, when they were needed, and if the cost did not exceed $2.75 or $3.00 per hundred. "If these conditions could be met," a Mississippi report said, "a great many machines would remain idle." These conditions represented an ideal, but an increasingly unlikely combination. By 1962 the Mississippi Farm Labor Report indicated that mechanization had reduced labor demands, but at the same time conceded that a dwindling workforce helped increase mechanization.[41]

While mechanization has received blame for displacing farm labor, some observers pointed to federal acreage programs that continued the effort to raise prices and restrict production. These programs forced drastic cutbacks in cotton acreage in the 1950s. Price supports and cotton allotments were discontinued during World War II, and farmers operated without any controls from 1944 to 1952. Federal acreage controls for cotton were reimposed in 1953 and reduced acreage by 25 percent compared to 1949. In 1956 the Soil Bank program further reduced acreage in the name of soil conservation. Thus cotton acreage remained low (fig. 8.3). Under the Soil Bank, Arkansas's cotton acreage was 30 percent below the 1945–54 average and represented the state's smallest acreage since 1895. In 1957 the state's cotton acreage fell even lower, the smallest since 1883—a combination of both federal programs and wet weather. The cotton acreage rose in 1958, but the state had 391,000 acres in the Soil Bank program. Despite fewer acres in cotton, production per acre increased.[42] Federal programs allowed for expanded production between 1959 and 1963, but acreage restrictions resumed in the mid-1960s. The Federal Food and Fiber Act of 1965 offered a payment of 10.5 cents per pound on projected yields for land diverted from cotton production. Farmers were required to reduce their cotton acreage by at least 12.5 percent but allowed a reduction as high as 35 percent.

Most scholars have argued that federal acreage controls produced a significant decline in the demand for labor. In a 1966 study economist Roger Burford found that the reduction in cotton acreage under federal programs served to speed up migration from the farm.[43] More recently Mississippi historian James C. Cobb noted, "Delta planters became the prime beneficiaries of government initiatives, which not only boosted their incomes through acreage-control payments and price supports but reduced their labor needs and relieved them of their responsibilities as providers as well."[44] According to economist Frank Maier, federal acreage programs not only meant fewer jobs but also lower piece rates for handpicking cotton, double reasons to expect an increase in out-migration. Yet lower handpicking costs encouraged farmers to hire people rather than invest money in machines. Since federal acreage controls depressed labor costs, Maier also believed that they discouraged the adoption of mechanical pickers.[45] While the effect of the Soil Bank and similar programs were mixed, their inconsistency would not be the last time that federal programs produced dubious effects in southern agriculture.

In 1969 Leland DuVall, the longtime farm editor of the Little Rock *Arkansas Gazette,* summed up the recent changes in rural Arkansas after observing agriculture since the 1930s:

> In some quarters, it was argued that farmers were "forced" to mechanize their operations because the declining labor pool left them without an adequate supply of field hands. The more logical explanation is that plowing with a four-row tractor is more efficient than plowing with a horse-drawn cultivator and when it became possible—due to the development of chemicals, better seed and fertilizers—to increase yield and justify the investment, farmers extended their capitalization and enlarged the scope of their operation. In the process, they drove out the reserve labor pool needed for seasonal employment peaks and so they were forced to accelerate the mechanization process.[46]

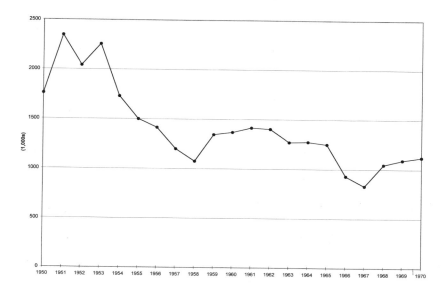

FIGURE 8.3. Acres planted in cotton in Arkansas, 1950–1970.

Source: Based on data in U.S. Department of Agriculture, Economic Research Service, *Statistics on Cotton and Related Data, 1920–1973,* Statistical Bulletin No. 535 (Washington, D.C.: USDA, 1974), 66.

DuVall suggested that the mechanical cotton picker did not compose the only source of change. The AAA provided the essential breakthrough from the old sharecropper system in moving many farms toward day labor. But the Cotton South was still locked into labor surpluses and low wages, which blocked any real attempt to modernize. Fortunately, though, World War II pulled workers out of the South and created a farm labor shortage that lasted until the mid-1960s. This labor shortage proved to be the most important factor in subsequent developments.

When the war was over, no one wanted to do hard, low-paying farmwork anymore; everyone wanted more out of life, and they knew they could find new opportunity outside the South. Some migrants undoubtedly were disappointed, but overall they found the better life that they sought. Labor continued to leave the South for opportunities elsewhere throughout the 1950s and 1960s. Cotton producers responded to labor shortages with mechanization, but at the same time they faced pressure from foreign cotton and synthetics. Archaic hand-labor methods were too expensive to compete with cheap, foreign cotton and synthetics, and farmers had to produce cheaper cotton in order to stay in business.

While the last labor-intensive task to be conquered was weeding, the belief in the superiority of handpicked cotton remained strong. So did its price. These two factors ensured a demand for hand labor. The decline in sharecropping resulted in a reorganization of plantations based on day labor, a more flexible arrangement that freed growers from annual contracts. The 1959 census of agriculture was the last census to record sharecroppers, signaling the death of this institution. As sharecropping disappeared and farms consolidated, the Cotton South at last threw off the institutional handicaps that had blocked mechanization. While the shift from traditional sharecrop operations varied from farm to farm, the Mississippi River Delta took the lead in making the transition in the old Cotton Belt. As long as the problem of weeding remained unresolved, however, growers were unable, even afraid, to push for full mechanization. Though day laborers were in demand, they were offered fewer and fewer days of work; and as a result the prime labor pool, especially young males, disappeared in search of better opportunities. This was DuVall's point.

Migration rates during the 1950s matched those of World War II. When possible, the South imported foreign labor to shore up its declining labor force. At the same time, the loss of labor evoked worry about how to meet labor needs for weeding and harvesting, thus motivating further mechanization based on the fear that labor might not be available. Other factors intervened too. First in the late 1950s and again in the 1960s the Soil Bank and other programs dramatically reduced cotton acreage, thus eliminating unskilled jobs. But these jobs were increasingly rejected in preference to non-agricultural work. And even welfare checks increasingly removed the motivation for some people to look for work.[47]

Everything turned around in the 1960s, as the labor market again changed from shortage to labor surplus. The speed of social change in the Cotton South had increased exponentially, with the region becoming increasingly urbanized and the civil rights movement breaking down Jim Crow barriers to public accommodations. The booming economy meant increased opportunities beyond agriculture for black workers. The passage of the Voting Rights Act in 1965 made black voters a significant political power, but also altered white attitudes. A large black population with the ballot posed a threat to white control. By 1965 black farm labor had not only become economically superfluous but also, because of civil rights and especially the passage of the Voting Rights Act, a political liability.

In *The Most Southern Place on Earth* James C. Cobb reported a growing inclination during the 1960s on the part of Mississippi Delta planters to reduce the black population. The regional power structure, he contended, "adopted an unwritten but generally accepted policy to eliminate the Negro Mississippian either by driving him out of the state or starving him to death."[48] Local welfare officials, according to Cobb, cut back on payments to blacks who registered to vote and informed them of the generous welfare benefits available in Chicago and other northern cities. White Mississippians hoped to redistribute blacks more evenly over the United States.

Economists Lee J. Alston and Joseph P. Ferrie have also argued that southerners in the 1960s hoped to encourage black out-migration as a means of limiting the impact of civil rights and preserving the traditional southern way of life. As the core of Lyndon B. Johnson's War on Poverty, the Economic Opportunity Act (1965) initially contained provisions for grants aimed at land reform, namely proposals to purchase land for resale to tenants and sharecroppers. Southern congressmen, however, stripped these provisions from the final version of the bill and instead focused the program on poverty in northern ghettos. Alston and Ferrie saw the debate over the bill as a "last-ditch effort to maintain the Southern way of life by encouraging out-migration of blacks." Without mechanization, they noted, migration would have increased labor costs. But with mechanization, black labor was superfluous.[49]

According to one story that circulated during the 1960s, southern black workers were given bus tickets, a few dollars, and the address of the welfare office in New York City. Former New York mayor and congressman John Lindsey recalled that "his Southern colleagues would clap him on the back and say, 'John, we're sending 'em right up to you.'"[50]

Charles Aiken also found evidence that the southern "white power structure" retaliated against blacks for civil rights activities. One of the most famous such cases occurred when Fannie Lou Hamer was evicted from the Marlowe plantation in Sunflower County, Mississippi, after she went to the courthouse at Indianola in 1962 to register to vote. Hamer went on to become one of the most effective leaders of the civil rights movement in Mississippi.[51]

By the late 1960s, though black labor had decreased in value, black workers were still employed. They were poor, and the work was not full time, but it was better than no work at all. Then the demand for unskilled agricultural workers came suddenly to a full stop. When northern liberals applied the federal minimum wage to agricultural workers in 1967, they achieved exactly the opposite of what they intended. On February 1, agricultural labor came under the minimum wage of $1.00 an hour on farms with five or more employees.[52] For a family of workers, all members, even children, were covered. One plantation manager in Mississippi responded that labor at $1.00 an hour was a "luxury we can't afford."[53] That was especially true since the price of cotton for Mississippi farmers was falling in the mid-1960s, dropping from over 35 cents a pound in 1961 to a low of 22.71 cents in 1966.[54] At $10.00 for a ten-hour day, assuming an average picker picked 150 pounds, the cost of picking equaled $6.60 per hundredweight compared to the going rate of $2.50. Instead of paying $8.00 to $10.00 a day for chopping cotton, planters purchased more chemicals. While full mechanization had virtually been completed anyway, the minimum wage killed the demand for hand labor in the Cotton South.[55]

Here was a classic case of unintended consequences. As Cobb wrote, "The role of the federal government in exacerbating the problems it was committed to solving was but one of the interlocking ironies that emerged from the upheaval that shook the Mississippi Delta during the 1960s."[56]

The social, political, and economic changes of the period 1945–70 were the products of many forces. Mechanization was one factor in the changes that reduced labor demand and caused migration. But it was not the only factor. Farmers switched to less labor-intensive enterprises such as growing soybeans and raising cattle. The federal minimum wage made hand labor too costly; and welfare, a kind of "urban furnish," reduced the available labor supply by giving people an alternative to work.[57] Even civil rights legislation played a surprising and unexpected role.

The postwar Cotton South was the product of migration, mechanization, and federal agricultural programs. Migration produced labor shortages that ended the plantation system and forced farmers to turn to mechanization. Of all the forces at work in the Cotton South after World War II, mechanization has been the most misunderstood.

The wartime demand for labor in northern and western defense industries carried the Great Migration to record levels. The resulting labor shortage marked the end of the South's plantation system. When the war was over, labor did not return to the cotton fields, and the out-migration continued throughout the 1950s and into the 1960s. As the South found itself facing a new world of high labor costs and cheap foreign cotton, mechanization offered farmers the only hope of reducing production costs and remaining competitive.

Chapter 9

The Great Migration and the Mechanical Cotton Picker: Cause or Effect?

In the summer of 1963 a young black man named Clifton L. Taulbert boarded an Illinois Central (IC) passenger train at Greenville, Mississippi, for St. Louis, Missouri. He had just graduated from O'Bannon High School in Greenville as class valedictorian, and he was anxious to seek his fortune in the promised land of the North. Since other members of his family had made the same trip, he had always dreamed about when it would become his turn to escape the cotton fields of Washington County.[1]

As Taulbert's train left the Mississippi Delta, the end of an era was fast approaching. Less than a year later, the Illinois Central Railroad ended passenger service to Greenville. Over the previous decades, thousands of migrants—black and white—had ridden the IC tracks from the Delta to northern cities like Chicago and Detroit. Starting in New Orleans, the Illinois Central rolled through Mississippi, with its largest stops at Jackson and Greenville before going on to Memphis, then followed the Mississippi River northward, and finally traveled to the shores of Lake Michigan.

The trip was relatively comfortable. Passengers could board the train at Greenville in the evening, ride all night, and wake up the next morning in Chicago. Quickly and easily, black migrants were on the doorstep of a new world, far away from the cotton fields of the Deep South. A new life with higher wages and better schools was not so distant after all.[2]

Those who made this journey on the Illinois Central and on other routes were part of the Great Migration, one of the largest population movements of the twentieth century. Between 1915 and 1970 almost seven million black migrants left the rural South in search of jobs in the industrial North and West. Like Taulbert, many were literate and from southern cities.

In fleeing the South, they changed the entire nation. Northern factories took advantage of their labor, but more importantly black migrants gained access to new opportunities and they forged new lives. In the Cotton South out-migration weakened the basis of the plantation system as it had existed since the Civil War.[3] When migration peaked during World War II, the old plantation system of cheap, docile labor collapsed.

White migrants also fled the South in hope of finding a new life away from the region's cotton fields. They followed the same pattern as black migration, but were smaller in absolute numbers, more than four million.[4] Like black migrants they sought areas where they could take advantage of higher-paying jobs and better schools for their children.

Push or Pull?

The dynamics of black migration, like any population movement, involved the simultaneous interaction of push and pull forces, whose relative importance varied from time to time. Push factors were negative incentives for leaving an old place (problems people hoped to escape), while pull factors were positive reasons for going to a new place (gains they expected to reap). When both forces were operative, migration was virtually certain. For black migrants, push factors included low cotton prices, oppressive crop liens and high interest rates, the boll weevil's ravages of cotton plants—all of which handicapped blacks in southern agriculture. Other push factors were lynchings and racial violence used to maintain social control and to keep blacks dependent.[5]

While push forces may have been at work, pull factors were usually more powerful, drawing people to brighter horizons with the promise of higher wages, better housing, more educational opportunities, or the absence of violence and discrimination.

The commonsense view was that mechanical pickers pushed people off the land, intensifying the Great Migration. As was said over and over, machines were labor-saving devices. The image of the mechanical cotton picker as a Frankenstein monster that displaced workers and cast them adrift from their cultural heritage had a powerful appeal. For depression America, the southern sharecropper became a sympathetic figure who was widely depicted as the victim of the increasing use of tractors.

As expected, inventors and implement companies have refused to accept the role of scapegoats in the Great Migration. They did not want to be criticized for massive dislocations of populations and the trauma that such dislocations entailed. They always maintained that they had no responsibility for the picker's social consequences. The Rust brothers explored several options for lessening the impact of their mechanical picker on labor but failed to find a way to do so and still remain in business.

Cotton growers were adamant in claiming that the cotton harvester did not push sharecroppers, tenants, and day laborers off the land; mechanization simply replaced workers who were already gone in pursuit of higher paying jobs in the cities. In other words, pull factors like economic advancement played the dominant role. A collateral view was that technological progress could not be stopped, or even slowed down; it must go wherever developments lead. If population readjustments were required, then that was the price of progress.[6]

The literature on the Great Migration contains support for both push and pull explanations. According to some scholars, black migration formed a direct response to rising job opportunities in northern industry. The accelerated demand for industrial production and the end of European immigration in the early 1920s increased the demand for labor while at the same time disrupting the flow of immigrants from Europe. During the war the draft also dried up normal labor pools. These conditions suddenly caused northern employers to open their doors to black workers. World War II created unprecedented opportunities for black Americans to contribute to the war effort by serving in the military and by working in defense industries. This emphasis on economic factors in pulling black migrants from the South usually played down potential push forces such as Jim Crow discrimination and adverse educational conditions. Some writers discounted the impact of Jim Crow, since blacks faced discrimination for extended periods without resorting to migration.[7]

In contrast, push factors like lynching and racial violence also played a predominant role in motivating a large out-migration. At the end of the nineteenth century, white southerners struggled to regain control over blacks who enjoyed a limited but marvelous sense of liberation during Reconstruction. In the 1880–1930 period, lynching was usually a retaliation for rape and other crimes, but it was also part of a system of racial control. The explanation for lynching lay in racial prejudice and psychological insecurities, as well as in political conflict; but the key motivation was the need to ensure a sufficient supply of cheap, docile labor during the peak periods of labor demand in the cotton season.[8] According to one study, the relationship between migration and violence was reciprocal. In other words, out-migration was heaviest from counties where lynchings had occurred, while counties with less out-migration experienced fewer lynchings. Mob violence, then, was a significant force pushing blacks from certain areas.[9]

In recent literature on the Great Migration, mechanization has played the starring role as the villain in the drama. One version of this view depicts tractors as playing the key role in the transition to full agricultural mechanization, meaning that the rural poor were "tractored" off the land.[10] In *The Promised Land,* journalist Nicholas Lemann began his story of Mississippi migrants with an International Harvester demonstration on the Hopson plantation in 1944, conveying the message that the adoption of mechanical pickers underlay the dispossession of poor, defenseless people.[11]

Other historians blamed mechanization both for replacing labor and destroying the South's "agrarian values" in the transition to capital-intensive agribusiness. Pete Daniel called the spindle cotton picker the "central engine of transformation." But he also conceded, "Mechanization caused part of the rural exodus, but, as so many studies reiterated, it was not clear whether people were pushed off the land by machines, fled in anticipation of them, or were lured away by factory jobs. No matter what the cause, farmers who needed labor feared that they would not find it."[12]

The view of mechanization as an evil force has been surprisingly persistent over time. In 1999 journalist Anthony Walton claimed that the black exodus from the South was "largely a result of the invention of the mechanical cotton picker, which enabled three or four workers to perform a task that on some farms had required hundreds if not thousands of hands."[13] This statement, made fifty years after cotton harvesters were produced commercially, demonstrates the enduring power of the picker's popular image as Frankenstein's monster.

While this literature is informative, it is not conclusive. The movement of great masses of people is hardly a topic that can be studied like a unique historical event. Indeed, it was composed of millions of discrete events as ordinary people for a variety of reasons decided to leave their homes. As the product of millions of actions, migration can be seen as a quantifiable pattern of human behavior. The relationship between mechanization and migration can be posed as a testable hypothesis and then analyzed using the best available empirical data and statistical tools. There have been only a few attempts to approach the problem in this manner.

In an article entitled "The Mechanical Cotton-Picker, Negro Migration, and the Integration Movement," sociologists Harry C. Dillingham and David F. Sly first sought to establish the relationship between mechanization and migration. Using data on Arkansas Delta counties for the period 1952–59, they reported that the number of mechanical pickers increased from 482 to 3,254, or from a county average of 28.3 to 191.4. Meanwhile, these counties lost 15,275 black tenants. Their calculation produced a correlation (Spearman rho) of .74 between black tenants and the number of mechanical pickers. In contrast, the correlation between mechanical pickers and white tenants was .39. Dillingham and Sly concluded that this evidence supported the hypothesis that mechanical pickers displaced tenants.[14]

Yes, the relationship between black tenants and mechanical pickers was highly correlated, but did mechanical pickers drive out tenants or was a labor shortage the cause of mechanization? Dillingham and Sly's evidence was not sufficient to form a judgment. Unfortunately, their data were limited to a few counties. In addition a reanalysis of their data using modern statistical software produces a different result. The relationship between the change in the number of black tenants from 1950 to 1959 in fifteen Arkansas counties yields a Pearson correlation of -.608, which is statistically significant at the .05 level. This correlation, however, explains only 37 percent of the variance between the two variables (.608 squared). The correlation for white tenants in seventeen counties is -.330 and is not statistically significant from zero.

Taking the opposite view, economist Craig Heinicke denied that the cotton harvest mechanization was the key cause of migration between 1950 and 1960. Heinicke wondered why no one had ever tried to estimate the number of people displaced by the mechanical cotton harvester. In his view, the picker played a part in migration decisions but was only one of a combination of forces. According to his estimate the picker accounted for only 24 percent of the black migration out of the South during this period. Other machines, especially tractors, may have a greater impact on displacements. In addition, he argued, the reduction in cotton acreage that took place in the 1950s played a large role. Finally, he said, black migrants were motivated primarily by better opportunities available in the North.[15]

In another analysis economists Willis Peterson and Yoav Kislev created a statistical model of the cotton labor market in an effort to determine whether the cotton harvester was a source of "labor displacement or replacement."[16] They used a two-equation model to estimate simultaneously both push and pull effects on wages and employment and concluded that human cotton pickers were pulled out of the South by higher wages in nonfarm occupations.

Peterson and Kislev focused on the impact of changes in custom rates for machine picking and in manufacturing wages on the quantity of available labor. Their analysis revealed that the effect of wages accounted for 79 percent of the change in labor supply, while 21 percent was explained by the cost of machine rates of picking. The common assertion that rural people were "tractored off" of their land was wrong, they found. As wages in industrial jobs increased, farmworkers left to take advantage of new opportunities; and farmers who were still in agriculture had no choice except to switch from hand labor to machines if they wanted to stay in business.

Peterson and Kislev's work constituted the first empirical evidence of the relative influence of the supply and demand sides of the cotton labor market. But their work contained critical weaknesses. They used data for custom picking for the period 1930–64; but since no data actually existed for custom picking between 1930 and 1948, they substituted a version of custom labor rates based on the Kansas wheat harvest. All custom picking work done from 1930 to 1949 was experimental work. Except for prototypes and a few early production models, no machines were available for commercial picking until 1949. A better approach would have been to limit the analysis to 1949–64, which covers the earliest period that saw the use of commercial pickers.

Fortunately, the problem of the lack of data has been solved by Warren C. Whatley, who devised a new set of data for custom cotton picking. Whatley noted that the impact of mechanical cotton pickers had existed in an "empirical vacuum."[17] In devising his cost estimates, he considered an exhaustive list of considerations: (1) expected operating costs including repairs, lubricants, fuel, and labor; and (2) expected fixed costs ranging from depreciation, interest, insurance, taxes, shelter for the machine, and a share of tractor depreciation for tractor-mounted machines as well as the cost of mounting and dismounting the picker mechanism. In addition Whatley included (3) the grade loss of cotton picked by machine compared to handpicked cotton; and finally (4) the expected market value of cotton left in the field by the machine. Hand pickers picked cotton cleaner than machines, which always experienced some loss in cotton left in the field. Whatley dug into obscure agricultural publications for cost estimates and insights into operational procedures, and he drew heavily on Frank Maier's dissertation, a vast fund of information.[18] Whatley and Maier's attention to detail give unusual confidence in these estimates. Thus the appearance of new data makes another statistical test possible.

We propose a replication of the Peterson-Kislev test of the relative importance of push and pull factors in migration. Here we build on and extend their work in that we use the new Whatley data and limit the analysis to the years 1949 to 1964, the earliest period that saw the actual use of commercially produced mechanical cotton pickers in large and growing numbers. No machine could affect the labor market before it was available for use on a wide scale.

The proposed hypothesis is that the quantity of labor needed to harvest cotton decreased as mechanization costs declined and as nonfarm wages increased. In a dynamic set of interrelationships, labor quantity depended on piece rates for handpicking and on custom rates for machine picking, which should have moved lower together, controlling for the effect of cotton prices. But piece and custom rates also depended on manufacturing wages, which should have driven up piece rates and driven down custom rates, controlling for the effect of cotton yields. To analyze these relationships, we will focus on the relative impact of mechanization costs (custom rates) and manufacturing wages—that is, push versus pull factors. While testing the interaction of these factors, we are primarily interested in which factor was most important.

The analysis employs time series data from 1949 to 1964 for twelve states: Arkansas, Arizona, Alabama, California, Georgia, Louisiana, Missouri, Mississippi, New Mexico, North Carolina, South Carolina, and Tennessee. These states, though admittedly diverse, all used the spindle-type picker. Texas and Oklahoma were omitted because they used predominately cotton strippers.

The definition and sources of variables used in this analysis of the cotton harvesting labor market are as follows:

- Q, or quantity of labor, used in harvesting cotton is measured as the number of bales of cotton picked by hand, a product of multiplying the number of bales of cotton harvested in each of the twelve states by the percentage picked by hand. The source for this and all cotton data is U.S. Department of Agriculture, *Statistics on Cotton and Related Data, 1920–1973,* Statistical Bulletin No. 535 (Washington, D.C.: GPO, 1974), 63–79, 218.
- P, or piece rate, is the price paid in each of the twelve states to handpick one hundred pounds of seed cotton. From the 1920s to 1964 the U.S. Department of Agriculture recorded the cost of handpicking cotton. This analysis ends in 1964 because this data was unavailable after that year. *Statistics on Cotton and Related Data, 1920–1973,* 63–79, 82.
- C, or custom rate, is the price paid by farmers in each of the twelve states to harvest by machine one hundred pounds of lint cotton, twice-over coverage. The source of the data is Warren C. Whatley, "New Estimates of the Cost of Harvesting Cotton, 1949–1964," *Research in Economic History,* 13 (1991): 220.
- M, or manufacturing wage, is the national average hourly wage in manufacturing jobs as cited in the *Economic Report of the President* (Washington, D.C.: GPO, 1969), 261.

- CP, or price, is the average price per pound of lint cotton paid in each of the twelve states. *Statistics on Cotton and Related Data,* 63–79.
- Y, or yield of cotton, is the number of bales harvested in each of the twelve states. *Statistics on Cotton and Related Data,* 63–79. Cotton production is a crucially important variable, as cotton production was under government regulation throughout the period under study. In Arkansas, for example, the number of harvested cotton acres fell more than half between 1953 and 1958, potentially having the same effect on tenants and day laborers as the AAA had during the 1930s.[19]

Using Peterson and Kislev as a guide, this analysis proposes the following two-equation model to estimate the relative importance of push and pull effects on labor in cotton harvesting:

- Quantity of labor used in harvesting cotton = piece rates + custom rates + cotton prices + state dummy variables + error factors. Or Q = P + C + CP + SD + e.
- Quantity of labor used in harvesting cotton = piece rates + manufacturing wages + cotton yields + state dummy variables + error factors. Or Q = P + M + Y + SD + e.

These equations estimate the effect of hand- and machine-picking rates and manufacturing wages on labor, controlling for cotton prices and yields. Q and P are assumed to be endogenous, all other variables are exogenous. Q, the dependent variable, is a proxy measure of labor, the product of multiplying the total number of bales of cotton harvested in each state by the percentage picked by hand per year. The independent variables measure factors that could influence the quantity of labor used to harvest cotton, including the impact of handpicking costs, machine-picking costs, and the level of manufacturing wages. In addition, two control variables were used: the price of cotton and cotton yields. A series of state dummy variables (SD) is used (but not shown in the results) to control for differences that may have existed among the twelve cotton states.

The two-equation model was estimated simultaneously using two-stage least squares regression corrected for auto-correlation with the Cochrane-Orcutt method.[20] All price variables were deflated by the Consumer Price Index (1960 = 100), and the equations were estimated in log form. Piece rates were adjusted for the cost of recruiting and organizing hand pickers in the Mississippi River Delta and the southeastern states.[21]

Mississippi illustrates the trends among the variables that dominated the quantity of labor required in picking cotton (fig. 9.1). The cost of piece rates for handpicking and custom rates for machine picking tracked closely during the early 1950s, while in 1959 machine picking rates fell below handpicking for the first time. These price trends were consistent with the dramatic increase in machine picking experienced in the 1960s. Handpicking costs remained relatively constant as the trend line for machine-picking rates sloped downward. But manufacturing wages soared higher and higher throughout the period under study, suggesting that the pull of nonfarm wages overrode any other reason for changes in labor markets (fig. 9.2).

The correlation matrix of the variables used in the models provides a preliminary view of their relationships (table 9.1). The percentage of handpicked cotton and piece rates are surprisingly unrelated: changes in piece rates had no impact on the amount of cotton that was handpicked. While this finding runs counter to expectations, the price for handpicking demonstrated little variation until the end of the period under study. However, the percentage of handpicked cotton and custom rates for machine picking show a moderately strong, positive correlation (.367). In other words, when custom rates rose, farmers turned to hand pickers (fig. 9.1). The correlation between custom rates and piece rates (-.439) also indicates that farmers turned to hand pickers when custom-picking rates increased. As expected, custom rates and manufacturing wages are negatively associated (-.561) and statistically significant from zero. Similarly, manufacturing wages show a negative relationship with percentage of cotton handpicked (-.464). The rising trend in manufacturing wages offered workers an incentive to earn better wages outside of agriculture. The strongest relationship in table 9.1 is between cotton yields and percentage handpicked. When yields were high, farmers turned to hand pickers. The reason may have been the lack of an adequate number of machines available until the 1960s coupled with a reluctance to abandon traditional methods of production.

The two-stage least squares solutions for both push and pull equations is shown in table 9.2. On the push side of the labor market, all variables are significant, and the standardized coefficients indicate that custom rates (.988) are the most powerful factor. This equation accounts for 74 percent of the variance in the model. Piece rates and cotton prices have a similar effect on the labor supply but in opposite directions.

The pull-side equation indicates that manufacturing wages and cotton yields are statistically significant. The standardized coefficients point to manufacturing wages (0.828) as the variable that plays the strongest role in the equation. The piece rate variable is the weakest in both equations and apparently fails to achieve significance because of the presence of two more powerful

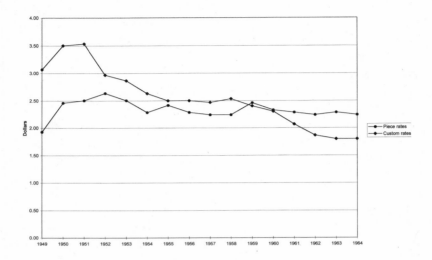

FIGURE 9.1. Piece and customs wage rates for harvesting cotton in Mississippi, 1949–1964.

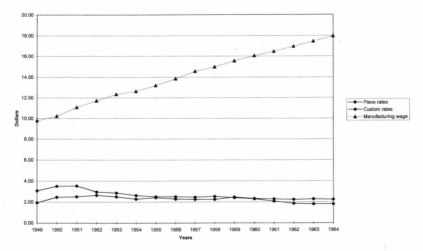

FIGURE 9.2. Piece and custom wage rates for harvesting cotton in Mississippi and average weekly national manufacturing wage, 1949–1964.

Source: U.S. Department of Agriculture, Economic Research Service, *Statistics on Cotton and Related Data, 1920–1973,* Statistical Bulletin No. 535 (Washington, D.C.: USDA, 1974), 86; Warren C. Whatley, "New Estimates of the Cost of Harvesting Cotton, 1949–1964," *Research in Economic History* 13 (1991): 220; *Economic Report of the President* (Washington, D.C.: GPO, 1969), 261.

TABLE 9.1. Correlation Coefficients for the Cotton Harvesting Labor Market, 1949–1964

	Percentage Handpicked	Piece	Custom	Price	Manufacturing Wage	Yield
Percentage handpicked		-.072	.367*	.002	-.464*	.623*
Piece	-.072		-.439*	.186*	.165*	.344*
Custom	.367*	-.439*		.192	-.561*	-.260*
Price	.002	.186*	.192*		-.221*	-.107
Manufacturing wage	-.464*	.165*	-.561*	-.221*		.015
Yield	.623*	.344*	-.260*	-.107	.015	

* $p < .05$
N= 192

predictors, manufacturing wages and cotton yields, which account for most of the variance. The pull-side equation explains over 70 percent of the variance in the model. Based on the standardized coefficients, the two-equation model identifies custom rates and manufacturing wages as the strongest influences on changes in the supply of labor for cotton harvesting.

Using the Peterson-Kislev method, we can now compare the impact of changes in mechanization and manufacturing wages on the labor available for picking cotton. Less than 40 percent of the total decrease in handpicking was due to the decline in labor demand caused by mechanization (table 9.3, column 4). The other 60 percent of the decline can be attributed to the decrease in the supply of labor caused by higher wages in manufacturing industries, which depleted the labor supply. In summary, the pull effect in reducing the labor supply was more important than the push that mechanical harvesters created in displacing labor.

This conclusion supports the contention that hand labor was pulled out of the Cotton South by higher industrial wages rather than displaced by job-destroying cotton pickers. The results are consistent with those reported by Peterson and Kislev, but show that the mechanical cotton picker played a larger role in displacing labor than they reported.[22] This analysis also attributes to mechanical cotton pickers a greater impact than Heinicke found. While both push and pull forces operated simultaneously, the attraction of manufacturing wages formed the decisive factor over and above the push effect of mechanical cotton harvesters. As cotton farmers in increasing numbers mechanized their

TABLE 9.2 Regression Results (2SLS) from Analysis of Demand and Supply of Labor on Piece and Custom Wage Rates for Cotton Picking, 1949–1964

	PUSH EQUATION			PULL EQUATION		
	Estimate	T-ratio	Standardized Estimate	Estimate	T-ratio	Standardized Estimate
Piece	2.246*	3.224	.242	1.716	1.270	.214
Custom	2.594*	15.551	.988			
Cotton price	-1.551*	-5.824	-.255			
Manufacturing wage				-3.062*	-8.514	-.828
Cotton yield				.863*	9.139	.486
R^2	.740			.705		
Adjusted R^2	.712			.681		
Durbin-Watson	1.886			1.858		
N	191			191		

Note: State dummy variables have been omitted.
*$p < .05$

operations during the 1950s and 1960s, they were largely responding to labor that had already left in search of higher wages in manufacturing jobs.

Mechanization and Migration in the Mississippi River Delta

The concepts of push and pull forces are valuable in illustrating the interplay of motives on the part of potential migrants. We can extend our understanding of the relationship between mechanization and migration by focusing on specific conditions in the Mississippi River Delta itself. The relationship between migration, mechanization, and federal programs in this region can be subjected to an empirical analysis.

This time we use county-level data for the period 1950–1969, focusing on seventy-nine counties that reported cotton pickers in the 1969 census of agriculture. These counties, identified in figure 9.3, were the leading cotton-producing counties with large numbers of tenants. They accounted for most of the cotton grown in the Delta and led the region in the transition from labor-intensive to capital-intensive agriculture. These seventy-nine sample counties produced on the average between 84 and 94 percent of the cotton grown in Arkansas, Louisiana, and Mississippi between 1950 and 1969 (table 9.4).

The selected counties experienced all of the trends that shook the Cotton South between 1950 and 1969. The use of tractors increased over these years; the number of tenants, both white and black, declined decisively; the amount of land in cotton also declined, but was already low; and the use of hired farm labor increased (table 9.5).

TABLE 9.3. Estimated Labor Market Model for Custom and Piece Wage Rates for Picking Cotton and Manufacturing Wages* (Annual Percentage)

	Change in Variable (1)	Change in Piece Rates (2)	Change in Labor (3)	Share Explained (4)
Custom picking rates	-.0409	-.1999	-.3430	39.85
Manufacturing wages	.0399	-.2305	-.5177	60.15
Totals			-.8607	100.00

Column 1: Annual rate of change estimated from regression equation: log(x)= a + rt + sd + e.
Column 2: Column 1 times coefficients (table 9.2) times 1/(a - b)
Column 3: Column 2 times coefficients in table 9.2.
Column 4: Column 3 divided by -.8607.

*Based on Peterson and Kislev, "The Cotton Harvester in Retrospect: Labor Displacement or Replacement?" *Journal of Economic History* 46 (March 1986): 214.

TABLE 9.4. Cotton Production in Seventy-Nine Cotton Counties Compared to Statewide Production, 1950–1969 (Bales in 1,000's)

	1950	1954	1959	1964	1969
Sample counties	3,117	2,889	3,211	3,964	2,870
State totals	3,688	3,381	3,524	4,288	3,050
Percentages	0.84	0.85	0.91	0.92	0.94

Source: For statewide figures on cotton production, see U.S. Department of Agriculture, Economic Research Service, *Statistics on Cotton and Related Data, 1920–1973,* Statistical Bulletin No. 535 (Washington, D.C.: USDA, 1974), 66, 70, 71. For cotton production in sample counties, see U.S. Bureau of the Census, *Census of Agriculture, 1959, Area Reports Parts, Arkansas, Louisiana, and Mississippi* (Washington, D.C.: GPO, 1961), tables 1, 5; U.S. Bureau of the Census, *Census of Agriculture, 1969, Area Reports Parts, Arkansas, Louisiana, and Mississippi* (Washington, D.C.: GPO, 1972), tables 1, 3; U.S. Bureau of the Census, *Census of Agriculture, 1992,* vol. 1, *Geographic Area Series, Arkansas, Louisiana, and Mississippi* (Washington, D.C.: GPO, 1994), table 1.

TABLE 9.5. Means and Standard Deviations (in parentheses) of Selected Variables for Cotton Counties in Arkansas, Louisiana, and Mississippi, 1950–1969

	1950	1954	1959	1964	1969
Tractors	.193	.321	.484	.625	.814
	(.094)	(.134)	(.147)	(.145)	(.073)
White tenants	.415	.373	.257	.209	.177
	(.129)	(.137)	(.123)	(.111)	(.096)
Black tenants	.780	.764	.656	.541	.236
	(.111)	(.140)	(.161)	(.197)	(.104)
Land in cotton	.218	.158	.128	.137	.123
	(.124)	(.088)	(.073)	(.071)	(.066)
Hired farm labor	.404	.457	.474	.545	.616
	(.105)	(.120)	(.129)	(.137)	(.124)

Source: See table 9.4.

For each of these selected counties, we estimate net migration for blacks and whites over two decades, 1950 to 1960 and 1960 to 1970. These estimates are based on county-level population data for age, sex, and race drawn from the 1950, 1960, and 1970 population censuses.[23] The census survival method, a standard approach used by demographers, forms the basis of the calculations (see appendix for a discussion of the methodology used in calculating migration estimates as well as specific migration estimates for each county).

A comparison between statewide migration estimates reported by the census bureau and the new estimates for the seventy-nine selected counties supports the belief that the county estimates are valid (table 9.4). In Arkansas and Mississippi these seventy-nine counties in most cases accounted for half or more than half of the total estimated statewide black migration. This fact in itself makes evident that mechanization accounted for only part of all migration. Even if we assume that mechanization accounted for all of the net migration in the seventy-nine cotton-producing counties, statewide migration estimates show that population losses also occurred in non-cotton counties. This migration, then, must have had other causes.

These estimates of migration from county to county constitute the dependent variable. Since they represent net migration, with positive and negative values,

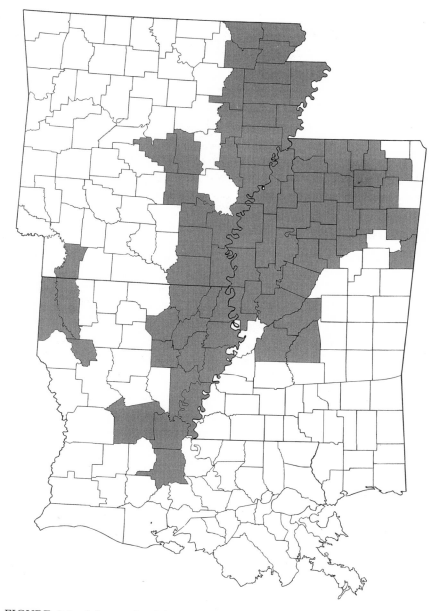

FIGURE 9.3. Arkansas, Louisiana, and Mississippi counties used in estimating migration, 1950–1970.

TABLE 9.6. Estimated Statewide Migration, Arkansas, Louisiana, and Mississippi, Compared to Estimates of Cotton Counties, 1950–1959, 1960–1969

	1950–1959			1960–1969		
	State	Selected Counties	Percentage	State	Selected Counties	Percentage
White						
Arkansas	-283,000	-106,388	37.6	38,000	-26,026	68.5
Louisiana	43,000*	-15,769	36.7	26,000	-28,949*	111.3
Mississippi	-110,000	-50,997	46.4	10,000	-771	7.7
Totals	-350,000	-173,154	49.5	74,000	-55,746	75.3
Black						
Arkansas	-150,000	-74,297	49.5	-112,000	-64,445	57.5
Louisiana	-93,000	-42,151	45.3	-163,000	-62,290	38.2
Mississippi	-323,000	-175,577	54.4	-279,000	-152,357	54.6
Totals	-566,000	-292,025	51.6	-554,000	-279,092	50.4

*The selected counties lost population, but Louisiana statewide recorded a population gain for the decade.
Note: For statewide migration estimates see table 8.2.

negative values indicate out-migration. By using the absolute value of the net migration estimate, we allow for in-migration as well as for out-migration. Most Delta counties lost population between 1950 and 1960; only a few urbanized counties saw gains. In order to simplify the interpretation of the result, however, migration estimates were multiplied by -1, so that positive numbers indicate out-migration.

Since data on cotton pickers were not available until 1969, this analysis uses tractors as a proxy for mechanization. Every farmer who purchased a picker already owned a tractor and used it in preharvest operations.

The proposed model regresses migration against the percentages of farms that reported tractors and the average number of acres in cotton—all data taken from the agricultural censuses of 1950, 1954, 1959, 1964, and 1969. These variables tap the influence of two key factors that might have affected migration. The percentage of tractors tests the extent to which mechanization caused migration. The hypothesized relationship is that counties with farms reporting larger number of tractors experienced greater out-migration, since tractors replaced tenants and their families. As out-migration increased, the number of farms using tractors in Delta counties presumably also increased as farmers made an effort to accommodate a smaller labor force.

The cotton variable is used to control for the influence of declining cotton acreage as government programs restricted cotton production. Between 1950 and 1969, federal farm policy accelerated the reduction of cotton acres, which in turn presumably eliminated jobs. Yet the impact of these programs was mixed. If they eliminated jobs, they also depressed wages, which may have created more demand for hand labor.[24] Cotton production, however, held steady as farmers employed more efficient methods and increased their yields per acre. As a result, the percentage of acres in cotton is a better variable than cotton yield. We expect to find a negative relationship between migration and cotton acreage. When acres in cotton declined and eliminated jobs, out-migration should have increased. Other variables, including the percentage of tenants, might have been used but were eliminated in an effort to avoid problems with multi-collinearity. Finally we compare separately the impact of these variables on both black and white migrants.

The results of this analysis are presented in tables 9.7 and 9.8. The regression format allows us to compare the relative importance of tractors on migration while holding constant the effect of cotton acreage. Across the sample counties during the 1950s tractors demonstrate a consistently positive relationship with white migration (table 9.7). In other words, counties that lost a large percentage of white migrants were also counties that reported a large percentage of tractors. These results confirm the expected relationship. Yet white migrants also tended to leave counties that were heaviest in cotton production. The positive coefficients for cotton acreage not only run counter to the expected relationship, but based on the standardized coefficients they also indicate that cotton acreage had twice the impact as tractors. Since the cotton coefficients are positive, this finding does not confirm federal programs as a cause of migration. Instead, white migration was associated with counties in which cotton production remained highest. These models, however, are relatively weak with R^2s that average only .300. We may speculate that while some whites were pushed off farms, most white migrants were not people who were leaving agriculture at all.

The results of the analysis of black migration in the 1950s are decidedly different, pointing to the existence of fundamental racial differences in the two migration streams. Unlike whites, black migrants demonstrate a stronger but *negative* relationship with tractors, while having a consistently positive relationship with the percentage of land in cotton. While whites were leaving counties with high levels of mechanization, blacks were staying in such counties. Black out-migration was lowest in counties with large percentages of tractors. Mechanization, then, was not pushing blacks out of cotton counties in the Mississippi River Delta. Blacks in large numbers were leaving the area, but the largest black losses were associated with counties having low levels of mechanization.

The black migration models achieved R^2s averaging .594, about twice as strong as the white models. This added explanatory power increases confidence in the results of the analysis. The standardized coefficients, however, show that both migrant groups left when cotton acreage increased, a factor wielding twice the influence of tractors. This finding again does not confirm the expected impact of federal program in stimulating out-migration. Migrants were apparently fleeing cotton farming's hard work, low wages, and poor living conditions. We can speculate that other factors, such as lack of economic opportunities, poor land, or perceptions of better opportunity outside of agriculture, played a part in migration decisions.

When we extend the analysis to the 1960–70 decade, we may expect to find more powerful models since the use of tractors and cotton pickers had reached a more advanced stage. By 1960 machines picked 40 percent of Mississippi River Delta cotton. Within a decade, the percentage soared to 100 percent. Did this final rush to mechanize produce a heavy out-migration? This part of the analysis continues the same technique described earlier but uses data from the 1960 and 1970 population censuses. This time we can take advantage of the 1969 census of agriculture, which reported the number of farms by county that used mechanical cotton pickers. Thus we can create a direct test of the impact of mechanical pickers on estimated net migration.

In contrast to the 1950s the percentage of tractors across selected counties had no bearing on white migration (table 9.8). The cotton acreage variable shows that whites, like blacks, were being lost from the counties that were the heaviest cotton producers, again failing to show that federal acreage reductions produced out-migration. The R^2s again, however, indicate very weak models for this period. By the 1960s white migration was essentially over.

The results for the 1960s black migration models again demonstrate a marked contrast with white migration. The heavy use of tractors from county to county tended to be associated with a low migration of blacks while controlling for cotton acreage. The standardized coefficients indicate that cotton acreage had twice the impact on black migration as did the percentage of tractors. The models still achieved decent R^2s, but their explanatory power declined throughout the decade.

The regression results can be used to show the average change in black net migration across counties with each 1-percent change in tractors, while controlling for a 1-percent change in the percentage of cotton acreage. In 1950, for example, each percentage point increase in tractor use in a county corresponded with 3,326 fewer black migrants.[25] As tractor use rose, black out-migration declined. In other words, the counties with the highest population losses had the lowest tractor usage. Conversely, counties that reported larger percentages of tractors lost relatively few black migrants. Whatever

TABLE 9.7. Regression of Migration on Percentage of Farms with Tractors and Percentage of Land in Cotton, 1950–1959

	1950	1954	1959
White			
Tractors	10055*	15446*	10338*
	(.397)	(.439)	(.338)
Cotton acreage	10346*	20352*	22831*
	(.287)	(.398)	(.382)
Intercept	-3963*	-5879*	5814*
R^2	.276	.355	.270
Adjusted R^2	.256	.338	.250
Black			
Tractors	-17170*	-12854*	-8925*
	(-.474)	(-.504)	(-.397)
Cotton Acreage	17842*	22669*	28904*
	(.686)	(.611)	(.658)
Intercept	3320*	4429*	4571*
R^2	.591	.619	.572
Adjusted R^2	.580	.609	.560
N	75	76	75

Note: Standardized coefficients shown in parentheses.
* $p < .05$

was driving black migrants out, it was not mechanization per se. Black migrants responded to a list of inducements, only part of which related directly to agriculture.

The final model (table 9.8, column 1969B) uses mechanical cotton pickers as a variable for the first time, since the census of agriculture first recorded mechanical pickers by county in 1969. The relationship between mechanical pickers and white migration was not statistically significant. The model for

TABLE 9.8. Regression of Migration on Percentage of Farms with Tractors/Cotton Pickers and Percentage of Land in Cotton, 1964–1969

| | 1964 | 1969 | |
		A Tractors	B Pickers**
White			
Tractors/pickers	3261	2154	6612
	(.159)	(.059)	(.278)
Cotton acreage	14887*	15687*	4973
	(.341)	(.328)	(.104)
Intercept	-3205*	-2833	-978
R^2	.153	.132	.141
Adjusted R^2	.130	.107	.117
Black			
Tractors/pickers	-7582*	-12483*	-1520
	(-.375)	(-.352)	(-.066)
Cotton acreage	28904*	36856*	30954*
	(.672)	(.790)	(.663)
Intercept	4615*	9526*	533
R^2	.537	.453	.364
Adjusted R^2	.525	.437	.347
N	75	74	74

Note: Standardized coefficients shown in parentheses.
* $p < .05$
** The 1969B models use the percentage of cotton pickers rather than tractors as the machine variable. County level data for cotton pickers is not available prior to 1969.

black migration offers only one significant variable, the percentage of land in cotton. Black migrants continued to leave cotton areas during the 1960s, but not because of the percentage of mechanical pickers in use.

Between 1950 and 1970 the Mississippi River Delta entered its most dramatic period of change—a period in which the region was buffeted by forces that had been building intensity for a generation. Mechanization and migration played complementary, not contradictory, roles. The South's poverty lay in its overpopulated rural economy based on inefficient hand labor. When the Great Migration began to draw excess population out of the region, this movement averted the disaster that many observers had feared since the 1930s. Luckily, the long-needed reduction in the farm population took care of itself as people voluntarily left the region during World War II and afterward. But most of the migrants were not pushed out by mechanical cotton pickers; they were pulled out in a search for better economic opportunities. If they were pushed out at all, they were trying to escape the hard work and low pay associated with southern cotton fields. At last the South's path to modernization lay open.

Chapter 10

The Consequences of Cotton Mechanization

The mechanical cotton picker played an indispensable role in the transition from the pre–World War II South of overpopulation, poverty, and sharecropping to the postwar, modern South. This transformation was a triumph over the region's endemic problems that went back for more than a century. Yet many of the developments of this period are surrounded with misconceptions. Conventional wisdom holds that the mechanical picker eliminated jobs and pushed poor blacks and whites off the land, forcing them into urban ghettos and welfare dependency. This view is wrong. The Great Migration had been under way for decades before the development of the mechanical cotton picker. While the mechanization of cotton did replace some workers, most migrants responded to a desire to improve their lives by taking advantage of better opportunities outside of agriculture, not to an "enclosure" movement motivated by landowners who mechanized as rapidly as possible.[1] The South's cotton farmers were often reluctant to make the transition from hand labor, which was familiar and workable, to machines, which were expensive and untried.

From 1940 to 1970 the Great Migration reduced the South's oversupply of small farmers and forced the Cotton Belt to switch from labor-intensive to capital-intensive agriculture. Though southern farmers faced enormous changes after World War II, mechanization made possible the continuation of cotton farming in the post-plantation era. While the Civil War freed the slaves, the mechanical cotton picker emancipated workers from backbreaking labor and emancipated the South itself from its dependence on cotton and sharecropping. Cotton acreage declined as farmers switched to rice and soybeans, crops that were already mechanized, creating a more diversified agricultural economy.

In the course of modernization every society must face a time when its subsistence farmers are forced to move to urban areas and to accept commercial values. The predictable result is untold hardship. But the values of subsistence labor also exact a heavy price in privation, illiteracy, high birthrates, and over-population. When we blame machines and the landowners who used them for the hardship of labor displacement, we ignore the benefits that resulted. Migration and subsequent mechanization ended the South's plantation system, a system with problems ranging from inefficiency to racism. If this antiquated system had continued, it would have only perpetuated its flaws for an indefinite future.[2]

The transformation of the South originated in a series of dramatic changes produced by the Great Depression and World War II. Some historians have suggested that the climactic changes that occurred during the Second World War were more important than were those of the Civil War.[3] While the Civil War and Reconstruction were dramatic events in themselves, they left the structure of the southern economy fundamentally unchanged. Slavery was gone, but the plantation system remained. The South made progress in the late nineteenth century, but it could not break away from its heritage of hand labor and develop a modern agricultural economy. That development did not occur until some seventy years later. World War II rather than the Civil War marked the transition from an Old South to a New South.

During the postwar era southern agriculture rushed to catch up with twentieth-century technology. In the Mississippi River Delta the impact of technological change can be measured in the number of farms, farm acreage, and farm size. Over the past sixty years the drop in the number of farms has been precipitous (table 10.1). In Arkansas, for example, the number of farms reached a high point in 1935 at more than 253,000, but afterward nosed into a consistent dive dropping to 45,142 in 1997, while the amount of land in farms remained relatively constant. As the number of farms declined, the size of farms increased almost five times. The most precipitous drop occurred in Mississippi, where the number of farmers plunged from 363,529 to 31,318 in the past half century.

More specifically, the Arkansas Delta lost 83,693 farms between the end of World War II and 1992 (table 10.2). At the same time, the average farm size increased from 77.7 acres to 620.2 acres. The total land area being farmed again remained relatively constant. The decline in the number of farm operators confirmed the collapse of labor-intensive agriculture.

TABLE 10.1. Farms in Arkansas, Louisiana, and Mississippi, 1930–1997

	ARKANSAS			LOUISIANA			MISSISSIPPI		
	Number	Land (1,000s)	Average Size	Number	Land (1,000s)	Average Size	Number	Land (1,000s)	Average Size
1930	242,334	16,053	66.2	161,445	9,355	57.9	312,663	17,332	55.4
1935	253,013	17,742	70.1	170,216	10,444	61.4	311,683	19,655	63.1
1940	216,674	18,045	83.3	150,007	9,996	66.6	291,092	19,156	65.8
1945	198,769	17,456	87.8	129,295	10,040	77.7	263,529	19,617	74.4
1950	182,429	18,871	103.4	124,181	11,202	90.2	251,383	20,711	82.4
1954	145,076	17,944	123.7	111,127	11,441	103.0	215,915	20,702	95.9
1959	95,007	16,459	173.2	74,438	10,347	139.0	138,142	18,630	134.9
1964	79,898	16,565	207.3	62,466	10,411	166.7	109,141	17,752	162.7
1969	60,433	15,695	259.7	42,269	9,789	231.6	72,577	16,040	221.0
1974	50,959	14,642	287.3	33,240	9,133	274.8	53,620	14,301	266.7
1978	51,751	15,075	291.3	31,370	9,295	296.3	44,104	13,211	299.5
1982	50,525	14,683	290.6	31,629	8,929	282.3	42,415	12,422	292.9
1987	48,242	14,356	297.6	27,350	8,007	292.8	34,074	10,746	315.4
1992	43,937	14,128	321.6	25,652	7,838	305.6	31,998	10,188	318.4
1997	45,142	14,365	318.2	23,823	7,877	330.6	31,318	10,125	323.2

Source: U.S. Bureau of the Census, *Census of Agriculture, 1959, Area Reports Series, Arkansas, Louisiana, and Mississippi* (Washington, D.C.: GPO, 1961), table 3; U.S. Bureau of the Census, *1997 Census of Agriculture, Louisiana State and Parish Data,* vol. 1, *Geographic Area Series, Part 18* (Washington, D.C.: GPO, 1999), table 1; U.S. Bureau of the Census, *1997 Census of Agriculture, Arkansas State and County Data,* vol. 1, *Geographic Area Series, Part 4* (Washington, D.C.: GPO, 1999), table 1, p. 10.

TABLE 10.2. Farms in Arkansas Delta, 1945-1997

	Number of Farms	Acres in Farms	Average size
1945	98,727	7,668,872	77.7
1950	88,709	8,451,148	95.3
1954	62,524	7,230,040	115.6
1959	42,366	8,091,842	191.0
1964	31,090	8,304,798	267.1
1969	25,353	8,497,119	335.2
1978	18,401	8,426,527	457.9
1987	15,034	7,969,916	530.1
1992	11,141	6,910,101	620.2
1997	11,092	7,133,484	643.1

Source: U.S. Bureau of the Census, *1945–1997 Censuses of Agriculture* (Washington, D.C.: GPO, 1951–99). Here the Arkansas Delta is defined as consisting of Arkansas, Chicot, Clay, Craighead, Crittenden, Cross, Desha, Greene, Jackson, Jefferson, Lawrence, Lee, Lincoln, Lonoke, Mississippi, Monroe, Phillips, Poinsett, Prairie, St. Francis, White, and Woodruff Counties.

The racial makeup of Arkansas Delta farmers has also changed (table 10.3). The number of white farmers decreased in 1940, but the largest declines occurred between 1954 and 1964. The decline in the numbers of black farmers began in the 1930s and then accelerated. While the number of white farm operators in the Arkansas Delta dropped by about 2,000 in the 1940s, black farmers declined by 30,000. After 1950 the movement of black farmers out of agriculture registered declines of around 50 percent in most census intervals. Black operators continued to decline at a faster rate than did white operators. The 1997 census of agriculture found only 934 black farm operators in the entire state of Arkansas. Today over 95 percent of farmers across the entire Mississippi River Delta are white.[4]

Since the Civil War, tenants and sharecroppers had worked in increasing numbers on the South's farms. After 1945 the decline in the number of tenants was even more remarkable than the drop in the number of farmers. Arkansas farm tenancy has been dropping steadily since 1935, losing about 23 percent every five years (table 10.4). Between 1954 and 1959, 54 percent of the state's farm tenants disappeared.[5] By the 1970s the number of tenants who remained was negligible. The most dramatic decline in tenants occurred in Mississippi between 1964 and 1969. Mississippi has changed from the state in the region with the highest rate of tenancy to the state with the lowest.

TABLE 10.3. Race of Farm Operators in Arkansas Delta, 1920–1974

	White	Percentage Change	Black	Percentage Change	Total	Percentage Change
1920	39,772		47,291		87,063	
1930	51,828	30.3	54,085	14.4	105,913	21.7
1935	57,298	10.6	48,640	-10.1	105,938	.00
1940	52,472	-8.4	39,707	-18.4	92,179	-13.0
1945	51,877	-1.1	36,485	-8.1	88,362	-4.1
1950	50,136	-3.4	29,024	-20.4	79,160	-10.4
1954	40,447	-19.3	22,522	-22.4	62,969	-20.5
1959	27,071	-33.1	10,352	-54.0	37,423	-40.6
1964	21,202	-21.7	5,615	-45.8	26,817	-28.3
1969	19,398	-8.5	2,817	-49.8	22,215	-17.2
1974	15,299	-21.1	1,230	-56.3	16,529	-25.6

Source: U.S. Bureau of the Census, *Fourteenth Census of the United States: 1920, Agriculture,* vol. 5, pt. 2, *The Southern States* (Washington, D.C.: GPO, 1922); U.S. Bureau of the Census, *Census of Agriculture, 1925–1974* (Washington, D.C.: GPO, 1927–77). See table 10.2 for a list of Arkansas Delta counties.

Still another dramatic postwar change was the dethroning of King Cotton. Across the Mississippi River Delta, the number of cotton farms has plummeted from 600,000 to 5,000 in the past seventy years. Over 57 percent of Arkansas farms grew cotton in 1945 compared to less than four percent in the 1997 agricultural census (table 10.5). After 1950 Arkansas lost on average more than 2,400 cotton farms each year. Similarly, Louisiana cotton farms fell from 61.3 percent to 6.7 percent. In 1930 over 90 percent of Mississippi farms were cotton farms, but today only 5.4 percent of Mississippi farms grow cotton.

The decline in cotton, however, was only part of the story. A half century ago, cotton was grown widely throughout Arkansas, Louisiana, and Mississippi —in both the upland and lowland counties. Today most of the region's cotton is grown in alluvial bottomlands. The Arkansas Delta today harvests more acres of rice and soybeans than acres of cotton (table 10.6).[6] While the rice crop has increased, the largest increase has been in soybean acreage.

Soybeans had been introduced in the Mississippi River Delta before World War II and in the 1950s emerged as a major cash crop. The advantage of soybean production was that it was already mechanized—a crop planted and cultivated with tractors and harvested with combines.[7]

TABLE 10.4. Tenants and Farm Operators in Arkansas, Louisiana, Mississippi, 1930–1997

	ARKANSAS		LOUISIANA		MISSISSIPPI	
	Tenants	Percentage	Tenants	Percentage	Tenants	Percentage
1930	152,691	63.0	107,551	66.6	225,617	72.2
1935	151,759	60.0	108,377	63.7	217,564	69.8
1940	115,442	53.3	89,167	59.4	192,819	66.2
1945	88,610	44.6	63,541	49.1	156,255	59.3
1950	68,602	37.6	49,199	39.6	129,821	51.6
1954	48,263	33.2	37,524	33.7	99,197	45.9
1959	22,388	23.6	17,950	24.1	43,599	31.6
1964	13,907	17.4	12,151	19.5	25,634	23.5
1969	7,670	12.7	6,765	16.0	6,580	9.1
1974	5,436	10.7	4,347	13.1	3,824	7.1
1978	5,792	11.2	4,252	13.6	3,700	8.4
1982	5,154	10.2	3,878	12.3	3,212	7.6
1987	5,404	11.2	3,686	13.5	3,113	9.1
1992	5,116	11.6	3,883	15.1	2,974	9.3
1997	4,875	10.8	3,240	13.6	2,543	8.1

Source: U.S. Bureau of the Census, *Census of Agriculture, 1959, Area Reports Series, Arkansas, Louisiana, and Mississippi* (Washington, D.C.: GPO, 1961), table 3; U.S. Bureau of the Census, *1974 Census of Agriculture, State and County Data, Arkansas, Louisiana, and Mississippi* (Washington, D.C.: GPO, 1972), table 5; U.S. Bureau of the Census, *1997 Census of Agriculture, Geographic Area Series, Arkansas, Louisiana, and Mississippi* (Washington, D.C.: GPO, 1994), table 10, p. 24.

As the region moved away from cotton, many farmers also turned away from row crops altogether. Cattle ranching became a major development after World War II, as did catfish farming and broiler production. But whatever they tried, postwar farmers preferred crops that were less labor intensive. In time, mechanization spread even to truck crops. In 1961 the Arkansas Farm Labor Report noted that hay, rice, wheat, and soybeans had been highly mechanized for a number of years. In addition, mechanical bean and spinach harvesters had appeared.[8]

Beyond agriculture, the consequences of mechanization included social and political changes. Rural areas lost population and with less population they suffered an erosion of political power, while urban areas gained population and accordingly political clout. This transfer of power had a direct impact

TABLE 10.5. Cotton Farms in Arkansas, Louisiana, and Mississippi; 1930–1997

	ARKANSAS			LOUISIANA			MISSISSIPPI		
	All Farms	Cotton Farms	Percentage of cotton farms	All Farms	Cotton Farms	Percentage of cotton farms	All Farms	Cotton Farms	Percentage of cotton farms
1930	242,334	192,209	79.3	161,445	128,537	79.6	312,663	282,175	90.2
1935	253,013	183,595	72.6	170,216	126,175	74.1	311,683	268,562	86.2
1940	216,674	150,667	69.5	150,007	114,291	76.2	291,092	259,529	89.2
1945	198,769	114,070	57.4	129,295	79,319	61.3	363,529	210,737	58.0
1950	182,429	100,234	54.9	124,181	64,097	51.6	251,383	190,732	75.9
1954	145,076	67,767	46.7	111,127	51,348	46.2	215,915	156,249	72.4
1959	95,007	34,888	36.7	74,438	24,374	32.7	138,142	77,390	56.0
1964	79,898	21,704	27.2	62,466	16,184	25.9	109,141	50,796	46.5
1969	60,433	15,079	25.0	42,269	10,281	24.3	72,577	28,584	39.4
1974	50,959	7,585	14.9	33,240	4,486	13.5	53,620	11,277	21.0
1978	51,751	4,064	7.9	31,370	2,531	8.1	44,104	4,860	11.0
1982	50,525	2,019	4.0	31,628	2,371	7.5	42,415	3,710	8.7
1987	48,242	2,479	5.1	27,350	2,675	9.8	34,074	4,225	12.4
1992	43,937	2,279	5.2	25,652	2,599	10.1	31,998	3,344	10.5
1997	45,142	1,730	3.8	23,823	1,586	6.7	31,318	1,701	5.4

Source: U.S. Bureau of the Census, Census of Agriculture, 1959, Area Reports Parts, Arkansas, Louisiana, and Mississippi (Washington, D.C.: GPO, 1961), tables 1, 5; U.S. Bureau of the Census, Census of Agriculture, 1969, Area Reports Parts, Arkansas, Louisiana, and Mississippi (Washington, D.C.: GPO, 1972), tables 1, 3; U.S. Bureau of the Census, Census of Agriculture, 1997, vol. 1, Geographic Area Series, Arkansas, Louisiana, and Mississippi (Washington, D.C.: GPO, 1994), table 1, pp. 10–11.

TABLE 10.6.   Acres Harvested of Cotton, Rice, and Soybeans in Arkansas Delta, 1950–1992 (in 1,000s)

	Cotton	Rice	Soybeans
1950	1,432	339	494
1955	1,300	428	1,142
1960	1,266	379	2,287
1965	1,168	429	3,068
1970	1,017	431	4,010
1975	662	860	4,357
1980	828	1,240	3,960
1985	427	1,020	3,413
1990	736	1,168	3,119
1992	962	1,335	2,965

Source: Statistical Reporting Service, U.S. Department of Agriculture and Agricultural Extension Service, University of Arkansas, *1950–1992 Agricultural Statistics for Arkansas* (Fayetteville: Division of Agriculture, 1951–93). This table defines the Arkansas Delta as the counties in Arkansas Extension Service's Districts 3, 6, and 9.

on congressional representation. After the 1950 census, for example, Arkansas's population loss forced a congressional redistricting in which the state lost representation. From 1900 to 1950 Arkansas had seven congressional districts, but the state lost one district in 1950 and two more in 1960, dropping from seven to four districts.[9] The largest losses after 1950 occurred in the rural farm population; and most of the migrants were higher-income, better-educated farmers rather than down-and-out sharecroppers and farmworkers.[10] Mississippi lost two congressional districts, and Louisiana was unchanged (table 10.7). Overall, population losses after World War II resulted in the loss of five congressional seats for the Mississippi River Delta states.[11]

The growth of urban areas was a postwar phenomenon throughout the region. By the 1970 census, Arkansas, one of the most rural states in the nation, had an urban majority, if only a bare majority.[12] The U.S. Supreme Court's *Baker* v. *Carr* (1962) decision confirmed the loss of rural power by affirming the one-man, one-vote principle, which equalized the populations of rural and urban congressional districts.

Though traditionally rural and agricultural, the states of the Mississippi River Delta sought to stabilize their populations by creating industrial jobs. In

Mississippi the Balance Agriculture with Industry (BAWI) plan began to sub-sidize industrial development in the 1930s; and the BAWI idea, including the use of municipal bonds to construct factories and the offer of tax exemptions, soon spread across the South.[13] The Arkansas Industrial Development Commission, established in 1954 with Winthrop Rockefeller as director, made a conscious effort to industrialize the state's economy and reverse its heavy population losses. The Mississippi River Delta slowly achieved a small degree of industrialization.

In forty critical years from the late 1930s to the 1970s, mechanization and migration transformed the Mississippi River Delta. The depression and World War II produced the Second Great Emancipation, as machines took over work that for a century and a half had been done by hand labor, thus making agri-culture capital intensive rather than labor intensive.

"Lincoln emancipated the Southern negro," W. E. Ayres wrote John Rust in 1934. "It remains for cotton-harvesting machinery to emancipate the Southern cotton planter. The sooner this is done, the better for the entire South."[14]

The Second Great Emancipation actually accomplished far more. The mechanical cotton picker freed farmers from inefficient hand labor, making cotton a more competitive crop in international markets. After World War II cotton as an industry had to reduce costs and become more efficient, and mechanization was the only way that could happen. The competition of cheap foreign cotton and synthetic fibers made the ancient, inefficient production methods of southern farms impractical and indefensible. Mechanization made

TABLE 10.7. Congressional Districts, Arkansas, Louisiana, and Mississippi, 1950–1970

	1950	1970
Arkansas	7	4
Louisiana	8	8
Mississippi	7	5
Totals	22	17

Source: *Official Congressional Directory, 81st Cong., 2d sess.* (Washington, D.C.: GPO, 1950), 819, 832, 838; *Official Congressional Directory, 91st Cong., 2d sess.* (Washington, D.C.: GPO, 1970), 29–31, 129–33, 165–68.

possible the continuation of large-scale cotton farming after the collapse of the plantation system—a system destroyed by migration-induced labor shortages.

Even in the early 1930s Ayres looked for ways to help farmers grow cotton cheaper. He emphasized the need to reduce labor costs, and he advised farmers to adopt machines as rapidly as possible.[15] After World War II mechanization freed cotton farmers from their dependence on expensive labor and ended their struggles against labor shortages. The transition from hand labor to machine labor required not only the development of the mechanical picker, but also the related development of herbicides for weed control. The invention of the mechanical cotton picker encouraged scientists and engineers to perfect such ancillary requirements and opened the way to modern, capital-intensive farming.

Ayres's insight that the mechanical picker would free the southern cotton farmer has come true, but the picker was also a Second Great Emancipation for southern blacks, as well. The picker freed them from their dependence on poorly paid agricultural work. It freed them from the agricultural system that had enslaved them for more than three centuries.[16] In fact, all southerners, white and black, were freed of an onerous form of stoop labor. Yet this freedom sometimes had negative consequences. For most, freedom was obtained by moving to Chicago and other industrial cities. Those who did not join the migration were often trapped into another form of dependency. They accepted government handouts, with attendant problems of drugs, crime, and illegitimacy.

The mechanization of cotton had another positive, though unintended, consequence. Mechanization meant that farming could continue without the presence of a kind of rural peasantry. So ended the South's need for cheap labor and its corollaries, labor control and Jim Crow repression. The end of the plantation system constituted an essential precondition that facilitated the civil rights movement of the 1950s. It was not accidental that Jim Crow began in the 1890s as the postbellum plantation system took its final form in the waning century; nor was it accidental that the civil rights movement coincided with the collapse of the plantation system and agricultural mechanization. In large part the civil rights agitation focused on breaking down the Jim Crow barriers erected to sustain the plantation system's need for cheap labor and deference in social relations. When civil rights leaders demanded the vote and access to public accommodations, they were really attacking the archaic institutions of the plantation. With the collapse of the plantation economy, the South could move beyond its repressive Jim Crow system into a more tolerant racial atmosphere.

Historian Jay Mandle has argued that the "emergence of the civil rights movement had its roots in the breakdown of the plantation economy."[17] The plantation system required the rigid enforcement of social controls, which ranged from racial segregation to lynchings. Capital-intensive agriculture meant that the need for labor control no longer existed, thus paving the way for civil rights protests. In the post–World War II South, blacks experienced both greater geographic mobility and increased economic opportunity. The old constraints quickly became intolerable. In addition traditional segregation was incompatible with the needs of an industrializing and urbanizing social organization.[18]

In an article on paternalism in southern agriculture, economists Lee J. Alston and Joseph P. Ferrie elaborated on Mandle's argument. They defined paternalism as an implicit agreement in which workers exchange dependable work for nonmarket services including protection from acts of violence. "Even before the movement for civil rights at the federal level," they wrote, "technological forces were working to undermine the South's traditional system of race relations—what we have called its system of social control—and the paternalistic relations that it fostered."[19] With mechanization the demand for hand labor disappeared, and so did the requirements of paternalism and social control.

Indeed, the success of the civil rights movement was made possible because the South had less investment in the need to restrict the role of blacks in southern society. If every revolution has amounted to kicking in a rotten door, the collapse of the plantation system and the mechanization of cotton were the forces that rotted the wood; concealed in the background, these forces accounted for the success of the civil rights movement. True, other causes played a role, including the military service of blacks during World War II, but the mechanical cotton picker was an indispensable factor. The positive role that black masses played in the civil rights movement demonstrated that they were responding to forces that had reached the grassroots level.

Despite the ugly violence that civil rights marches provoked, the South's resistance to the challenge to Jim Crow was less vicious than it might have been. The creation of the Jim Crow system was accompanied by the lynching of 2,500 blacks between 1890 and 1910. While civil rights activists lost their lives in the 1960s, the South failed to display the last-ditch defense that the region would have mustered if the need for unskilled black labor had remained as great as before World War II. The mechanical cotton picker's role in creating the Second Great Emancipation was one with many nuances.

The technological basis of the Old South's economy was Eli Whitney's cotton gin, which enabled cotton plantations and slavery to spread across the lower South and into the Mississippi River Valley. The First Great Emancipation destroyed slavery but produced sharecropping as the source of plantation labor, keeping the South poor and unmechanized. The post–Civil War economy, still too much like that of the Old South, struggled with sharecropping, overpopulation, and a declining share of the international cotton market until it crashed in the early 1930s. Only a government bailout prevented total collapse.

Out of the matrix of depression and world war came a Second Great Emancipation. The out-migration of World War II destroyed the cheap labor supply that plantation agriculture required. The future of the Cotton South still looked precarious after World War II; but again, as in the late eighteenth century, a machine molded the region's future. The technological basis of the postwar South was the mechanical cotton picker, the centerpiece of the South's belated shift from labor-intensive to capital-intensive agriculture. The Second Great Emancipation not only freed southerners from backbreaking labor, but also paved the way for the modernization of the South. Between 1930 and 1970 the Mississippi River Delta underwent a revolution that was unattainable and even unimaginable without the existence of the mechanical cotton picker.

Where Are They Now?

The Smithsonian's National Museum of American History on the Mall in Washington, D.C., contains an exhibit featuring Old Red, a one-row International Harvester model H-10-H cotton picker manufactured in 1943. This machine picked an estimated eight thousand bales of cotton in California's San Joaquin Valley over sixteen seasons before it was retired in 1959. It sits today in an area that most tourists overlook. Agricultural machinery lacks the drawing power of flashier exhibits like the Enola Gay, the B-29 that dropped the atomic bomb on Hiroshima.

How this machine came to be in the Smithsonian is a curious story. In 1969 the Smithsonian Institution planned an exhibit on cotton across the entire scope of American history. Believing that International Harvester developed the first "effective spindle picker," John T. Schlebecker, curator of the Smithsonian's Division of Agriculture and Mining, contacted John J. Dierbeck Jr., International Harvester's director of public relations, to ask for help in locating one of the early machines.[1] After a search Dierbeck referred him to James B. Mayer, president and CEO of Producers Cotton Oil Company of Fresno, California, a company that owned a picker fondly called Old Red. Schlebecker contacted Mayer about the loan of Old Red to the Smithsonian for a three-year exhibit, offering to pay all transportation costs between California and Washington.[2] Mayer immediately agreed to the loan.[3]

On February 5, 1970, Old Red left Fresno after an elaborate send-off ceremony. In his speech Mayer gave International Harvester credit for inventing the cotton picker and for being the first to mass-produce it. This point was a sensitive one, because Rust partisans felt strongly that he was the rightful inventor. Mayer's assertion greatly pleased International Harvester, and the company enjoyed the good publicity. With the audience sitting on cotton bales and sipping "Old Reds" (Bloody Marys) the occasion featured speeches, television coverage, and a pep band.[4]

Attending the ceremony was Clarence R. Hagen of Chicago, the retired chief engineer for International Harvester who had headed the development effort. He was honored as the man who decided to run the picker tractor in reverse, creating the mechanical cotton picker as it came to be known.[5]

International Harvester was proud of its success in developing a mechanical cotton picker over a twenty-year odyssey. Company officials liked to point out that they spent $4.5 million on the development of the picker—in the words of J. W. Wegener, Memphis Works manager—"without any assurance that we would be able to market a cotton picker IF and WHEN we did develop it."[6]

Loaded on a new International flatbed trailer truck, Old Red departed on its transcontinental journey. The route took Old Red through some of the nation's prime cotton growing country: Bakersfield, San Bernardino, El Centro, Yuma, Casa Grande, Phoenix, Tucson, El Paso, Odessa, Big Springs, Abilene, Texarkana, Little Rock, Memphis, and on to Washington. International Harvester wanted to route the picker through these cotton areas to increase promotional possibilities. As Old Red traveled across the country, the machine became a mechanical celebrity with local news media. At the Memphis stopover on February 17, the significance of the machine was most clearly felt. International Harvester's Memphis Works owed its existence to the picker's success. Memphis Mayor Henry Loeb, Memphis Works officials, and media representatives all attended a news conference to honor the mechanical cotton picker and its contribution to the local economy.[7] Compared to current pickers, however, Old Red seemed frail and diminutive.

At the National Museum of History and Technology on February 24, 1970, Old Red received a formal presentation. In the program, the machine was described as "the first successful mechanical cotton picker." A cocktail-and-supper party followed. Attire was informal. The Smithsonian's newest celebrity had arrived home.

On May 14, however, the Old Red story took a surprising twist. John W. Nance Jr. telephoned Ed Wilborn, editor of the *Progressive Farmer,* to complain about a statement in the magazine's May issue that "the No. 1 IH cotton picker was donated to the Smithsonian Institution by Producers Cotton Oil Company."[8] Nance stated that *he* had owned the original International Harvester picker. Most of all, however, he objected to the statement that the first picker came from California when, in fact, he claimed, it came from

Mississippi. The *Progressive Farmer*'s article was based on information from an International Harvester news release. Wilborn offered to print a correction if the story was wrong.[9]

International Harvester officials defended the choice of the California machine over a Mississippi machine. The Smithsonian picker was one of an "emergency" run of twenty-five cotton pickers made with a special allocation of materials in late 1943. It arrived in the San Joaquin Valley for the 1944 harvest. Robert Massey, an IH executive, reported: "So far as we know it is the only one of that first run of machines still in existence, and this is one reason it went to the Smithsonian. Another, and perhaps better, reason is that it is very definitely the oldest Harvester picker we know of that is still operational. In fact, it still picks cotton and," Massey boldly overstated, "may even have been able to make the trip from California on its own if it had been given a chance." The machine Nance mentioned was a later machine, an M-10-H probably manufactured in 1945, according to Massey. He believed the machine had not been operational for several years.[10]

Nance's claim was far more solid than IH officials realized. Nance had married Mary Hopson, the daughter of Howell H. Hopson Sr., one of the owners of the Hopson plantation. Nance claimed that the original three cotton pickers were purchased by the Hopson Planting Company, and he reminded Harvester officials that IH did a great deal of their engineering and testing on Hopson land. The original picker, according to Nance, had been in use on their plantation until a few years earlier. As he recalled, he gave it to International Harvester's Memphis Works, but learned later that it had been cut up for scrap. Another Hopson machine, which Nance called the "No. 2 picker," went to the Delta Experiment Station Museum at Stoneville, Mississippi, and was still there. Massey confessed to Nance that the Stoneville picker was originally recommended for the Smithsonian but the decision was made to take the California machine.

Harvester officials sought to find out what happened to the picker that Nance returned to Memphis Works. C. R. Hagen, who had retired, had no recollection of the Hopson plantation's returning a picker. Nor did he recall after twenty-five years what the machine's fate was.[11] But it was learned that the Nance machine was an experimental model, which would not have qualified it for the Smithsonian since Schlebecker wanted a commercial model.[12] The Smithsonian's criteria had specifically stated that the machine not be an experimental model, that it must be in excellent condition to meet aesthetic requirements, and if possible it should be in operating condition.

In a telephone call to Chicago, Nance objected strongly to IH and the Smithsonian's selection. According to a memorandum of the conversation, Nance was very "exercised" because he felt that the Hopson family was due the recognition that went to the Producers Cotton Oil Company of California. Nance reported that the Hopson Plantation had operated as many as fourteen cotton pickers at one time, and they still owned a large number of International Harvester pickers and tractors. If the entire matter was not corrected, Nance threatened to get rid of all his Harvester equipment.[13] As he reminded one official, "the boys who sell the 'green stuff' were continually after him, and that if International Harvester didn't get this thing straightened out, he was going to switch."[14]

Harvester officials initially saw Nance as a cranky old man who was making trouble for them, until they realized that he was a valuable customer who for years had equipped his farm with Harvester (that is, "red") equipment. They took seriously his threat to go "green" and telephoned Nance to arrange a meeting with him at his home in Sardis, Mississippi. As the man who made the decision to recommend the California picker, Dierbeck offered to go to Mississippi and talk directly to Nance as the "sacrificial lamb" and take any abuse he wanted to hand out.[15] At Nance's home, however, Harvester employees were cordially received.

International Harvester made a series of concessions in the hope of placating Nance. David C. Haney, a Harvester vice president, sent him a note reassuring him of the company's appreciation for the association with the Hopson plantation and promising a full investigation into the matter. For their visit with Nance, officials armed themselves with a battery of arguments to explain the California choice. After the Smithsonian's request, they recalled, the company's search turned up two machines, one an M-10-H on display at the Delta Experiment Station Museum, and the other was the H-10-H found in Fresno. The Fresno machine was preferred because it had been completely refurbished in 1964, it was the earliest commercial model, and it was in working condition. (The Stoneville picker was no longer the original delivered to Clarksdale anyway, because the H tractor which originally powered the picker had been upgraded to a larger M tractor.) Smithsonian officials also felt it was presumptuous to ask one museum to give up its exhibit for another museum; in addition, the Stoneville machine would need to be refurbished and made operable before the Smithsonian would accept it. In any event, Harvester officials claimed that they did not represent Old Red as the oldest machine in existence, although some newspapers and magazines did describe it as *the* only, or oldest, machine in existence.

International Harvester Farm, a corporate publication, printed an article that played up the role of the Hopson plantation.[16] The article noted that IH engineers used the plantation's resources in performing "a major portion of the field testing and experimentation work." A photograph of John and Mary Nance appeared on the cover.

As for the Smithsonian, Schlebecker agreed to place an additional plaque on the exhibit reading:

> The First Successful Spindle Cotton Picker. This machine represented over 30 years of development by International Harvester in cooperation with plantation owners in the South, Southwest and West. One of the principal contributors to the success of this machine was the H. H. Hopson plantation in Clarksdale, Mississippi.

In a booklet Schlebecker was writing on early cotton production, he promised to give the Hopson plantation "appropriate mention."[17]

The Smithsonian's cotton exhibit opened in 1972. In the end, Nance seemed satisfied, and he did not "go green."[18] An attempt to preserve an important part of recent history had unfortunately generated hard feelings.

The Inventor of the Mechanical Cotton Picker

Nance's disagreement over which machine was the original picker suggested that the rightful inventor of the mechanical cotton picker could also be a controversial question. International Harvester has a solid claim to being the first to develop a successful picker and take it into full commercial production in 1949. The company had a workable picker as early as 1942, and indeed might have produced it earlier if not constrained by wartime shortages. For more than twenty years, Harvester had carried on their own development work creating many innovations in picking technology. Memphis Works produced a few commercial models in 1948, but full production began in 1949. Deere and Company entered the market in 1950 and successfully produced pickers using advanced designs. As a result, Deere can make no claim for being first.

The alternate contender was, of course, John Rust. He applied for his first patent on a mechanical picker in 1928, and it was granted in 1933. During the 1930s, Rust was widely hailed as the inventor of the mechanical cotton picker, and indeed he saw himself as the rightful inventor. However, many inventions have been claimed by more than one inventor, who, working separately, arrived at similar discoveries at the same time. Such conflicting claims usually produced patent lawsuits, including especially Elias Howe Jr. versus Isaac Merritt

Singer over the sewing machine; Cyrus McCormick versus Obed Hussey over the reaper; and Alexander Graham Bell versus Elisha Gray, Thomas Edison, and Emilé Berliner over the telephone.[19]

Rust was not the first inventor to work on a spindle picker. Samuel S. Rembert and Jedediah Prescott's 1850 patent utilized the spindle principle. In 1895, Angus Campbell took out the first patent on a modern cotton picker spindle. Hiram Berry as well as others experimented with variations of the spindle idea.[20] Rust's claim to fame was based on his insight that cotton had an affinity for moistened metal surfaces. Indeed, moistened spindles are used on all pickers today. Rust's machines set the first picking records in the 1930s while astonishing and scaring the nation. Rust always insisted on using long, straight, smooth spindles; however, short, tapered, and barbed spindles proved to be the most efficient.[21]

Today most scholars give John Rust credit for the invention of the mechanical cotton picker. He is not only the inventor most mentioned in standard reference works on the history of technology, but also he is identified as "the first one to show the world that the idea [of mechanical picking] would work" and is credited with the "breakthrough" that had eluded other inventors for a century.[22] Only rarely are other inventors even mentioned. International Harvester's role is largely unnoticed except in the work of agricultural historians.[23]

Ultimately, the invention of the mechanical cotton picker must be shared. The basic ideas that led to the mechanical cotton picker came from individual inventors, but the task was too much for one man. Only a major implement company like International Harvester commanded the necessary resources to develop a commercially successful mechanical picker.[24] The Rust brothers, however, produced the first workable picker, a machine that actually picked cotton and picked it well in trial runs under field conditions. But they were unable to put their machine into production because of a lack of resources. While reference works associate Rust with the mechanical picker, his name and what he accomplished in improving southern life has faded from the public consciousness compared to his reputation a half century ago.

Historian Raymond Arsenault bemoaned the fact that the development of air conditioning had been ignored by historians despite its obvious role in making life in the modern South tolerable. He also complained about the lack of mention of the air conditioner in standard historical works.[25] But Arsenault need not have felt that his topic had been singled out. In more than three thousand combined pages, neither David C. Roller and Robert W. Twyman's *Encyclopedia of Southern History* nor Charles Reagan Wilson and William

Ferris's *Encyclopedia of Southern Culture* even mentioned John Rust at all.[26] Nor did they mention International Harvester. In fact, they omitted any reference whatever to the part mechanical cotton pickers played in shaping southern agricultural history.

The Second Great Emancipation involved a varied cast of characters—individual, group, corporate, and even geographic. Since the transition to capital-intensive agriculture in the Cotton South is now complete, we naturally want to know the outcome of their separate stories.

As an industry, agriculture has continued to oscillate between good times and bad. The late 1970s saw an agricultural depression that hit all segments of the cotton industry.[27] Farmers were caught in a cost-price squeeze as their production costs rose and cotton prices stagnated, a process that generated a domino effect in the industry. With many farmers slipping into bankruptcy, farm implement dealers were caught with excessive inventory, and in turn equipment manufacturers saw their profits diminished. After International Harvester entered bankruptcy, Tenneco Inc., a conglomerate based in Houston, Texas, purchased Harvester's farm machinery division. Tenneco had previously acquired J. I. Case, a farm machinery manufacturer that originally produced grain combines.[28] In 1985 Tenneco merged the Harvester unit with its J. I. Case division, producing Case-International Harvester. The Case IH division took over Harvester's extensive network of dealers and continued the manufacture of cotton pickers painted the traditional red. Tenneco enjoyed the advantage of diversification that a single-industry company like IH lacked.

With Harvester's demise, Deere and Company dominated the farm machinery industry, one increasingly burdened with risk as the number of farms declined. Deere, of course, still manufactures the ubiquitous green farm machinery, and most of the cotton pickers seen today in the Mississippi River Delta are green. Through the agricultural depression and corporate mergers of the 1970s, Deere and Company survived and prospered. In 1989 Deere built a five-row cotton picker, and in 1997 the company introduced a six-row machine. Designed for high-yielding cotton (three bales per acre) with a basket capable of handling 8,100 pounds of lint cotton, the six-row machine provided faster picking speeds and greater picking capacity. In addition, Deere still produces cotton strippers for use in high-plains cotton.[29]

Modern mechanical cotton pickers operate more efficiently with a smaller differential in cotton grade between machine and handpicked cotton; they also leave less unpicked cotton in the field.[30] But the most amazing feature of mechanical cotton pickers today is their price tag. Rust had initially planned to sell his cheapest machine for $995. In 1949 the first one-row International Harvester picker sold for $4,738.[31] Burnice Frizzell paid $9,100 for an IH picker in 1953, and he thought he paid a high price. A new six-row John Deere picker today, however, carries a price tag of $200,000. Even tractors cost $90,000 in their deluxe models, featuring enclosed cabs, air-conditioning, and cassette tape players.

The two companies that manufactured cotton pickers with the Rust patents have discontinued their interest in the market. Allis-Chalmers (A-C) produced cotton pickers under the Rust patents from 1949 to 1985. The first production model was a two-row machine mounted on a tractor, but A-C also manufactured cheaper one-row models that were aimed at the low end of the market. By the 1960s A-C produced larger spindle machines designed for taller, higher-yielding cotton, as well as cotton strippers. Allis-Chalmers engineers took their pickers beyond Rust's designs. While originally using smooth spindles, they later adopted a spindle with recessed-barbs. In addition, A-C experimented with a variety of stripper designs, including models that were equipped with multiheads and a burr extractor that produced cleaner cotton. In 1982 Allis-Chalmers Corporation split into several components, with various divisions merging with other concerns. The farm equipment division became Deutz-Allis in 1985 and Allis Gleaner Corporation in 1990, which today manufactures farm equipment under the name AGCO Allis.[32]

Ben Pearson Manufacturing Company at Pine Bluff, Arkansas, was the smallest firm to manufacture cotton harvesters. The Ben Pearson-Rust pickers were more successful in the California-Arizona market than in the old Cotton South. Pearson machines also sold well in South American markets.[33] Like Allis-Chalmers, the company experimented with unconventional designs. In 1970, under the leadership of G. E. Powell, Ben Pearson introduced the "cotton combine," a machine that used a small-grain type cutting header to harvest cotton grown in narrow rows. The machine cut down the cotton stalks, and spindles mounted horizontally picked the lint, leaving the stalks on the ground. This design was intended to reduce labor costs to a minimum; since the use of herbicides eliminated chopping and made the use of standard forty-inch rows unnecessary, cotton seed could be planted more densely or even broadcast by airplane. While the cotton combine attracted attention, it was not the breakthrough it seemed. Today part of Quest Corporation, Ben Pearson is out of the cotton picker business.[34]

John Rust lived his last years in Pine Bluff, Arkansas. His association with Ben Pearson brought him financial security at last; and true to his philanthropic nature, he endowed scholarships at several agricultural colleges and universities to assist young men and women from rural areas with their education.[35] He was also involved in lawsuits toward the end of his life. He and his brother Mack had gone their separate ways during World War II, and when John achieved success with Ben Pearson, Mack sued for what he regarded as his rightful share. John Rust also became involved in a dispute with Ben Pearson over royalties.[36]

Rust's life was cut short. At age sixty-one John Rust died of a heart attack in Pine Bluff on January 20, 1954, at a time when only 15 percent of cotton in the Mississippi River Delta was machine picked.[37] Mack Rust died on January 11, 1966, at Coalinga, California.[38] The other lone inventors passed into obscurity well before the story of cotton mechanization played out.

The Delta itself, which James C. Cobb called "the most southern place on earth," has undergone greater change in its landscape than any other part of the Cotton South. A century ago virgin hardwood forests covered this region, but they have gradually given way to an open, virtually treeless vista. The 1970s saw additional land clearing, and the landscape now is more stark than ever.

Today the sights of Delta agriculture present a markedly different image than they did in the era before World War II.[39] Then, at chopping and picking time the fields were populated with people working in small groups, moving slowly down the cotton rows. In the late 1950s and early 1960s people and machines worked in fields together. Today, the fields at harvest time are empty except for a few machines that slowly move back and forth, eating up four or more rows at a time. Even the ubiquitous cotton wagons used to haul seed cotton to the gin are gone. The mechanical pickers dump the cotton lint into large compactors that compress it hydraulically into huge, rail-car-sized modules of seed cotton. Since each module consists of about sixteen bales, they allow mechanical cotton pickers to operate without regard for ginning capacity. The gins send special equipment to transport the modules for ginning.

The organizational structure of Delta agriculture has also changed. In 1955 geographer Merle C. Prunty Jr. used the term *neoplantation* to describe a new type of plantation organization he saw evolving in the South. As a geographer, Prunty was interested in spatial changes. The highly mechanized neoplantations adopted a nucleated settlement pattern after sharecropper families left agriculture. As the scattered tenant houses were torn down, the plantation community moved into a cluster or nucleus where machines and workers came together—a spatial arrangement not unlike that of the old slave plantation in which the owner's residence was near the slave cabins. The more traditional plantations retained the fragmentation that had characterized the post–Civil War South—the land divided into separate units with each family working its own separate acreage from land-breaking to harvest. In a study of Mississippi during the early 1960s, Charles Aiken, a student of Prunty's, observed plantations in various stages of the transition from the fragmented plantation to the neoplantation.[40] By the 1970s, the tenant shacks had all disappeared, and today the fields stretch without interruption to the distant tree line.

The modern Mississippi River Delta is a region where agribusiness dominates, unlike the Alabama Black Belt and the old Piedmont cotton areas of Georgia, where cotton is no longer a major crop. But with high production costs along with the usual unpredictability of prices, insects, and weather, Delta agriculture carries increasing risks. Many farmers, even large ones, lost out in the cost-price squeeze of the 1970s, their costs rising dramatically but the prices they received stagnating. In the late 1990s they again faced low cotton prices.

The Mississippi River Delta remains a poor region. Charles Aiken was surely correct when he called the South's old plantation areas "depressing" and "dysfunctional."[41] Unlike Appalachian poverty, Delta poverty has never received full national attention, but it is there for anyone to see. Tourists who drive down the Mississippi side of the river from Memphis, cutting across the rich Yazoo-Mississippi bottomland, to Greenville and on to Vicksburg—the traditional end of the Mississippi Delta—see poverty and hopelessness in the eyes of many residents. Schools struggle against alienation, and small towns reek of idleness, indolence, and stagnation. This drive takes visitors through the modern Cotton South, including the cotton fields around Clarksdale where the experimental pickers of John Rust and International Harvester once operated. The rusting hulk of an old picker still stands in front of the Hopson commissary. At Scott visitors can see the old headquarters of the Delta and Pine Land Company; and at Stoneville the Delta Research and Extension Center, as it is now known, continues its research.[42]

For a diversion travelers often stop at the riverboat casinos near Tunica or in Greenville and amuse themselves gambling.[43] In a desperate search for economic activity, the Mississippi side of the river has become gambling country. The casinos have created new jobs, but they have not eliminated poverty. Many blacks who live in Tunica County, for example, have such a poor work ethic they have been replaced by outsiders in casino jobs.[44] In 1989, 56.8 percent of the county's people lived below the poverty level, making Tunica County one of the nation's poorest.[45]

If tourists drive southward from St. Louis through the Missouri boot heel, or cross the river at Memphis and drive down U.S. River Road 1 through Arkansas, they will see a flat, virtually empty region, marked by a series of stagnating dowager towns, including Marianna, Helena, McGehee, Lake Village, Eudora, and Lake Providence, Louisiana, which *Time* magazine once described as "the poorest place in America."[46] Along their main streets, dark and empty store windows stare back blankly, but the neon signs in liquor stores still glow their welcome. Unemployment rates sometimes rise as high as 40 percent in eastern Arkansas.

The Delta economy today offers little more than farming and gambling. There has been economic growth and even a degree of industrialization. In 1987, Nucor-Yamato Corporation built a steel mill near Osceola, in Mississippi County, Arkansas.[47] The Grand Gulf nuclear power plant is located south of Port Gibson, Mississippi, near where U.S. Grant's Army of the Tennessee crossed the river prior to the siege of Vicksburg. There are other success stories too, but not enough of them.

In 1988 Congress created a Lower Mississippi Delta Development Commission with the ambitious goal of revitalizing the region in a ten-year effort. The commission, headed by Arkansas Gov. Bill Clinton, did a good job identifying the region's problems and recommended a comprehensive road-building program. "We don't expect a big government check," Clinton said.[48] Within two years the commission was defunct. The cost of lifting the Delta out of its poverty, even if theoretically possible, was too great in an era of high government deficits.

The Delta has always been a region of contrasts—rich land and poor people. But agricultural mechanization did not cause Delta poverty. The region is poor today for the same reason it was poor a half century ago; it lacks an economic base to support all of the people who live there.

Those who left the region on the Great Migration are the ones who found a solution to Delta poverty. They are the heroes of one of the greatest success stories of the modern South. Many of those who stayed behind subsisted on government handouts. If it had not been for welfare, which convinced them that they could stay and eke out an existence, they too might have gone on to a better life instead of exchanging plantation paternalism for government paternalism. Even Third World countries do not have higher rates of illegitimacy and family breakdown than the Delta.[49]

While mechanization did not cause poverty in the Delta, it did change the relationship between the races. Before mechanization, whites depended on blacks, and as a result subjugated and controlled them. But today blacks are no longer needed to chop and pick cotton. "By the end of the 1960s," James C. Cobb wrote, "Delta blacks [were] largely superfluous to the economic interest of Delta whites."[50] Here is the key to race relations in the Delta today. Despite the Great Migration, blacks still make up 70 percent of the population of the Delta. According to Benjamin and Christina Schwarz, "The paramount problem in Tunica, from the point of view of many whites, is what to do with this group that stayed behind—a black majority disproportionately unemployed, dependent, and miserably educated, a population that many whites regard as dross."[51] For their part, many blacks seem resigned to poverty, which whites sometimes interpret as an unwillingness to improve their lot.

The black migrants who left the South invaded northern cities, where the pessimists of the 1930s predicted they would exacerbate social problems. During the 1960s, some commentators believed that the naysayers were right, arguing that former sharecroppers were the cause of crime, welfare, poverty, and especially urban riots. These commentators maintained that the problems of northern cities originated with the arrival of a large, uneducated black population from the South. These migrants presumably composed the basis of the urban underclass. "The slums are in large part a result of the malaise of the rural and small town South;" said Roger Beardwood in 1968, "The violence in northern streets is a product of frustration born in southern fields."[52]

According to former Secretary of Agriculture Orville L. Freeman in 1970,

> [D]isplacement of large numbers of rural people by mechanization is more responsible for the big city problems which resulted in the burning of cities in the United States in the 1960s than any other factor. For my part, I have no hesitation in confirming this analysis. I have visited cotton plantations in the American Southland where in one year labor supported by the plantation dropped from one hundred families to five families.[53]

This viewpoint, a sharecropper-to-underclass thesis, still has it advocates. In a more recent version, journalist Nicholas Lemann asserted that plantation workers and former sharecroppers who migrated to the North brought with them illegitimacy, crime, and alcoholism. "The black underclass did not just spring into being over the past twenty years," Lemann wrote in 1986. "Every aspect of the underclass culture in the ghettos is directly traceable to roots in the South—and not the South of slavery but the South of a generation ago. In fact there seems to be a strong correlation between underclass status in the North and a family background in the nascent underclass of the sharecropper South."[54]

This negative view may be politically correct, but it unfortunately ignores the positive qualities of southern sharecroppers. Scholars have long downplayed their work ethic, their strong family structure, and their willingness to take risks to better themselves. They have forgotten that sharecropping was a labor system that kept families together. In *The Truly Disadvantaged* sociologist William Julius Wilson challenged the sharecropper-to-underclass thesis. Research on urban poverty and migration after 1950, he said, "consistently shows that southern-born blacks who have migrated to the urban North experience greater economic success in terms of employment rates, earnings, and [less] welfare dependency than do those urban blacks who were born in the North."[55]

Nor did former sharecroppers cause the urban riots of the 1960s. As journalist David Whitman pointed out in a review of Lemann's work, former sharecroppers and cotton pickers from the South constituted a major success story. They were less likely to live in poverty than native urban blacks, less likely to have criminal records, and more likely to have a high-school education.[56] As Whitman quipped, high-school graduates in the Delta moved to Chicago, those who failed to graduate stayed behind. In summary, the urban riots were the work of people who were natives of northern cities.

Even the Kerner Commission in 1968 described urban rioters as follows: "Characteristically, the typical rioter was not a hoodlum, habitual criminal, or riffraff; nor was he a recent migrant, a member of an uneducated underclass, or a person lacking broad social and political concerns. Instead, he was a teenager or young adult, a lifelong resident of the city in which he rioted."[57] This view absolved former sharecroppers of blame for urban riots and proved the pessimists wrong.

Despite its problems or because of them, the Mississippi River Delta, though poor, is today a region with a strong sense of its culture. Indeed, even the region's poverty conveys a sense of accomplishment, of having suffered, endured, and overcome. Many former migrants or their descendants have returned to the Delta, where their roots still are, because they are tired of the crime, gangs, drugs, and congestion of large northern cities.[58] Overall, however, the Delta lost population in the 1990s as people still seek economic opportunity elsewhere.[59]

The Mississippi Delta is proud of its musical heritage. Greenville celebrates the Delta Blues Festival every September, and insiders still like the atmosphere of edge-of-a-cotton field juke joints for the good music and good food. Mississippi's Highway 61, which runs from Natchez to Memphis, is famous as the route that musicians like B.B. King, Muddy Waters, and other regional artists traveled out of the Delta and into national fame.[60]

On the Arkansas side of the river, the Delta Cultural Center at Helena offers its own commemoration of the region's life and culture. Arkansas Delta spokesmen claimed their region was being ignored while the Ozark Folk Center in Mountain View drew on a large tourist trade and kept Ozark arts and crafts alive. Opened in 1990, the Delta Cultural Center operates a museum to showcase the culture and history of the Arkansas side of the river. Not to be outdone by Greenville, Helena also holds its own annual blues celebration called the King Biscuit Blues Festival.

Besides music, the Delta has a rich literary tradition in writers ranging from William Alexander Percy, who wrote *Lanterns on the Levee,* to David L. Cohn, Hodding Carter, Eudora Welty, and Willie Morris. The civil rights era has also added rich nuances to the history of the region.[61]

Agriculture has continued to change. While the sharecroppers have disappeared, tenants remain, though in small numbers, usually paying cash rent. Often the only way for farmers to acquire land is to rent it. Today, however, it is tenants who are often prosperous; and they, not landowners, are the ones who own mechanical cotton pickers. They may custom pick other farmers' cotton.[62]

The plantations themselves have also vanished at least semantically.[63] While the word *plantation* is still used in a historical context—for example, the Plantation Agriculture Museum at Scott, Arkansas, or Florewood River Plantation near Greenwood, Mississippi—Delta agriculture today involves *farms,* not plantations. No matter how large their size, all operations are called farms. Plantations belong to the past, and the term is no longer in current use because of its pejorative connotation.[64]

The process of social and technological change has not been easy. But the pessimists of fifty and sixty years ago proved to be poor prophets. Agriculture in the Mississippi River Delta has undergone an astonishing transformation from hand labor to machine labor. As a result, its poorest people are not performing stoop labor each fall. Nor are they prohibited from using schools, restaurants, and other public facilities. Many "New" Souths have come and gone, but the modern South that emerged after the Second Great Emancipation offers the Mississippi River Delta its best hope yet for progress and prosperity.

Appendix

The migration figures analyzed in chapter 9 (see fig. 9.3 and tables 9.4–9.8) are based on new estimates of county-level migration from seventy-nine cotton counties and parishes in Arkansas, Louisiana, and Mississippi between 1950 and 1970. I created new estimates because migration estimates are available for states and regions but not for counties or parishes.

Demographers employ two methods for estimating migration:

- The census survival method uses survival ratios to determine state survival data over ten-year periods. This method yields an estimate for decades as opposed to annual estimates.
- The components of change method can be used to produce an annual migration estimate for either states or counties but requires detailed information on the number of births and deaths for the geographic area and for each year. This information tends to be readily available for states, but is more difficult to obtain for counties. It is probably the most accurate method if the birth and death data are available.

This analysis uses the census survival method to estimate net migration by age, sex, and race, following the procedure reported in Everett S. Lee et al., *Population Redistribution and Economic Growth, United States, 1870–1950.*[1] While Lee and his colleagues estimated state migration rates, here I extended their procedure to the county level. Since the Mississippi River Delta lost population through out-migration during the 1950s and 1960s, state ratios could not be used because the census survival method assumes that populations are closed (those entered only by birth and left only by death); instead, I relied on national survivor ratios. I can assume that the national population was closed in the absence of major waves of immigration. The second assumption is that specific mortality rates are the same for each state—and county or parish—as for the nation. These assumptions create the potential for a degree of error, but this method offers the most practical way for estimating migration at the county level.

As Lee explained, "A forward census survival ratio is a fraction in which the numerator is the number of persons in an age-sex group of a closed population at a given census and the denominator is the number ten years younger at the preceding census."[2] For example, the forward census survival ratio for white males aged ten to fourteen in 1950 and twenty to twenty-four in 1960 in the United States was:

White males aged 20–24, 1960 = 4,949,357
White males aged 10–14, 1950 = 4,545,822

Using these data the ratio is:

$$\frac{4,545,822}{4,949,357} = 0.938672$$

In other words, 93.9 percent of males age ten to fourteen in 1950 survived as twenty- to twenty-four-year-olds in 1960.

When multiplied by the enumerated white males aged ten to fourteen in each county in 1950, this ratio produces an estimate of the number of persons who presumably would have lived to be enumerated in 1960. The difference between this expected population and the 1960 population actually enumerated in each county is defined as net migration.[3] This calculation is represented by following equation:

net migration = p' - rp

where p' is the county's white male population aged twenty to twenty-four in 1960, p is the county's white male population aged ten to fourteen in 1950, and r is the forward census survival ratio.

For example, Ashley County, Arkansas, recorded 386 white males aged twenty to twenty-four in 1960 and 829 white males aged ten to fourteen in 1950. The net migration estimate for this group of white males is:

386 - 0.938672 (829) = -392.

Between 1950 and 1960, then, Ashley County lost 392 white males who would have been twenty to twenty-four years old in 1960.

This procedure was followed for each five-year age bracket ten years old and older for males and females, black and white, in the seventy-nine selected counties. These estimates were then totaled to produce an estimated migration for the 1950–60 decade for each county or parish. The same process was repeated for the 1960–70 decade.

The Arkansas and Mississippi counties and Louisiana parishes for which migration estimates were made are listed in table A.1 (see also fig. 9.3). These counties were selected for the migration study because they reported the use of mechanical cotton pickers in the 1969 Census of Agriculture. In other words, they were the leading cotton producing counties of the Mississippi River Delta.

In addition, this table shows the estimated population changes between 1950 and 1960 and between 1960 and 1970 based on the census survival method. Note that migration estimates may be either positive or negative numbers, indicating in-migration and out-migration respectively. The estimated net population loss from these counties between 1950 and 1970 was 1,221,332 people.

TABLE A.1. Estimated Migration by County and Race, Arkansas, Louisiana, and Mississippi, 1950–1970

County	1950–1960			1960–1970		
	White	Black	Total	White	Black	Total
Arkansas						
Ashley	-2,799	-2,655	-5,454	-167	-2,335	-2,502
Chicot	-3,126	-2,918	-6,044	-669	-1,962	-2,631
Clay	-7,830	-3	-7,833	-3,404	-4	-3,408
Craighead	-10,036	-167	-10,203	-391	-108	-499
Crittenden	-523	-9,388	-9,911	1,363	-8,822	-7,459
Cross	-5,130	-3,130	-8,260	-991	-1,300	-2,291
Desha	-4,042	-3,822	-7,864	-1,314	-4,877	-6,191
Drew	-2,554	-1,714	-4,268	-112	-1,104	-1,216
Greene	-7,051	-38	-7,089	-2,267	0	-2,267
Jackson	-5,556	-856	-6,412	-3,424	-728	-4,152
Jefferson	133	-8,643	-8,510	-1,624	-7,681	-9,305
Lafayette	-1,564	-1,782	-3,346	-563	-1,155	-1,718
Lawrence	-6,188	-101	-6,289	-1,818	2	-1,816
Lee	-3,022	-4,097	-7,119	684	-3,254	-2,570
Lincoln	-1,503	-3,077	-4,580	-598	-2,127	-2,725
Lonoke	-4,309	-2,100	-6,409	664	-1,689	-1,025
Mississippi	-20,436	-6,025	-26,461	-9,766	-6,665	-16,431
Monroe	-2,388	-2,694	-5,082	-920	-2,316	-3,236
Phillips	-3,412	-7,064	-10,476	-2,529	-6,583	-9,112
Poinsett	-13,387	-762	-14,149	-6,023	-1,169	-7,192
Pulaski	11,662	-4,535	7,127	10,202	-2,222	7,980
Randolph	-4,931	-20	-4,951	-663	-37	-700
St. Francis	-3,951	-6,303	-10,254	-437	-6,410	-6,847
Woodruff	-4,445	-2,403	-6,848	-1,259	-1,899	-3,158
Totals	-106,388	-74,297	-180,685	-26,026	-64,445	-90,471

TABLE A.1. (continued)

County	1950–1960			1960–1970		
	White	Black	Total	White	Black	Total
Louisiana						
Avoyelles	-5,197	-1,752	-6,949	-2,534	-1,945	-4,479
Bossier	6,017	-2,381	3,636	-1,985	-3,374	-5,359
Caddo	7,477	-2,056	5,421	-11,478	-9,736	-21,214
Caldwell	-1,617	-862	-2,479	154	-531	-377
Catahoula	-1,583	-903	-2,486	-101	-978	-1,079
Concordia	2,499	-966	1,533	436	-1,899	-1,463
East Carroll	-1,897	-2,662	-4,559	-1,042	-2,412	-3,454
Franklin	-5,457	-2,742	-8,199	-1,425	-3,453	-4,878
Madison	-1,101	-2,891	-3,992	-585	-2,738	-3,323
Morehouse	-1,857	-3,278	-5,135	-1,365	-4,229	-5,594
Natchitoches	-3,304	-4,229	-7,533	319	-3,851	-3,532
Ouachita	5,994	560	6,554	3,773	-6,137	-2,364
Rapides	2,635	-2,371	264	-3,653	-5,534	-9,187
Red River	-1,337	-2,095	-3,432	-179	-1,291	-1,470
Richland	-4,468	-2,793	-7,261	-1,419	-3,010	-4,429
St. Landry	-6,683	-7,817	-14,500	-5,973	-7,796	-13,769
Tensas	-1,209	-2,282	-3,491	-536	-2,356	-2,892
West Carroll	-4,681	-631	-5,312	-1,356	-1,020	-2,376
Totals	-15,769	-42,151	-57,920	-28,949	-62,290	-91,239
Mississippi						
Attala	-4,250	-3,760	-8,010	-532	-2,766	-3,298
Benton	-1,198	-1,197	-2,395	-88	-1,116	-1,204
Bolivar	-5,004	-14,176	-19,180	-725	-11,783	-12,508
Calhoun	-3,583	-1,137	-4,720	-1,223	-1,233	-2,456
Carroll	-2,256	-3,518	-5,774	-185	-2,334	-2,519
Chickasaw	-1,373	-2,970	-4,343	-437	-1,420	-1,857
Coahoma	-1,571	-10,536	-12,107	-1,878	-9,526	-11,404
De Soto	-249	-5,206	-5,455	9,423	-4,338	5,085
Grenada	-1,050	-2,510	-3,560	730	-1,750	-1,020

TABLE A.1. (continued)

County	1950–1960			1960–1970		
	White	**Black**	**Total**	**White**	**Black**	**Total**
Hinds	13,291	-5,831	7,460	2,955	-6,275	-3,320
Holmes	-1,814	-8,402	-10,216	-427	-5,734	-6,161
Humphreys	-2,112	-5,909	-8,021	-1,118	-5,363	-6,481
Issaquena	-602	-1,288	-1,890	-251	-937	-1,188
Lafayette	-2,108	-2,360	-4,468	1,805	-1,626	179
Lee	-1,330	-2,257	-3,587	1,846	-2,093	-247
Leflore	-2,324	-11,557	-13,881	-755	-9,808	-10,563
Lowndes	4,122	-4,244	-122	109	-4,262	-4,153
Madison	-863	-6,421	-7,284	830	-7,866	-7,036
Marshall	-1,010	-4,597	-5,607	841	-4,918	-4,077
Monroe	-3,806	-3,877	-7,683	-777	-3,127	-3,904
Montgomery	-1,509	-1,592	-3,101	-482	-1,041	-1,523
Panola	-2,724	-4,736	-7,460	-467	-4,666	-5,133
Pontotoc	-3,524	-1,096	-4,620	-575	-636	-1,211
Prentiss	-3,534	-562	-4,096	446	-274	172
Quitman	-3,749	-5,496	-9,245	-1,740	-5,635	-7,375
Rankin	2,822	-2,487	335	5,448	-1,841	3,607
Sharkey	-947	-3,385	-4,332	-423	-2,730	-3,153
Sunflower	-5,177	-14,098	-19,275	-2,017	-11,752	-13,769
Tallahatchie	-3,547	-7,447	-10,994	-1,313	-5,917	-7,230
Tate	-729	-2,629	-3,358	1,105	-3,296	-2,191
Tippah	-3,117	-1,147	-4,264	-111	-495	-606
Tunica	-1,022	-7,167	-8,189	-607	-6,010	-6,617
Union	-2,843	-886	-3,729	-600	-720	-1,320
Washington	3,853	-12,532	-8,679	-7,948	-11,001	-18,949
Webster	-1,670	-642	-2,312	-420	-723	-1,143
Yalobusha	-1,892	-2,137	-4,029	20	-1,361	-1,341
Yazoo	-2,598	-6,785	-9,383	-1,230	-5,984	-7,214
Totals	-50,997	-176,577	-227,574	-771	-152,357	-153,128
Grand Totals	-295,311	-409,473	-704,784	-110,721	-405,827	-516,548

Notes

Chapter 1: Mules and Tenants

1. Whitney's cotton gin was a wooden cylinder with wire teeth that passed through slots in a bar. As raw cotton pressed against the bar, the gin's teeth tore away at the lint, stripping it from the seeds, and revolving brushes removed the lint from the teeth. Jeannette Mirsky and Allan Nevins, *The World of Eli Whitney* (New York: Macmillan, 1952), 64–69.

2. National Bureau of Economic Growth, *Trends in the American Economy in the Nineteenth Century* (Princeton: Princeton University Press, 1960), 97–104.

3. Jay R. Mandle, *The Roots of Black Poverty: The Southern Plantation Economy after the Civil War* (Durham: Duke University Press, 1978). See also U.S. Bureau of the Census, *Plantation Farming in the United States* (Washington, D.C.: GPO, 1916).

4. Eugene D. Genovese, *Roll, Jordan, Roll: The World the Slaves Made* (New York: Pantheon, 1974), argued that the expansion of slavery created a distinctive, noncapitalistic southern society.

5. Gilbert C. Fite, *Cotton Fields No More: Southern Agriculture, 1865–1980* (Lexington: University Press of Kentucky, 1984).

6. Donald Crichton Alexander, *The Arkansas Plantation, 1920–1942* (New Haven: Yale University Press, 1943), 55–57. See also E. L. Langsford and B. H. Thibodeaux, *Plantation Organization and Operation in the Yazoo-Mississippi Delta Area,* Technical Bulletin No. 682 (Washington, D.C.: U.S. Department of Agriculture, May 1939), 4–7.

7. Harold D. Woodman, *New South, New Law: The Legal Foundations of Credit and Labor Relations in the Postbellum Agricultural South* (Baton Rouge: Louisiana State University Press, 1995).

8. Warren C. Whatley, "Southern Agrarian Labor Contracts as Impediments to Cotton Mechanization," *Journal of Economic History* 47 (March 1987): 51–52; Vaiden, M. G., J. O. Smith, and W. E. Ayres, *Making Cotton Cheaper: Can Present Production Costs Be Reduced?* Bulletin No. 290 (Starkville: Mississippi Agricultural Experiment Station, February 1931), 3–4.

9. E. L. Langsford and B. H. Thibodeaux, *Plantation Organization and Operation in the Yazoo-Mississippi Delta Area,* Technical Bulletin No. 682 (Washington, D.C.: U.S. Department of Agriculture, May 1939), 58. See table 7.1 in this volume. A simple calculation revealed that fifteen acres of cotton required 2,254.5 hours of labor. If we assumed that a year's worth of labor (ten-hour days for

fifty weeks) consisted of 3,000 hours, a cotton farmer needed only 75 percent of the available hours to bring in his cotton. He was idle the remaining 25 percent of the time. This finding indicated the existence of substantial labor inefficiency, which prevented landowners from obtaining the full use of available labor and reduced the income of workers not employed full time.

10. Fite, *Cotton Fields No More*, 22. See also Gilbert C. Fite, "Southern Agriculture since the Civil War: An Overview," *Agricultural History* 53 (January 1979): 3–21.

11. Lee J. Alston, "Tenure Choice in Southern Agriculture, 1930–1960," *Explorations in Economic History* 18 (July 1981): 211–32; Lee J. Alston and Robert Higgs, "Contractual Mix in Southern Agriculture since the Civil War: Facts, Hypotheses, and Tests," *Journal of Economic History* 42 (July 1982): 327–53.

12. "Cotton," *Fortune* 7 (June 1933): 27. Emphasis added.

13. William C. Holley and Lloyd E. Arnold, *Changes in Technology and Labor Requirements in Crop Production: Cotton*, National Research Project Report No. A-7 (Philadelphia, Pa.: Works Progress Administration, September 1937), 19–54. See also Alexander, *The Arkansas Plantation*, 102–4; Ronald E. Seavoy, *The American Peasantry: Southern Agricultural Labor and Its Legacy: A Study in Political Economy, 1850–1995* (Westport, Conn.: Greenwood Press, 1998), 37–47.

14. Alexander, *The Arkansas Plantation*, 103–12; Holley and Arnold, *Changes in Technology and Labor Requirements in Crop Production: Cotton*, 19–21.

15. In the 1930s crop dusting by airplanes became popular. See Benjamin F. Red, "Dixie's Dawn Patrol," *Arkansas Gazette Sunday Magazine*, October 20, 1935.

16. Rupert B. Vance, *Human Factors in Cotton Culture* (Chapel Hill: University of North Carolina Press, 1929), 108.

17. While the average picker, including children, picked 45.5 pounds per day in the Mississippi River Delta, 150 pounds was considered a day's work for adults. Holley and Arnold, *Changes in Technology and Labor Requirements in Crop Production: Cotton*, 50–51.

18. Roman L. Horne and Eugene G. McKibben, *Changes in Farm Power and Equipment: Mechanical Cotton Picker*, National Research Project Report No. A-2 (Philadelphia, Pa.: Works Progress Administration, 1937), 5.

19. These figures are based on 1930s prices.

20. Gavin Wright, *Old South, New South: Revolutions in the Southern Economy since the Civil War* (New York: Basic Books, 1986), 34.

21. U.S. Department of Agriculture, Economic Research Service, *Statistics on Cotton and Related Data, 1920–1973*, Statistical Bulletin No. 535 (Washington, D.C.: USDA, 1974), 1–3. See Wright, *Old South, New South*, 118.

22. Robert Higgs, "The Boll Weevil, the Cotton Economy, and Black Migration, 1910–1930," *Agricultural History* 50 (April 1975): 335–50.

23. See Graeme Quick and Wesley Buchele, *The Grain Harvesters* (St. Joseph,

Michigan: American Society of Agricultural Engineers, 1978); Stewart Hall Holbrook, *Machines of Plenty: Pioneering in American Agriculture* (New York: Macmillan Co., 1955).

24. Wayne D. Rasmussen, "The Mechanization of Agriculture," *Scientific American* 247 (September 1982): 77–89.

25. Allen G. Bogue, *From Prairie to Corn Belt: Farming on the Illinois and Iowa Prairies in the Nineteenth Century* (Ames: Iowa State University Press, 1994), 165.

26. Jeremy Atacks and Fred Bateman, *To Their Own Soil: Agriculture in the Antebellum North* (Ames: Iowa State University Press, 1987); and Bogue, *From Prairie to Corn Belt,* 148–68.

27. Holley and Arnold, *Changes in Technology and Labor Requirements in Crop Production: Cotton,* 98–106. See also Langsford and Thibodeaux, *Plantation Organization and Operation in the Yazoo-Mississippi Delta Area,* 58.

28. Holley and Arnold, *Changes in Technology and Labor Requirements in Crop Production: Cotton,* 2–10.

29. Moses Senkumba Musoke and Alan L. Olmstead, "The Rise of the Cotton Industry in California: A Comparative Perspective," *Journal of Economic History* 42 (June 1982): 385–412.

30. The lateness of cotton's progress toward mechanization is mentioned in Horne and McKibben, *Changes in Farm Power and Equipment,* 1; Holley and Arnold, *Changes in Technology and Labor Requirements in Crop Production: Cotton,* xv. See Warren C. Whatley, "A History of Mechanization in the Cotton South: The Institutional Hypothesis," *Quarterly Journal of Economics* 100 (November 1985): 1191–1215; and Whatley, "Southern Agrarian Labor Contracts as Impediments to Cotton Mechanization," *Journal of Economic History* 47 (March 1987): 45–70.

Chapter 2: "Too Much Land, Too Many Mules, and Too Much Ignorant Labor"

1. See Gilbert C. Fite, "Southern Agriculture since the Civil War: An Overview," *Agricultural History* 53 (January, 1979): 3–21. See also Heywood Fleisig, "Mechanizing the Cotton Harvest in the Nineteenth-Century South," *Journal of Economic History* 25 (December 1965): 704–6.

2. See Harold D. Woodman, "Sequel to Slavery: The New History Views the Postbellum South," *Journal of Southern History* 43 (November 1977): 523–54. See also Peter Temin, "The Postbellum Recovery of the South and the Cost of the Civil War," *Journal of Economic History* 36 (December 1976): 898–907.

3. Robert Higgs, *Competition and Coercion: Blacks in the American Economy, 1865–1914* (Cambridge: Cambridge University Press, 1977); and Higgs, *The Transformation of the American Economy, 1865–1914: An Essay in Interpretation* (New York: Wiley, 1971).

4. Jonathan M. Wiener, *Social Origins of the New South: Alabama, 1860–1885* (Baton Rouge: Louisiana State University Press, 1978); and Jay R. Mandle, *The Roots of Black Poverty: The Southern Plantation Economy after the Civil War* (Durham: Duke University Press, 1978).

5. Ronald E. Seavoy, *The American Peasantry: Southern Agricultural Labor and Its Legacy: A Study in Political Economy, 1850–1995* (Westport, Conn.: Greenwood Press, 1998), 4, 6.

6. See James C. Cobb, *Industrialization and Southern Society, 1877–1984* (Lexington: University Press of Kentucky, 1984); and Cobb and Michael V. Namorato, eds., *The New Deal and the South* (Jackson: University Press of Mississippi, 1984).

7. In 1870 the Census Bureau counted each sharecropper or tenant as operating a separate farm, inflating the number of southern farms and understating the average size of operational units. C. Vann Woodward, *Origins of the New South, 1877–1913* (Baton Rouge: Louisiana State University Press, 1951), 178–79. In explaining the lack of mechanization, however, the operational farm unit in the South remained the tenant farm, not the plantation.

8. David C. Roller and Robert W. Twyman, eds., *The Encyclopedia of Southern History* (Baton Rouge: Louisiana State University Press, 1979), 301. Louisiana cotton production did not exceed its 1860 level until 1900.

9. Seavoy, *American Peasantry*, 202.

10. Carl H. Moneyhon, *The Impact of the Civil War and Reconstruction on Arkansas: Persistence in the Midst of Ruin* (Baton Rouge: Louisiana State University Press, 1994), 264–69.

11. Roger L. Ransom and Richard Sutch, *One Kind of Freedom: The Economic Consequences of Emancipation* (Cambridge: Cambridge University Press, 1977), chap. 3.

12. Most white southerners were skeptical of the freedmen. See Carl Schurz, *Report on the Condition of the South* (New York: Arno Press, 1969), 16–32; and J. T. Trowbridge, *The South: A Tour of Its Battlefields and Ruined Cities* (New York: Arno Press, 1969), 362–68. Some southerners, however, found that free labor was superior to slave labor. See Charles Nordhoff, *The Cotton States in the Spring and Summer of 1875* (New York: D. Appleton, 1876), 36–39.

13. Ransom and Sutch, *One Kind of Freedom*, 44–47; Seavoy, *American Peasantry*, 205–6, 215.

14. Ibid.

15. *Little Rock Arkansas Gazette,* January 15, 1867.

16. Frederick A. Bode and Donald E. Ginter, *Farm Tenancy and the Census in Georgia* (Athens: University of Georgia Press, 1987), 185. See also Seavoy, *American Peasantry,* 152.

17. See, for example, Naresh Sharma and Jean Dreze, "Sharecropping in a North

Indian Village," *Journal of Development Studies* 33 (October 1996): 1–39. For tenancy in the Midwest, see Donald L. Winters, *Farmers without Farms: Agricultural Tenancy in Nineteenth-Century Iowa* (Westport, Conn.: Greenwood Press, 1978).

18. For the debate over the origins of sharecropping, see Jonathan M. Wiener, "Class Structure and Economic Development in the American South," *American Historical Review* 84 (October 1979): 970–1006; Harold D. Woodman, "Sequel to Slavery: The New History Views the Postbellum South," *Journal of Southern History* 43 (November 1977): 523–54; Ronald L. F. Davis, *Good and Faithful Labor: From Slavery to Sharecropping in the Natchez District, 1860–1890* (Westport, Conn.: Greenwood Press, 1982); Joseph D. Reed Jr., "Sharecropping as an Understandable Market Response: The Postbellum South," *Journal of Economic History* 33 (March 1973): 106–30; Ralph Shlomowitz, "The Origins of Southern Sharecropping," *Agricultural History* 53 (July 1979): 557–75; Jonathan M. Wiener, *Social Origins of the New South: Alabama, 1860–1885* (Baton Rouge: Louisiana State University Press, 1978); and Michael Wayne, *The Reshaping of Plantation Society: The Natchez District, 1860–1880* (Baton Rouge: Louisiana State University Press, 1983).

19. Ransom and Sutch, *One Kind of Freedom,* 56–57, 61.

20. Davis, *Good and Faithful Labor,* 6–12.

21. Edward Royce, *The Origins of Southern Sharecropping* (Philadelphia: Temple University Press, 1993), 220–22.

22. Seavoy, *American Peasantry,* 184, 468.

23. See, for example, Warren C. Whatley, "Labor for the Picking: The New Deal in the South," *Journal of Economic History* 43 (December 1983): 905–29.

24. See William Cohen, *At Freedom's Edge: Black Mobility and the Southern White Quest for Racial Control, 1861–1915* (Baton Rouge: Louisiana State University Press, 1991); Pete Daniel, *The Shadow of Slavery: Peonage in the South, 1901–1960* (Lexington: University Press of Kentucky, 1978).

25. William F. Holmes, "The Arkansas Cotton Pickers Strike of 1891 and the Demise of the Colored Farmer's Alliance," *Arkansas Historical Quarterly* 32 (summer 1973): 107–19.

26. C. Vann Woodward, *The Strange Career of Jim Crow* (New York: Oxford University Press, 1955). See also Vernon Lane Wharton, *The Negro in Mississippi, 1865–1890* (New York: Harper and Row, 1965), 216–27.

27. Walter White, *Rope and Faggot: A Biography of Judge Lynch* (New York: Arno Press, 1969), 254; *World Almanac and Book of Facts for 1927* (New York: New York World, 1927), 322. A recent study that connects racial violence and migration is Stewart E. Tolnay and E. M. Beck, "Racial Violence and Black Migration in the American South, 1910–1930," *American Sociological Review* 57 (February 1992): 103–16. See also Stewart E. Tolnay and E. M. Beck, *A Festival of Violence: An Analysis of Southern Lynching, 1882–1930* (Urbana: University of Illinois Press,

1995). W. Fitzhugh Brundage, *Lynching in the New South: Georgia and Virginia, 1880–1930* (Urbana: University of Illinois Press, 1993), 108–13, links cotton and lynching.

28. Carl H. Moneyhon, *Arkansas and the New South, 1874–1929* (Fayetteville: University of Arkansas Press, 1997), 107–8. See Richard C. Cortner, *A Mob Intent on Death: The NAACP and the Arkansas Riot Cases* (Middletown, Conn.: Wesleyan University Press, 1988).

29. Gilbert C. Fite, "Southern Agriculture since the Civil War: An Overview," *Agricultural History* 53 (January 1979): 3–21.

30. See Harold D. Woodman, *King Cotton and His Retainers: Financing and Marketing the Cotton Crop of the South, 1800–1925* (Lexington: University of Kentucky Press, 1968).

31. Gavin Wright, *Old South, New South: Revolutions in the Southern Economy since the Civil War* (New York: Basic Books, 1986), 12.

32. Wright, *Old South, New South,* 117–18.

33. Warren C. Whatley, "Labor for the Picking: The New Deal in the South," *Journal of Economic History* 43 (December 1983): 905–29.

34. U.S. Department of Agriculture, Bureau of Agricultural Economics, *Farm Tenancy in Arkansas* (Washington, August 1941), 7. See Donald Crichton Alexander, *The Arkansas Plantation, 1920–1942* (New Haven: Yale University Press, 1943), 62–63; and William H. Metzler, *Population Trends and Adjustments in Arkansas,* Bulletin No. 388 (Fayetteville: Arkansas Agricultural Experiment Station, May 1940).

35. Gilbert C. Fite, *Cotton Fields No More: Southern Agriculture, 1865–1980* (Lexington: University Press of Kentucky, 1984), 22.

36. U.S. Department of Agriculture, *Suggestions to Southern Farmers,* Farmers' Bulletin No. 98 (Washington, D.C.: GPO, 1904), 25. Emphasis added.

37. M. G. Vaiden, J. O. Smith, and W. E. Ayres co-authored two bulletins: *Making Cotton Cheaper: Can Present Production Costs Be Reduced?* Bulletin No. 290 (Starkville: Mississippi Agricultural Experiment Station, February 1931); and *Making Cotton Cheaper: Can Present Production Costs Be Reduced?* Bulletin No. 298 (Starkville: Mississippi Agricultural Experiment Station, June 1932).

38. See Lawrence Goodwyn, *Democratic Promise: The Populist Moment in America* (New York: Oxford University Press, 1976).

39. Gilbert C. Fite, "Southern Agriculture since the Civil War: An Overview," *Agricultural History* 53 (January, 1979): 9–10.

40. See H. Thomas Johnson, *Agricultural Depression in the 1920s: Economic Fact or Statistical Artifact?* (New York: Garland, 1985).

41. Wright, *Old South, New South,* 12.

42. The concept of the demographic transition originated in Warren S. Thompson, "Population," *American Journal of Sociology* 34 (May 1929): 959–75. For criticisms,

see Donald O. Cowgill, "Transition Theory as General Population Theory," *Social Forces* 41 (March 1963): 270–74; David M. Heer, *Society and Population,* 2d ed. (Englewood Cliffs, N.J.: Prentice-Hall, 1975), 13–16; and Dennis H. Wrong, *Population and Society,* 4th ed. (New York: Random House, 1977), 21–26.

43. Stewart E. Tolnay, "Structural Change and Fertility Change in the South, 1910 to 1940," *Social Science Quarterly* 77 (September 1996): 559–76; and Tolnay and Patricia J. Glynn, "The Persistence of High Fertility in the American South on the Eve of the Baby Boom," *Demography* 31 (November 1994): 615–31. See U.S. Bureau of the Census, *Sixteenth Census of the United States: 1940. Population Differential Fertility 1940 and 1910. Standardized Fertility Rates and Reproduction Rates* (Washington, D.C.: GPO, 1944).

Chapter 3: Inventions and Inventors

1. The seminal work on cotton mechanization is James H. Street, *The New Revolution in the Cotton Economy: Mechanization and Its Consequences* (Chapel Hill: University of North Carolina Press, 1957). For contemporary views, see J. L. Watkins, *King Cotton: A Historical and Statistical Review, 1790–1908* (New York: J. L. Watkins and Sons, 1908), 149, 175, 259; H. P. Smith et al., *The Mechanical Harvesting of Cotton,* Bulletin No. 452 (College Station: Texas Agricultural Experiment Station, August 1932); Roman L. Horne, "Cotton Picker," in National Resources Committee, *Technological Trends and National Policy, Including the Social Implications of New Inventions* (Washington, D.C.: GPO, 1937), 142–43; Stewart Hall Holbrook, *Machines of Plenty: Pioneering in American Agriculture* (New York: Macmillan, 1955).

2. See John Jewkes, David Sawers, and Richard Stillerman, *The Sources of Invention* (New York: St. Martin's Press, 1959).

3. Calculated from Jacob Schmookler, *Patents, Inventions, and Economic Change: Data and Selected Essays* (Cambridge, Mass.: Harvard University Press, 1972), 100–103.

4. Arthur W. Page, "A Cotton-Harvester at Last," *World's Work* 21 (December 1910): 13750.

5. *Jackson (Miss.) Clarion-Ledger,* reprinted in Monticello, Arkansas, *Monticellonian,* November 16, 1894.

6. Wayne D. Rasmussen, "The Mechanization of Agriculture," *Scientific American* 247 (September 1982): 77–89; C. R. Hagen, "Twenty-Five Years of Cotton Picker Development," *Agricultural Engineering* 32 (November 1951): 593–96, 599; R. Douglas Hurt, "Cotton Pickers and Strippers," *Journal of the West* 30 (April 1991): 30–42.

7. Ralph C. Hon, "The Rust Cotton Picker," *Southern Economic Journal* 3 (April 1937): 381–91.

8. Eugene Butler, "And Then He Said," *Progressive Farmer* 45 (February 8, 1930): 4.

9. "W. E. Ayres 1922–1937," in Donald H. Bowman, *A History of the Delta Branch Experiment Station, 1904–1985,* Special Bulletin 86-2 (Starkville: Mississippi Agricultural and Forestry Experiment Station, August 1986), 11–24.

10. M. G. Vaiden, J. O. Smith, and W. E. Ayres, *Making Cotton Cheaper: Can Present Production Costs Be Reduced?* Bulletin No. 290 (Starkville: Mississippi Agricultural Experiment Stations, February 1931), 22–25.

11. James H. Street, *The New Revolution in the Cotton Economy* (Chapel Hill: University of North Carolina Press, 1957), 107–8; Hurt, "Cotton Pickers and Strippers," 30–31.

12. Smith, *Mechanical Harvesting of Cotton,* 5–6.

13. Donald Holley, "'The Prince of the Powers of the Air': Charles McDermott and His Flying Machine," *Drew County Historical Journal* 9 (1994): 46–53. See *Little Rock Arkansas Gazette,* May 3, 1873, July 7, 1874. Adding to his reputation as an eccentric, McDermott went on to secure a patent on a flying machine thirty years before the Wright brothers. Obviously it too failed to meet the test of performance.

14. Street, *New Revolution,* 109, 110, 112.

15. "An Improved Cotton Picker," *Scientific American* 67 (November 5, 1892): 291. See also William Dale, "A Machine for Picking Cotton," *Scientific American* 94 (May 5, 1906): 371–72; "New Mechanical Cotton Picker," *Literary Digest* 103 (November 16, 1929): 32. The Thurman machine is described in "Cotton Picking by Suction," *Literary Digest* 78 (August 4, 1923): 29.

16. F. D. McHugh, "Machines Pick Cotton, But—," *Scientific American* 159 (November 1938): 243.

17. The Thurman Vacuum Cotton Harvester (St. Louis: Vacuum Cotton Harvester Company, 1922), with item 19406, Deere Archives, Deere and Company, Moline, Ill.

18. "The Eyes of the Cotton World Are on the Success," n.d., ibid.

19. "The Successful Cotton Picker," *Scientific American* 126 (March 1922): 179; M. Tevis, "The Electrical Cotton-Picker," *St. Nicholas* 49 (April 1922): 655–57. See *Arkansas Gazette,* October 16, 1921.

20. "Cotton Mown Like Hay and Chemically Digested," *Science* 83, n.s. (May 22, 1936), 10; Alfred R. Macormac, "Utilization of the Whole Cotton Plant," *Scientific Monthly* 43 (September 1936): 285–86; "Scientia Omnia Vincit: Experiments in Turning the Whole Cotton Plant into Rayon," *Scientific American* 163 (November 1940): 243.

21. L. P. Gabbard and F. R. Jones, *Large-Scale Cotton Production in Texas,* Bulletin 362 (College Station: Texas Agricultural Experiment Station, 1927), 21.

22. Ibid.; *Dallas Morning News,* February 6, 1927.

23. Smith, *Mechanical Harvesting of Cotton,* 14–15.

24. Ibid., 13–24.

25. Smith, *Mechanical Harvesting of Cotton,* 15–17; H. P. Smith, "Cotton Harvesting Development to Date," *Agricultural Engineering* 12 (March 1931): 73–78.

26. Arthur W. Page, "A Cotton-Harvester at Last," *World's Work* 21 (December 1910): 13750.

27. "A Mechanical Cotton Picker," *Scientific American* 64 (January 17, 1891): 39.

28. Page, "A Cotton-Harvester at Last," 13748–13760.

29. John Jewkes, David Sawers, and Richard Stillerman, *The Sources of Invention* (New York: St. Martin's Press, 1959), 282–86.

30. R. Douglas Hurt, "P. P. Haring: Innovator in Cotton Harvesting Technology," *Agricultural History* 53 (summer 1979): 300–307.

31. Ibid., 302–3.

32. H. P. Smith, "Cotton Harvesting Development to Date," *Agricultural Engineering* 12 (March 1931): 76–77; W. Waterman, "Some Needs in Cotton Harvesting Development," *Agricultural Engineering* 19 (September 1938): 393–94; M. G. Vaiden, J. O. Smith, W. E. Ayres, *Making Cotton Cheaper: Can Present Production Costs Be Reduced?* (Starkville: Mississippi Agricultural Experiment Station, February 1931), 25–28.

33. Smith, *Mechanical Harvesting of Cotton,* 8.

34. C. H. Wendel, *150 Years of International Harvester* (Sarasota, Fla.: Crestline, 1981), 29. See also Barbara Marsh, *A Corporate Tragedy: The Agony of International Harvester Company* (Garden City, N.Y.: Doubleday, 1985).

35. Wendell, *150 Years of International Harvester,* 258–59, 310; Bureau of Agricultural Economics, U.S. Department of Agriculture, *Technology on the Farm* (Washington, D.C.: GPO, 1940), 9–13.

36. Hagen, "Twenty-Five Years of Cotton Picker Development," 593–96, 599.

37. "Pneumatic Cotton Picker," McCormick International Harvester Collection, 1881–1985, IHC Undocumented Series, box 142, State Historical Society of Wisconsin, Madison.

38. Hagen, "Twenty-Five Years of Cotton Picker Development," 594; E. A. Johnston, "The Evolution of the Mechanical Cotton Harvester," *Agricultural Engineering* 19 (September 1938): 383–85, 388. However, the earliest Harvester experimental pickers used serrated spindles. Over years of testing, Hagen tried spindles of every conceivable type, shape, and size.

39. Hagen "Twenty-Five Years of Cotton Picker Development," 593.

40. Ibid., 594.

41. E. A. Johnston, "The Evolution of the Mechanical Cotton Harvester," *Agricultural Engineering* 19 (September 1938): 384.

42. Ibid., 385.

43. Hagen, "Twenty-Five Years of Cotton Picker Development," 595.

44. "Deere & Co.," *Fortune* 14 (August 1936): 72–77, 152, 155, 159–60, 162, 164. See also Wayne G. Broehl, *John Deere's Company: A History of Deere and Company and Its Times* (New York: Doubleday, 1984).

45. R. Douglas Hurt, "Cotton Pickers and Strippers," *Journal of the West* 30 (April 1991): 30–42.

46. "Development of a Mechanical Spindle Type Cotton Picker," March 9, 1935, Deere Archives; Hurt, "Cotton Pickers and Strippers," 30–42.

47. "John Daniel Rust," *National Cyclopaedia of American Biography* (New York: James T. White and Co., 1958), 42:612–14. See also the forthcoming publication: "John Daniel Rust," *Arkansas Biography: A Collection of Notable Lives* (Fayetteville: University of Arkansas Press, 2000).

48. "Mack Donald Rust," *Who Was Who in America, 1961–1968* (Chicago: Marquis-Who's Who, 1968), 4:821.

49. Pine Bluff, Arkansas, High School *Pine Cone,* May 13, 1938.

50. John Rust, "The Origin and Development of the Cotton Picker," *West Tennessee Historical Society Papers* 7 (1953): 45–46. Rust told this story many times to reporters and others who would listen.

51. David Halberstam, *The Fifties* (New York: Villard Books, 1993), 447. See "Mr. Little Ol' Rust," *Fortune* 46 (December 1952): 150–52, 198–205. This article was reprinted as "John Rust Brings Home the Cotton," *Readers' Digest* 62 (April 1953): 73–77.

52. Rust, "The Origin and Development of the Cotton Picker," 46.

53. *Weatherford (Tex.) Democrat,* July 20, 1928; *Weatherford Daily Herald,* July 19, 1928.

54. Charles P. Steinmetz, *America and the New Epoch* (New York: Harper and Brothers, 1916); Robert Kenneth Straus, "Enter the Cotton Picker: The Story of the Rust Brothers' Invention," *Harpers* 173 (September 1936): 387.

55. *New Orleans (La.) Item-Tribune,* June 15, 1930.

56. W. E. Ayres to C. Williamson, March 4, 1935, Haring Papers. Ayres repeated this catchy observation many times because it appears in many contemporary articles. He also used several versions of it himself. See W. E. Ayres, "Machines to Replace Men as Dixie Farmers Cut Costs by Mechanization," *Memphis Commercial Appeal,* November 13, 1936.

57. Ibid., April 18, 1934.

58. *Arkansas Gazette,* May 5, 1935.

59. Kathryn Coe Cordell, "Mechanical Cotton Picker," *Arkansas Gazette Sunday Magazine,* June 30, 1935.

Chapter 4: The Agricultural Adjustment Administration and Structural Change in the Cotton South

1. U.S. Bureau of the Census, *Historical Statistics of the United States: Colonial Times to 1970* (Washington, D.C.: GPO, 1975), 517–18; U.S. Department of Agriculture, Economic Research Service, *Statistics on Cotton and Related Data, 1920–1973,* Statistical Bulletin No. 535 (Washington, D.C.: USDA, 1974), 145. In June 1932, cotton hit 4.6 cents on the New Orleans Cotton Exchange. George B. Tindall, *Emergence of the New South, 1913–1945* (Baton Rouge: Louisiana State University Press, 1967), 354.

2. "One-Fourth of a State Sold for Taxes," *Literary Digest* 112 (May 7, 1932): 10.

3. See Donald Holley, *Uncle Sam's Farmers: The New Deal Communities in the Lower Mississippi Valley* (Urbana: University of Illinois Press, 1975), 10–14.

4. Gavin Wright, *Old South, New South: Revolutions in the Southern Economy since the Civil War* (New York: Basic Books, 1986), 115–23.

5. Bennett S. White Jr., "The Shrinking Foreign Market for United States Cotton," *Quarterly Journal of Economics* 54 (February 1940): 255–76. See also Arthur Raper, *Machines in the Cotton Fields* (Atlanta, Ga.: Southern Regional Council, 1946).

6. Robert E. Snyder, *Cotton Crisis* (Chapel Hill: University of North Carolina Press, 1984); Gilbert C. Fite, "Voluntary Attempts to Reduce Cotton Acreage in the South, 1914–1933," *Journal of Southern History* 14 (November 1948): 481–99. See also Robert E. Snyder, "Huey Long and the Cotton-Holiday of 1931," *Louisiana History* 18 (spring 1977): 133–60; and Snyder, "The Cotton Holiday Movement in Mississippi, 1931," *Journal of Mississippi History* 40 (February 1978): 1–32.

7. *Historical Statistics of the United States,* series K 555, p. 517.

8. Snyder, "Huey Long and the Cotton-Holiday of 1931," 135–60.

9. T. Harry Williams, *Huey Long* (New York: Alfred A. Knopf, 1969), 530–33.

10. *Little Rock Arkansas Gazette,* October 5, 8, 1931.

11. Ibid., October 10, 1931.

12. Snyder, "The Cotton Holiday Movement in Mississippi, 1931," 1–32; Gilbert C. Fite, "Voluntary Attempts to Reduce Cotton Acreage in the South, 1914–1933," *Journal of Southern History* 14 (November 1948): 481–99. See Tindall, *Emergence of the New South,* 357.

13. Calculated from *Statistics on Cotton and Related Data, 1920–1973,* 66.

14. Nan Elizabeth Woodruff, *As Rare As Rain: Federal Relief in the Great Southern Drought of 1930–31* (Urbana: University of Illinois Press, 1985).

15. Holley, *Uncle Sam's Farmers,* 32–33. See also Berta Asch and A. R. Mangus, *Farmers on Relief and Rehabilitation,* WPA Research Monograph 8 (Washington, D.C.: GPO, 1937); and Sidney Baldwin, *Poverty and Politics: The Rise and Decline*

of the Farm Security Administration (Chapel Hill: University of North Carolina Press, 1967), 58–68.

16. Van L. Perkins, *Crisis in Agriculture: The Agricultural Adjustment Administration and the New Deal, 1933* (Berkeley and Los Angeles: University of California Press, 1969), 103–9; Lucy Wilmans, "The AAA and the Arkansas Cotton Farmer" (master's thesis, School of Business, University of Arkansas, 1935); *Arkansas Gazette,* July 28, 1933.

17. Wright, *Old South, New South,* 227.

18. U.S. Senate, *Payments Made under the Agricultural Adjustment Program,* 74th Cong., 2d sess., Doc. No. 274, pp. 26, 28.

19. Ibid.

20. *Arkansas Gazette,* August 31, December 13–16, 1934.

21. *Farm Tenancy: Report of the President's Committee.* (Washington, D.C.: GPO, 1937), 96–97.

22. Calculated from *Farm Tenancy: Report of the President's Committee* (Washington, D.C.: GPO, 1937), 96–99.

23. Fred C. Frey and T. Lynn Smith, "The Influence of the AAA Cotton Program upon the Tenant, Cropper, and Laborer," *Rural Sociology* 1 (December 1936): 498–99. For a discussion of this estimate, see David Wayne Ganger, "The Impact of Mechanization and the New Deal's Acreage Reduction Programs on Cotton Farms During the 1930s" (Ph.D. diss., University of California at Los Angeles, 1973), 284–91. Other scholars have made separate estimates of the AAA's impact. Economist Warren C. Whatley calculated that the AAA reduced the number of tenants by 22 percent; Warren C. Whatley, "Labor for the Picking: The New Deal in the South," *Journal of Economic History* 43 (December 1983): 905–29; Warren C. Whatley, "A History of Mechanization in the Cotton South: The Institutional Hypothesis," *Quarterly Journal of Economics* 100 (November 1985): 1191–1215. J. A. Baker and J. G. McNeely, *Land Tenure in Arkansas. I: The Farm Tenancy Situation,* Bulletin 384 (January 1940), 21–30.

When Frey and Smith broke down the figures by race, they found that white tenants dropped 14.7 percent while black tenants fell 19.1 percent. But white croppers suffered a loss of 18.2 percent, compared to a drop of 7.6 percent for black croppers.

24. Frey and Smith, "The Influence of the AAA Cotton Program upon the Tenant, Croppers and Laborer," 483–505.

25. Henry I. Richards, *Cotton and the AAA* (Washington, D.C.: Brookings Institution, 1936), 155, 161.

26. Wright, *Old South, New South,* 229–30.

27. Ganger, "The Impact of Mechanization," 270–71.

28. Richards, *Cotton and the AAA,* 160.

29. Harold Hoffsommer, "The AAA and the Sharecropper," *Social Forces* 13 (May 1935): 495–502.

30. Gilbert C. Fite, *George N. Peek and the Fight for Farm Parity* (Norman: University of Oklahoma Press, 1945); Christiana McFadyen Campbell, *The Farm Bureau and the New Deal: A Study of the Making of National Farm Policy, 1933–40* (Urbana: University of Illinois Press, 1962).

31. See "Biggest Cotton Plantation," *Fortune* 15 (March 1937): 125–32, 156–60. Lawrence J. Nelson's other work on the New Deal include "Oscar Johnston, the New Deal, and the Cotton Subsidy Payments Controversy, 1936–1937," *Journal of Southern History* 40 (August 1974): 399–416; "Welfare Capitalism on a Mississippi Plantation in the Great Depression," *Journal of Southern History* 50 (May 1984): 225–50; and *King Cotton's Advocate: Oscar G. Johnston and the New Deal* (Knoxville: University of Tennessee Press, 1999).

32. Richards, *Cotton and the AAA*, 138–39.

33. The STFU story is told in Donald H. Grubbs, *Cry from the Cotton: The Southern Tenant Farmers Union and the New Deal* (Chapel Hill: University of North Carolina Press, 1971); David Eugene Conrad, *The Forgotten Farmers: The Story of Sharecroppers in the New Deal* (Urbana: University of Illinois Press, 1965); and Howard Kester, *Revolt among the Sharecroppers* (New York: Covici-Friede, 1936). See also Paul E. Mertz, *New Deal Policy and Southern Rural Poverty* (Baton Rouge: Louisiana State University Press, 1978).

34. *Arkansas Gazette*, August 25, 1934. On tenant displacement, see Harold Hoffsommer, "The AAA and the Sharecropper," *Social Forces* 13 (May 1935): 494–502.

35. Theodore Saloutos, *The American Farmer and the New Deal* (Ames: Iowa State University Press, 1982), xv. See George S. Wehrwein, "How Many Farmers Do We Require?" *Land Policy Review* 3 (September 1940): 3–7.

36. Richards, *Cotton and the AAA*, 148.

37. Ibid., 148–49.

38. Richard H. Day, "The Economics of Technological Change and the Demise of the Sharecropper," *American Economic Review* 57 (June 1967): 427–49.

39. John Steinbeck, *The Grapes of Wrath* (New York: P. F. Collier, 1939); Erskine Caldwell, *Tobacco Road* (New York: Modern Library, 1947); James Agee and Walker Evans, *Let Us Now Praise Famous Men: Three Tenant Families* (New York: Houghton Mifflin, 1941). Dorothea Lange and Paul Schuster Taylor, *An American Exodus: A Record of Human Erosion* (New York: Reynal and Hitchcock, 1939); Charles S. Johnson, Edwin R. Embree, and Will W. Alexander, *The Collapse of Cotton Tenancy: A Summary of Field Studies and Statistical Surveys, 1933–35* (Chapel Hill: University of North Carolina Press, 1935).

40. Roy E. Stryker, *In This Proud Land: America 1935–1943 as Seen in the FSA Photographs* (Greenwich, Conn.: New York Graphic Society, 1973); F. Jack Hurley, *Portrait of a Decade; Roy Stryker and the Development of Documentary Photography in the Thirties* (Baton Rouge: Louisiana State University Press, 1972).

41. See Kirkpatrick Sale, *Rebels against the Future: The Luddites and Their War on the Industrial Revolution* (New York: Addison Wesley, 1996).

42. Archibald MacLeish, *Land of the Free* (New York: Harcourt Brace, 1938), 59; Dorothea Lange and Paul Schuster Taylor, *An American Exodus: A Record of Human Erosion* (New York: Reynal and Hitchcock, 1939), 41–42, 73. See D. G. Kehl, "Steinbeck's 'String of Pictures' in *The Grapes of Wrath*," *Image* (March 1974): 1–10.

43. John Steinbeck, *The Grapes of Wrath* (New York: Sun Dial Press, 1939), 44, 45, 47.

44. Donald Holley, "The Southern Tenant Farmers Union as a Social Movement," unpublished paper in author's possession. See Charles Tilly, *From Mobilization to Revolution* (Reading, Maine: Addison-Wesley, 1978).

45. Paul W. Bruton, "Cotton Acreage Reduction and the Tenant Farmer," *Law and Contemporary Problems* 1 (June 1934): 283–84; Harold D. Woodman, "Post-Civil War Southern Agriculture and the Law," *Agricultural History* 53 (January 1979): 319–37. See also Woodman, *New South, New Law: The Legal Foundations of Credit and Labor Relations in the Postbellum Agricultural South* (Baton Rouge: Louisiana State University Press, 1995).

46. Jeannie M. Whayne, *A New Plantation South: Land, Labor, and Federal Favor in Twentieth-Century Arkansas* (Charlottesville: University Press of Virginia, 1996), 159–67.

47. Bruton, "Cotton Acreage Reduction and the Tenant Farmer," 275–79, 280–86; Wright, *Old South, New South,* 229.

48. Bruton, "Cotton Acreage Reduction and the Tenant Farmer," 288.

49. Conrad, *Forgotten Farmers,* chap. 8; Grubbs, *Cry from the Cotton,* chap. 3.

50. Bruton, "Cotton Acreage Reduction and the Tenant Farmer," 290.

51. Wright, *Old South, New South,* 231–32.

52. Ibid., 228–29.

53. Richard H. Day, "The Economics of Technological Change and the Demise of the Sharecropper," *American Economic Review* 57 (June 1967): 427–49.

54. Ronald E. Seavoy, *The American Peasantry: Southern Agricultural Labor and Its Legacy: A Study in Political Economy, 1850–1995* (Westport, Conn.: Greenwood Press, 1998), 430.

55. Otis T. Osgood and John W. White, *Land Tenure in Arkansas: IV. Further Changes in Labor Used on Cotton Farms, 1939–44,* Bulletin No. 459 (Fayetteville: Arkansas Agricultural Experiment Station, August 1945).

56. J. A. Baker and J. G. McNeely, *Land Tenure in Arkansas. I: The Farm Tenancy Situation,* Bulletin No. 384 (Fayetteville: Arkansas Agricultural Experiment Station, January 1940), 30.

57. J. G. McNeely and Glenn T. Barton, *Land Tenure in Arkansas. II: Change in Labor Organization on Cotton Farms,* Bulletin No. 397 (Fayetteville: Arkansas Agricultural Experiment Station, June 1940), 13, 26.

58. M. G. Vaiden, J. O. Smith, and W. E. Ayres, *Making Cotton Cheaper: Can Present Production Costs Be Reduced?* Bulletin No. 298 (Starkville: Mississippi Agricultural Experiment Station, June 1932), 9, maintained that because labor was paid in advance, labor ran plantations in prosperous times and the owner ran it in bad times.

59. Alexander Yard, "'They dont regard my Rights at all': Arkansas Farm Workers, Economic Modernization, and the Southern Tenant Farmers Union," *Arkansas Historical Quarterly* 47 (autumn 1988): 201–29.

60. T. J. Woofter Jr., *Landlord and Tenant on the Cotton Plantation,* Research Monograph 5 (Washington, D.C.: Works Progress Administration, 1936), 156–57.

61. E. L. Langsford and B. H. Thibodeaux, *Plantation Organization and Operator in the Yazoo-Mississippi Delta Area,* Technical Bulletin No. 682 (Washington, D.C.: U.S. Department of Agriculture, May 1939), 3, 27, 52, 87. See Frank J. Welch, *The Plantation Land Tenure System in Mississippi,* Bulletin No. 385 (Starkville: Mississippi State Experiment Station, June 1943), 48, 53; Paul S. McComas and Frank J. Welch, *Farm Labor Requirements in Mississippi,* Agricultural Experiment Station Bulletin No. 387 (Starkville: Mississippi Agricultural Experiment Station, June 1943).

62. Wright, *Old South, New South,* 233.

Chapter 5: Impending Revolution

1. "If the Cotton Picker Proves Successful," *Christian Century* 49 (October 5, 1932): 1189.

2. *Little Rock Arkansas Gazette,* May 5, 1935.

3. "Cotton Picker," *Time* 25 (April 22, 1935): 36–37.

4. The Rust Cotton Picker Company was located at 2129 Florida Street, Memphis, Tennessee.

5. *Arkansas Gazette,* September 1, 1936; "Picker Problems," *Time* 28 (September 14, 1936): 47–49.

6. *Arkansas Gazette,* August 31, September 1, 1936; *Memphis (Tenn.) Commercial Appeal,* September 1, 2, 1936.

7. Mack Rust conducted the demonstration. John Rust had traveled to the Soviet Republic of Turkistan, which had purchased two of his machines. "Picker Problems," *Time* 28 (September 14, 1936): 47; Victor Weybright, "Two Men and Their Machine," *Survey Graphic* 25 (July 1936): 433; "Cotton-Gin Rival," *Literary Digest* 122 (September 5, 1936): 45–46.

8. *Arkansas Gazette,* September 1, 1936; *Commercial Appeal,* September 1, 2, 1936; "Picker Problems," 50.

9. Ibid.

10. *Jackson* (Miss.) *Daily News,* August 31, 1936. Emphasis added.

11. James H. Street, *The New Revolution in the Cotton Economy: Mechanization and Its Consequences* (Chapel Hill: University of North Carolina Press, 1957), 126; Paul R. Coppock, *Memphis Memoirs* (Memphis: Memphis State University Press, 1980), 107; "Picker Problems," 49.

12. Quoted in Jonathan Daniels, *A Southerner Discovers the South* (New York: Da Capo Press, 1970), 166–67. See also *Congressional Record,* 75th Cong., 1st sess., May 5, 1937.

13. Oliver Carlson, "The Revolution in Cotton," *American Mercury* 34 (February 1935): 129–36.

14. Henry Goddard Leach, "Humanizing Machines—I: The Rust Cotton Picker," *Forum* 96 (August 1936): 49–50.

15. Archibald MacLeish, "Machines and the Future," *Nation* 136 (February 8, 1932): 140–42; F. L. Allen, "What about Technocracy?" *American Mercury* 115 (March 1933): 34–35.

16. For a reference to Frankenstein in the contest of mechanical cotton pickers, see National Resources Committee, *Technological Trends and National Policy, Including the Social Implications of New Inventions* (Washington, D.C.: GPO, 1937), 139. For technocracy, see "Machines Won't Wait," *Collier's* 98 (October 17, 1936): 70.

17. B. O. Williams, "The Impact of Mechanization on the Farm Population of the South," *Rural Sociology* 4 (September 1939): 300–314; C. Horace Hamilton, "The Social Effects of Recent Trends in the Mechanization of Agriculture," *Rural Sociology* 4 (March 1939): 3–25; *Negro Year Book: An Annual Encyclopedia of the Negro, 1937–1938* (Tuskegee, Ala.: Negro Year Book Publishing Co., 1937), 41–42.

18. Dero A. Saunders, "Revolution in the Deep South," *Nation* 145 (September 11, 1937): 264–66.

19. James S. Bealle, "Dixie Needs No Cotton Picker," *Forum* 97 (April 1937): 224–29.

20. "Cotton Picking Machinery Perfected," *Scientific American* 146 (February 1932): 124.

21. "If the Cotton Picker Proves Successful," 1189. This article was a response to H. P. Smith et al., *The Mechanical Harvesting of Cotton,* Bulletin No. 452 (College Station: Texas Agricultural Experiment Station, August 1932).

22. Charles S. Johnson, Edwin R. Embree, and Will W. Alexander, *The Collapse of Cotton Tenancy: A Summary of Field Studies and Statistical Surveys, 1933–35* (Chapel Hill: University of North Carolina Press, 1935), 44.

23. Broadus Mitchell, "Southern Quackery," *Southern Economic Journal* 3 (October 1936): 146.

24. See *Reader's Guide,* vol. 10, for the appearance of the first articles concerning Rust.

25. Carlson, "The Revolution in Cotton," 129–36. Reprinted in *Readers' Digest* 26 (March 1935): 13–16. On Rust's view of the impact of the article, see Rust, "The Origin and Development of the Cotton Picker," 49. IH did not appear in *Readers' Guide* from 1935 to 1939. For Deere, see "Deere & Co.," *Fortune* 14 (August 1936): 72–77, 152, 155, 159–60, 162, 164.

26. Carlson, "The Revolution in Cotton," 129. Hand pickers were expected to pick 150 pounds a day.

27. Ibid., 132–33.

28. Ibid., 134–35.

29. See, for example, "Cotton Picker," 36–37.

30. "Program for Picker," *Time* 27 (March 23, 1936): 60.

31. Ibid.

32. *Arkansas Gazette,* March 12, 1936.

33. On Eddy, see Alva W. Taylor, "Rust Brothers Open New Path," *Christian Century* 53 (April 22, 1936): 607–8.

34. John and Mack Rust, "The Cotton Picker and Unemployment," Southern Tenant Farmers Union Papers, reel 6.

35. *Memphis (Tenn.) Press-Scimitar,* August 24, 1938; Jack Bryan, "The Rust Foundation," *Southern Workman* 67 (December 1938): 361–73. The publisher of this journal was Hampton Institute, Hampton, Virginia. See "Rust Foundation to Aid Labor," *Christian Century* 55 (October 5, 1938): 1210.

36. John Rust, "The Rust Cotton Picker," *Southern Workman* 67 (December 1938): 366.

37. The Rust Foundation was endowed only with the Rust brothers share of the income from the Rust Cotton Picker Company, which was to manufacture and market the machine. It did not affect the holdings or dividends of other stockholders. The Rust Cotton Picker Company was intended to be a profit-making concern. See *Arkansas Gazette,* March 12, 1936.

38. "New-Model Cotton Pickers," *Business Week,* October 2, 1937, 26; "These Are the New Models of the Rust Cotton Picker," *Business Week,* September 3, 1938, 24. Compare Kathryn Coe Cordell, "Mechanical Cotton Picker," *Arkansas Gazette Magazine,* June 30, 1935, 3.

39. John Clarence Petrie, "Rust Foundation to Aid Labor; Profits from Cotton Picker Will Pass to Society," *Christian Century* 55 (October 5, 1938): 1210. The *Christian Century* had expressed deep sympathy for tenants and sharecroppers. See Alva W. Taylor, "The Plight of the Southern Tenant," *Christian Century* 52 (April 3, 1935): 427–28. This article identified the Rust machine as a threat to tenant's livelihood.

40. Victor Weybright, "Two Men and Their Machine," *Survey Graphic* 25 (July 1936): 433.

41. Ibid., 432–33.

42. Henry Goddard Leach, "Humanizing Machines: The Rust Cotton Picker," *Forum* 96 (August 1936): 49–50.

43. "The Dilemmas of a Modern Man of Conscience," *Christian Century* 53 (April 1, 1936): 485.

44. John Clarence Petrie, "Rust Foundation to Aid Labor," *Christian Century* 55 (October 5, 1938): 1210.

45. *New York Times,* February 26, 27, 1997.

46. Robert Kenneth Straus, "Enter the Cotton Picker: The Story of the Rust Brothers' Invention," *Harper's* 173 (September 1936): 389–95. This article was reprinted in *Reader's Digest* 29 (October 1936): 43–47.

47. Ibid., 393.

48. "Machines Won't Wait," *Collier's* 98 (October 17, 1936): 70.

49. "Cotton Picker: Machine vs. Man Jitters Exaggerated in the South," *Newsweek* 12 (August 15, 1938): 32.

50. W. E. Ayres, "Machines to Replace Men as Dixie Farmers Cut Costs by Mechanization," *Commercial Appeal,* November 13, 1936. In 1935, Ayres wrote, "Personally, we consider the Rust cotton picker a better picking machine today than automobiles were after they had been in use for ten years." W. E. Ayres to C. Williamson, March 4, 1935, Haring Papers, National Museum of American History, Washington, D.C. Both Ayres and Mack Rust favorably compared the Rust picker with a Model T Ford. Mack Rust said, "We don't claim that this is the best possible cotton picker. But this machine is today a better cotton picker than the old Model T Ford was an automobile when it was first offered." "Picker Problems," 48.

51. W. E. Ayres, "Machines to Replace Men as Dixie Farmers Cut Costs by Mechanization," *Commercial Appeal,* November 13, 1936. Emphasis added. See also M. G. Vaiden, J. O. Smith, and W. E. Ayres, *Making Cotton Cheaper: Can Present Production Costs Be Reduced?* Bulletin No. 298 (Starkville: Delta Experiment Station, June 1932), 2.

52. This quotation was reconstructed from Carlson, "Revolution in Cotton," 136, and from "Rust Cotton Picker," STFU Papers, reel 6. See also Kathryn Coe Cordell, "Mechanical Cotton Picker," *Arkansas Gazette Magazine,* June 30, 1935, 3.

53. C. Horace Hamilton, "The Social Effects of Recent Trends in the Mechanization of Agriculture," 18, citing S. H. McCrory, R. F. Hendrickson, and Committee, "Agriculture," in *Technological Trends and National Policy,* 97. See *Arkansas Gazette* July 18, 1937. The actual quotation read: "Maximum efficiency in farm production has not been reached and is not in sight. It could not be reached without social cost; it cannot be stopped without social cost."

54. B. O. Williams, "The Impact of Mechanization on the Farm Population of the South," *Rural Sociology* 4 (September 1939): 300–313.

55. Ibid., 312.

56. Hamilton, "The Social Effects of Recent Trends in the Mechanization of Agriculture," 3–19.

57. Samuel I. Rosenman, *The Public Papers and Addresses of Franklin D. Roosevelt,* 13 vols. (New York: Russell and Russell, 1969), 7:421.

58. Clarence A. Wiley, "The Rust Mechanical Cotton Picker and Probable Land-Use Adjustment," *Journal of Land and Public Utility Economics* 15 (February 1939): 155–66.

59. Wiley estimated eighty cents per hundred for machine-picked compared with an average cost of about sixty cents per hundred for handpicked cotton.

60. Beginning with the Angus Campbell and Theodore H. Price collaboration, many inventors formed alliances with financial supporters. Berry had been joined by Charles Gamble and then by A. M. Hanauer. In addition, A. R. Nisbet and his son J. L. Nisbet joined with H. G. Wendland. F. D. McHugh, "Machines Pick Cotton, But—," *Scientific American* 159 (November 1938): 242–43; "Cotton Harvester," *Textile World,* January 31, 1931, 43.

61. McHugh, "Machines Pick Cotton, But—," 242–45. The cover of this issue showed an experimental model of an International Harvester picker.

62. H. P. Smith, "Progress in Mechanical Harvesting of Cotton," *Agricultural Engineering* 19 (September 1938): 389–91.

63. H. B. McKahin to C. D. Wiman, October 27, 1936, Deere Archives, Deere and Company, Moline, Ill.

64. "Deere & Co.," *Fortune* 14 (August 1936): 72–77, 152, 155, 159–60, 162, 164. This article failed to mention cotton pickers.

65. *Kiplinger Agricultural Letter,* No. 199, September 5, 1936, copy in Deere files.

66. "Deere & Co.," *Fortune* 14 (August 1936): 72–77, 152, 155, 159–60, 162, 164; C. R. Hagen, "Twenty-Five Years of Cotton Picker Development," *Agricultural Engineering* 32 (November 1951): 593–96, 599; and E. A. Johnston, "The Evolution of the Mechanical Cotton Harvester," *Agricultural Engineering* 19 (September 1938): 383–85, 388. See E. J. Gittins to P. P. Haring, October 14, 1932, August 24, 1934, Haring Papers. "New-Model Cotton Pickers," *Business Week,* October 2, 1937, 26, mentioned International Harvester's work.

67. See Ronald William Clark, *Edison: The Man Who Made the Future* (New York: Putnam, 1977); and Neil Baldwin, *Edison: Inventing the Century* (New York: Hyperion, 1995).

68. Straus, "Enter the Cotton Picker," 386.

Chapter 6: Cotton Harvester Sweepstakes

1. Cotton Harvester Season of 1942, McCormick International Harvester Collection, 1881–1985, IHC Undocumented Series, boxes 356 and 357, State Historical Society of Wisconsin, Madison. Hereafter cited as IHC Collection. James H. Street, *The New Revolution in the Cotton Economy: Mechanization and Its Consequences* (Chapel Hill: University of North Carolina Press, 1957), 120–21.

2. C. R. Hagen, "Twenty-Five Years of Cotton Picker Development,"
Agricultural Engineering 32 (November 1951): 593–96, 599.

3. Cotton Harvester Season of 1942, IHC Collection; *Little Rock Arkansas
Gazette,* August 15, 1942.

4. E. A. Johnston, "The Evolution of the Mechanical Cotton Harvester,
Agricultural Engineering 19 (September 1938): 383–85, 388; Hagen, "Twenty-Five
Years of Cotton Picker Development," 595–96.

5. "Cotton Harvester," *Newsweek* 20 (December 7, 1942): 68–69; "Six-Bale
Picker: International Harvester's Mechanical Cotton Picker," *Business Week,*
November 27, 1943, 69–70; "Perfected Cotton Picker Announced," *Science Digest*
13 (February 1943): 93. On McCormick, see "Fowler McCormick," *Fortune 34*
(September 1946): 111–15, 213–20.

6. C. H. Wendel, *150 Years of International Harvester* (Sarasota, Fla.: Crestline
Publishing, 1981), 82. Compare Johnson, Embree, and Alexander, *Collapse of
Cotton Tenancy,* 44.

7. McCormick's statement that IH had worked on the cotton picker for forty
years was wrong. Harvester's work began when the company purchased the
Campbell patents in 1924, eighteen years earlier. If McCormick meant to include
Campbell's work, then the development period went back fifty-seven years. See
Shirley Downing, "IH Traces Cotton Pickers to 1890 Patent," *Memphis (Tenn.)
Commercial Appeal,* April 24, 1977. See also chap. 3.

8. "Fowler McCormick Bares Plan to Pick Nation's Cotton by Machine," clip-
ping, no date, box 356, International Harvester Collection; *Arkansas Gazette,*
November 29, December 1, 1942.

9. *Business Week,* November 27, 1943, 69.

10. For a description of a 1944 demonstration, see Nicholas Lemann, *The
Promised Land: The Great Black Migration and How It Changed America* (New
York: Alfred A. Knopf, 1991), 3–5.

11. For migration figures, see table 8.2.

12. Calculated from U.S. Bureau of the Census, *Historical Statistics of the United
States, Colonial Times to 1970* (Washington, D.C.: GPO, 1975), series K 45, p. 458.

13. Ibid., series K 60, 62, 63, p. 458.

14. Calculated from ibid., series K 45, pp. 458, 459. See also table 10.3 for figures
on the Arkansas Delta. See Donald Holley, "The Second Great Emancipation: The
Rust Cotton Picker and How It Changed Arkansas," *Arkansas Historical Quarterly*
52 (spring 1993): 44–77.

15. See table 8.2 for migration estimates.

16. Calculated from *Historical Statistics of the United States,* series A 178–79,
195, 202, 203, pp. 22, 24, 28, 30. James D. Tarver, *Changes in Arkansas Population,
1940–1950,* Report Series 21 (Fayetteville: Agricultural Experiment Station,
December 1950), table 5, pp. 10–11.

17. *Commercial Appeal,* October 2, 30, 1944.

18. *Arkansas Gazette,* October 2, 1944.

19. Ibid., October 3, 1944. "It will be picked despite shortage of farm laborers in the South," *Business Week,* October 21, 1944, 52–53.

20. *Arkansas Gazette,* October 5, 1944.

21. Ibid., October 8, 1944.

22. Ibid., October 12, 1944. See Merrill Pritchett and William L. Shea, "The Afrika Korps in Arkansas, 1943–1946," *Arkansas Historical Quarterly* 37 (spring 1978): 16–18.

23. *Arkansas Gazette,* October 11, 1944.

24. Nan Elizabeth Woodruff, "Pick or Fight: The Emergency Farm Labor Program in the Arkansas and Mississippi Deltas During World War II," *Agricultural History* 64 (spring 1990): 74–85.

25. Jay R. Mandle, *The Roots of Black Poverty: The Southern Plantation Economy after the Civil War* (Durham: Duke University Press, 1978), 90.

26. Walter W. Wilcox, *The Farmer in the Second World War* (New York: DaCapo Press, 1973), 84–88. Report of Iowa University Press, 1947.

27. Sidney Baldwin, *Poverty and Politics: The Rise and Decline of the Farm Security Administration* (Chapel Hill: University of North Carolina Press, 1968), 221–25, 264.

28. Woodruff, "Pick or Fight," 74–85.

29. U.S. Department of Agriculture, Arkansas Wage Board, Ceiling Wage for Cotton Picking, Osceola, Ark., August 29, 1945, Records of the Office of Labor (War Food Administration), RG 224, entry 10, box 4, National Archives, Washington, D.C.; U.S. Department of Agriculture, Wage Stabilization for the Price of Picking Cotton in the Delta Section of Mississippi, Clarksdale, Mississippi, August 24, 1945, ibid.

30. H. L. Mitchell, statement read into the record, U.S. Department of Agriculture, Wage Stabilization for Chopping Cotton in Mississippi Delta Section, Greenwood, Miss., March 6, 1946, Records of the Office of Labor (War Food Administration), RG 224, entry 10, box 5, National Archives.

31. H. L. Mitchell, "A Ceiling on Cotton Pickers' Wages," [1945], ibid.

32. *Arkansas Gazette,* August 21, September 2, 4, 7, 18, 26, 1945.

33. See Walter W. Wilcox, *The Farmer in the Second World War* (Ames: Iowa University Press, 1947), 307; Otis T. Osgood and John W. White, *Land Tenure in Arkansas: IV. Further Changes in Labor Used on Cotton Farms, 1939–44,* Bulletin No. 459 (Fayetteville: Arkansas Agricultural Experiment Station, August 1945), 29–31; John R. Skates Jr., "World War II as a Watershed in Mississippi History," *Journal of Mississippi History* 37 (May 1975): 131–42.

34. Osgood and White, *Land Tenure in Arkansas: IV. Further Changes in Labor Used on Cotton Farms,* 30.

35. Harris P. Smith, "Late Developments in Mechanical Cotton Harvesting," *Agricultural Engineering* 27 (July 1946): 321. Emphasis added.

36. *Arkansas Gazette,* October 12, 1944; "Mechanical Crop: Mississippi Plantation Uses One-Row Pickers on Crop Raised Entirely with Machinery," *Business Week,* October 21, 1944, 54, 57.

37. Ibid.; H. H. Hopson Jr., "Mechanization of a Delta Cotton Plantation as applied to Hopson Planting Company" (Clarksdale, Miss.: Hopson Planting Co., 1944), copy in Special Collections Department, Mitchell Memorial Library, Mississippi State University Library, Starkville, Mississippi.

38. Ibid., 9.

39. Ibid., 10–11.

40. Ibid., 10.

41. Ibid., 12–13. Compare Frank J. Welch and D. Gray Miley, "Mechanization of the Cotton Harvest," *Journal of Farm Economics* 27 (November 1945): 933–36. Welch and Miley reported slightly different figures in a discussion of costs on the Hopson plantation. They gave the average cost per bale for 2,229 bales as $7.38.

42. J. D. Ratcliff, "Revolution in Cotton," *Collier's* 116 (July 21, 1945), 24.

43. Ibid.

44. Ibid., 42.

45. Ibid., 11.

46. *Commercial Appeal,* October 29, 30, November 3, 1944.

47. "Six-Bale Picker," *Business Week,* November 27, 1943, 69–70, 72.

48. "International Harvester Presents Memphis Works," International Harvesters Collection. *Chicago Daily News,* August 2, 1947. These figures are based on table 6.5. However, Hagen cited lower production figures: 3,175 pickers produced between 1949 and 1951, or 88 per month. Compare Hagen, "Twenty-Five Years of Cotton Picker Development," 599.

49. *International Harvester's Great New Cotton Picker: Now in Quantity Production* (Chicago: International Harvester Company, ca. 1949).

50. "Race for Pickers," *Business Week,* January 1, 1944, 61. See *Farm Implement News,* December 23, 1943.

51. "Cotton Harvesting: Development of a Mechanical Spindle Type Cotton Picker," 4–5, typescript dated March 9, 1956, Deere Archives, Deere and Company, Moline, Ill. See Hagen, "Twenty-Five Years of Cotton Picker Development," 593–96, 599.

52. *30 Seasons of Better Picking with John Deere* (Moline, Ill.: Deere and Co., 1979).

53. *Des Moines Register,* May 26, 30, 1961. In some articles the value of the shipment was placed at $4 million. "World's First Trainload of Cotton Pickers," *Atlantic Coast Line News,* July–August, 1961, 16–17; R. R. Smith, "John Deere Ships World's First Trainload of Cotton Pickers," *L & N Magazine* 37 (July 1961): 2–3.

54. Charles H. Wendel, *The Allis-Chalmers Story* (Sarasota, Fla.: Crestline Publishing, 1988), 15. See Norm Swinford, *Allis-Chalmers Farm Equipment, 1914–1985* (St. Joseph, Mich.: American Society of Agricultural Engineers, 1994), 41–42.

55. "A.-C. Goes South," *Business Week,* May 24, 1947, 18.

56. *Business Week,* May 24, 1947, 18. See ibid., October 21, 1944, 57–58; November 27, 1943, 70.

57. John Rust, "The Origin and Development of the Cotton Picker," *West Tennessee Historical Society Papers* 7 (1953): 53–54. "A.-C. Goes South," *Business Week,* May 24, 1947, 18. See David Halberstam, *The Fifties* (New York: Villard Press, 1993). See also Wendel, *Allis-Chalmers Story,* 90–91; Swinford, *Allis-Chalmers,* 354–62.

58. Rust, "The Origin and Development of the Cotton Picker," 54. See also Holley, "The Second Great Emancipation: The Rust Cotton Picker and How It Changed Arkansas," 68–71.

59. *Pine Bluff (Ark.) Commercial,* February 18, March 13, 1949.

60. Ibid., February 23, 1945.

61. On Ben Pearson's background, see Dallas T. Herndon, *Annals of Arkansas 1947* (Hopkinsville, Ky.: Historical Record Association, 1947), 3:1078–1080.

62. Interview with G. E. Powell, chairman of the board, Ben Pearson, Inc., Pine Bluff, Ark., June 5, 1992; *Pine Bluff Commercial,* March 23, April 1, 2, 1949. The deadline for delivery was extended to December 31, 1949.

63. Interview with G. E. Powell, June 5, 1992; *A Pictorial History of the Development of the Ben Pearson Rust Cotton Picker* ([Shreveport, La.]: Ben Pearson, Inc., [1962]); *The Rust Cotton Picker: Its Origin and Development* (Pine Bluff, Ark.: John Rust Co., 1951).

64. Ibid.

65. Calculated from data in "Ben Pearson, Inc. v. The John Rust Company," *Arkansas Reports, Cases Determined in the Supreme Court of Arkansas, January 1954–July 1954* (Little Rock: State of Arkansas, 1955), vol. 223, pp. 697–705. Rust sued Ben Pearson for $150,000. He would have been owed that amount under his contract if Pearson had sold four hundred pickers at a unit price of $3,750 for a total of $1,500,000.

66. *Memphis (Tenn.) Press-Scimitar,* June 15, 1953.

67. J. A. Hamilton, "A Study of the Market for Cotton Pickers," January 31, 1946, box 468, vol. 1, item 18, IHC Collection.

68. Without explanation, IH figures exaggerated the market slightly because 1,382,563/200 = 6,913. The number of acres used in their calculations varied slightly.

69. J. A. Hamilton, "A Study of the Market for Cotton Pickers," January 31, 1946, box 468, vol. 1, item 18, IHC Collection.

Chapter 7: The Cotton South's Gradual Revolution, 1950–1970

1. U.S. Bureau of the Census, *Historical Statistics of the United States: Colonial Times to 1970* (Washington, D.C.: GPO, 1975), Series K 555, p. 517

2. Gavin Wright, *Old South, New South: Revolutions in the Southern Economy since the Civil War* (New York: Basic Books, 1986), 12.

3. Frank H. Maier, "An Economic Analysis of Adoption of the Mechanical Cotton Harvester" (Ph.D. diss., University of Chicago, 1969), 263–64.

4. For the Pollyanna view see Louis Bromfield, "Go South, Young Man!" *Atlantic Monthly* 182 (November 1948): 57–62; idem, "The Rebirth of the South," *Reader's Digest* 55 (July 1949): 19–22; and idem, "The New South," *Life* 27 (October 31, 1949): 79–90.

5. Peter F. Drucker, "Exit King Cotton," *Harper's* 192 (May 1946): 473–74.

6. J. M. Morse, "Revolution in Cotton," *New Republic* 115 (August 19, 1946): 192–94.

7. A. G. Mezerik, "Dixie in Black and White: King Cotton Strikes Again," *Nation* 164 (June 21, 1947): 740–41.

8. David L. Cohn, *Where I Was Born and Raised* (Boston: Houghton, Mifflin, 1948), 329–30. For more of Cohn's views, see *The Life and Times of King Cotton* (New York: Oxford University Press, 1956).

9. Arthur Raper, *Machines in the Cotton Fields* (Atlanta: Southern Regional Council, 1946), 11. See also *Technology on the Farm, a Special Report by an Interbureau Committee of the Bureau of Agricultural Economics, United States Department of Agriculture* (Washington, D.C.: GPO, August 1940); and Rupert B. Vance, *All These People* (Chapel Hill: University of North Carolina Press, 1946), 210–12.

10. Raper, *Machines in the Cotton Fields*, 12.

11. Ibid., 21.

12. Oscar Johnston, "The Cotton Industry's Responsibility in Mechanization," *Report of the Proceedings of the Beltwide Cotton Mechanization Conference,* August 18–19, 1947, Stoneville and Greenville, Mississippi, 33.

13. Ibid., 36.

14. Frank J. Welch and D. Gray Miley, "Mechanization of the Cotton Harvest," *Journal of Farm Economics* 27 (November 1945): 933–39.

15. See David L. Cohn, "Lament for the South That Is No More," *New York Times Magazine,* January 22, 1950, 14, 41.

16. John Leonard Fulmer, *Agricultural Progress in the Cotton Belt since 1920* (Chapel Hill: University of North Carolina, 1950), 85, 106.

17. See chap. 1.

18. Charles S. Aiken, "The Decline of Sharecropping in the Lower Mississippi River Valley," *Geoscience and Man* 19 (June 30, 1978): 156. See Frank H. Maier, "An

Economic Analysis of Adoption of the Mechanical Cotton Harvester" (Ph.D. diss., University of Chicago, 1969), 99–100.

19. Kyle Engler, W. F. Buchele, and J. C. Newell, *Mechanized Production of Cotton, I.: Effect of Seedbed Preparation, Planting, and Cultivation on Mechanical Harvesting of Cotton,* Mimeograph Series No. 3 (Fayetteville: Arkansas Agricultural Experiment Station, April 1950); James H. Street, *The New Revolution in the Cotton Economy: Mechanization and Its Consequences* (Chapel Hill: University of North Carolina Press, 1957), 34.

20. "Goosing the Cotton," *Time* 81 (April 26, 1963): 60; Tom Hamburger, "Dramatic Population Reduction Inspires Technological Changes," *Arkansas Gazette,* May 19, 1977. See also ibid., May 16, 18, 1977.

21. Gilbert C. Fite, "Mechanization of Cotton Production since World War II," *Agricultural History* 54 (January 1980): 205–6.

22. Ibid., 191.

23. H. P. Smith, "Cotton Harvesting Development to Date," *Agricultural Engineering* 12 (March 1931): 74.

24. *Stat.* 1082–85 (1946).

25. Fite, "Mechanization of Cotton Production since World War II," 199–201.

26. Ibid., 200.

27. Fite, "Mechanization of Cotton Production since World War II," 201.

28. Ibid., 202.

29. Maier, "An Economic Analysis of Adoption of the Mechanical Cotton Harvester," 14, 19–20.

30. Street, *New Revolution,* 34.

31. Warren C. Whatley, "A History of Mechanization in the Cotton South: The Institutional Hypothesis," *Quarterly Journal of Economics* 100 (November 1985): 1191–1215; and Whatley, "Southern Agrarian Labor Contracts as Impediments to Cotton Mechanization," *Journal of Economic History* 47 (March 1987): 45–70.

32. Ibid., 52.

33. Moses Senkumba Musoke and Alan L. Olmstead, "The Rise of the Cotton Industry in California: A Comparative Perspective," *Journal of Economic History* 42 (June 1982): 385–412.

34. U.S. Department of Commerce, Bureau of the Census, *United States Census of Agriculture: 1959,* vol. 2, *General Reports: Statistics by Subjects* (Washington, D.C.: GPO, 1962), 829, 835. See Musoke and Olmstead, "The Rise of the Cotton Industry in California," 391.

35. This viewpoint was found in studies of the southern plantation economy conducted and published during the 1930s and 1940s. See Harald A. Pedersen and Arthur F. Raper, *The Cotton Plantation in Transition,* Bulletin No. 508 (Starkville: Mississippi State College, Agricultural Experiment Station, January 1954), 26 and David Wayne Ganger, "The Impact of Mechanization and the New Deal's Acreage

Reduction Programs on Cotton Farmers during the 1930s" (Ph.D. diss., University of California, Los Angeles, 1973).

36. Whatley, "Southern Agrarian Labor Contracts as Impediments to Cotton Mechanization," 45–70; and Whatley, "A History of Mechanization in the Cotton South: The Institutional Hypothesis," *Quarterly Journal of Economics* 100 (November 1985): 1191–1215.

37. In 1951, a two-row self-propelled Deere picker sold for $13,750. See prices in Maier, "An Economic Analysis of Adoption of the Mechanical Cotton Harvester," 100.

38. Any case study can be challenged on the grounds of how representative it is. In fact, most case studies are used not because they are representative at all; they are simply convenient examples because they are supported by available information. Of course other case studies could be cited with potentially different results, but the evidence points to small farmers as the earliest mechanizers.

39. "Biggest Cotton Plantation," *Fortune* 15 (March 1937): 125–32, 156–60.

40. Read P. Dunn Jr., *Mr. Oscar: A Story of the Early Years in the Life and Times of Oscar Johnston and of His Efforts in Organizing the National Cotton Council* (Memphis, Tenn.: National Cotton Council of America, 1991). See also Lawrence J. Nelson, *King Cotton's Advocate: Oscar G. Johnston and the New Deal* (Knoxville: University of Tennessee Press, 1999).

41. Oscar Johnston, "Will the Machine Ruin the South?" *Saturday Evening Post* 219 (May 31, 1947): 36–37, 94–95, 98.

42. "Biggest Cotton Plantation," *Fortune* 15 (March 1937): 125–32, 156–60.

43. See *Arkansas Gazette,* September 1, 1936, for his comments. See also chapter 3.

44. Quoted in Zhengkai Dong, "From Postbellum Plantation to Modern Agribusiness: A History of the Delta and Pine Land Company" (Ph.D. diss., Purdue University, 1993), 208.

45. Johnston made a practice of staggering the ages, even the age distribution of mules, phasing older mules into retirement. Jack Temple Kirby, *Rural Worlds Lost: The American South, 1920–1960* (Baton Rouge: Louisiana State University Press, 1987), 338–40.

46. Dong, "From Postbellum Plantation to Modern Agribusiness," 205–6. Johnston's observation may have referred to the possibility mechanizing cotton across the entire Cotton South. As we have seen, the Hopson plantation had already produced a crop "untouched by human hands." Scott and Clarksdale, Mississippi, are about thirty miles apart.

47. Oscar Johnston, "Delta & Pine Land Company of Mississippi," [1947], Delta and Pine Land Company Records, 1886–1982, box 27, p. 6, Special Collections

Department, Mitchell Memorial Library, Mississippi State University Library, Starkville, Mississippi.

48. In desperation Delta Pine and Land showed an interest in the Berry-Gamble picker, which was developed in the Greenville area. Though the Berry picker was never successful, Deere purchased the Berry patents in 1944. See chapter 6.

49. See Charles R. Sayre, "Cotton Mechanization since World War II," *Agricultural History* 53 (January 1979): 105–24.

50. "The Delta Pine Story," typescript in Delta and Pine Land Company Records, box 27. The last tenant crop was made in 1957. Early Ewing Jr., "The Delta and Pine Land Company," *Washington County Historical Society Programs of 1979*, 5. In comparison, Lee Wilson and Co., a 50,000-acre plantation in Mississippi County, Arkansas, operated with relatively little mechanization, still using hand pickers in preference to machines as late as the 1950s. Jim Crane, the plantation manager, conceded that mechanical cotton pickers were more economical than handpicking, but hand pickers produced premium cotton, which brought a higher price. "Industry on the Plantation," *Business Week,* October 23, 1948, 26. See Greg Warhurst, "Lee Wilson & Company: 100 Years of a Growing Tradition," May 1, 1992, typescript copy in Torreyson Library Archives, University of Central Arkansas, Conway, Ark.

51. U.S. Department of Agriculture, Economic Research Service, *Statistics on Cotton and Related Data, 1920–1973,* Statistical Bulletin No. 535 (Washington, D.C.: USDA, 1974), 218.

52. For the FSA, see Donald Holley, *Uncle Sam's Farmers: The New Deal Communities in the Lower Mississippi Valley* (Urbana: University of Illinois Press, 1975), 284. Crigler was officially known as the Arkansas Farm Tenant Security project.

53. Nelson farmed for a while but went on to other work.

54. Burnice Frizzell, statement at Farm Credit Conference, April 7, 1953, typescript in possession of Steve Frizzell, Star City, Ark.

55. "'Keeping Up' Is What It Takes to Keep Ahead," *Arkansas Union Farmer,* October 1960, 4–5.

56. See chap. 6.

57. Ibid.

58. At $2.50 per hundredweight, the Frizzells would have paid $37.50 per bale for handpicking, or $7,875 to pick 210 acres, assuming that the land produced a bale to the acre.

59. "'Keeping Up' Is What It Takes to Keep Ahead," 4–5.

60. Burnice Frizzell, statement at Farm Credit Conference, April 7, 1953.

61. "'Keeping Up' Is What It Takes to Keep Ahead," 4–5.

Chapter 8: Mechanization, Black Migration, and the Labor Supply in the Cotton South

1. Charles S. Aiken, *The Cotton Plantation South since the Civil War* (Baltimore: Johns Hopkins University Press, 1998), 131.

2. See, however, Nan Elizabeth Woodruff, "Pick or Fight: The Emergency Farm Labor Program in the Arkansas and Mississippi Deltas during World War II," *Agricultural History* 64 (spring 1989): 74–85. On pages 76–77, Woodruff stated, "It was not scarcity, but control over labor that lay at the center of the conflicts during the 1940s." See also Woodruff, "Mississippi Delta Planters and Debates over Mechanization, Labor, and Civil Rights," *Journal of Southern History* 60 (May 1994): 263–84.

3. Gilbert C. Fite, "Mechanization of Cotton Production since World War II," *Agricultural History* 54 (January 1980): 198.

4. Harris P. Smith, "Late Developments in Mechanical Cotton Harvesting," *Agricultural Engineering* 27 (July 1946): 321–22. See also Smith, "Mechanical Harvesting of Cotton Has Arrived," *Agricultural Engineering* 25 (May 1944): 167–68.

5. Dorothy Dickins, *The Labor Supply and Mechanized Cotton Production*, Bulletin No. 463 (Starkville: Mississippi Agricultural Experiment Station, June 1949), 5.

6. Oscar Johnston, "Will the Machine Ruin the South?" *Saturday Evening Post* 219 (May 31, 1947): 37.

7. Gilbert C. Fite, "Recent Changes in the Mechanization of Cotton Production in the United States," *Agricultural History* 24 (January 1950): 28. See also Fite, "Mechanization of Cotton Production since World War II," *Agricultural History* 54 (January 1980): 198–99.

8. "Cotton—Still the Deep South's Problem," *U.S. News and World Report* 40 (January 27, 1956): 66–68, 70, 72, 74.

9. Harald A. Pedersen and Arthur F. Raper, *The Cotton Plantation in Transition*, Bulletin No. 508 (Starkville: Mississippi Agricultural Experiment Station, January 1954), 8.

10. James H. Street, "The 'Labor Vacuum' and Cotton Mechanization," *Journal of Farm Economics* 35 (August 1953): 381–97. Street, *The New Revolution in the Cotton Economy: Mechanization and Its Consequences* (Chapel Hill: University of North Carolina Press, 1957), 175, 189–90, 229.

11. U.S. Department of Labor, Bureau of Employment Security, *Cotton Harvest Mechanization: Effect on Seasonal Hired Labor*, BES No. 209 (Washington, 1962), 6, 10.

12. "An Interview with Jere B. Nash [Sr.]," May 31, 1977, typescript, p. 17,

Washington County Library, Greenville, Miss. See also James Hand, F. H. "Slim" Holiman, and Jere Nash, interview with William Cash, Oral History Number 197, Delta State University Archives, Cleveland, Miss.

13. Charles S. Aiken, *The Cotton Plantation South since the Civil War* (Baltimore: Johns Hopkins University Press, 1998), 130–32; Woodruff, "Pick or Fight," 76–77; Gavin Wright, *Old South, New South: Revolutions in the Southern Economy since the Civil War* (New York: Basic Books, 1986), 247.

14. Woodruff, "Mississippi Delta Planters and Debates over Mechanization, Labor, and Civil Rights in the 1940s," 263–84.

15. Aiken, *Cotton Plantation South,* 131.

16. In 1948 Mississippi cotton sold for 31.08 cents a pound, while labor commanded $3.25 per hundred. The value of a bale was $155.40 less picking cost of $48.74, or 31.4 percent. These calculations are based on data in U.S. Department of Agriculture, Economic Research Service, *Statistics on Cotton and Related Data, 1920–1973,* Statistical Bulletin No. 535 (Washington, D.C.: USDA, 1974), 71, 86.

17. Street, *New Revolution,* 203–6.

18. *Statistics on Cotton and Related Data, 1920–1973,* 86.

19. Frank H. Maier, "An Economic Analysis of Adoption of the Mechanical Cotton Harvester" (Ph.D. diss., University of Chicago, 1969), 22.

20. Aiken, *Cotton Plantation South,* 131. Aiken wrote "scare."

21. Maier, "An Economic Analysis of Adoption of the Mechanical Cotton Harvester," 19–20, 22, 29, 42.

22. *Statistics on Cotton and Related Data, 1920–1973,* 218.

23. Maier, "An Economic Analysis of Adoption of the Mechanical Cotton Harvester," 7.

24. Arkansas Department of Labor, *Employment Security Division, Arkansas Farm Labor Report 1962* (Little Rock: Arkansas Department of Labor, 1963), 10.

25. *Cotton Harvest Mechanization: Effect on Seasonal Hired Labor,* 12.

26. M. J. Steitz, "The Current Cotton Picker Market," January 10, 1955, McCormick International Harvester Collection, 1881–1985. IHC Documented Series, Farm Machinery Reports, box 469, vol. 5, item 98, p. 11, State Historical Society of Wisconsin, Madison.

27. Ralph C. Hon, "The Rust Cotton Picker," *Southern Economic Journal 3* (April 1937): 391.

28. U.S. Bureau of the Census, *Historical Statistics of the United States: Colonial Times to 1970* (Washington, D.C.: GPO, 1975), Series K 17, 45, p. 458.

29. *Historical Statistics of the United States,* Series K 45, p. 458. For similar data, see Street, *New Revolution,* 185, 186, 187.

30. David Whitman, "The Great Sharecropper Success Story," *Public Interest,* 104 (summer 1991): 3–21.

31. Street, *New Revolution,* 179; U.S. Bureau of the Census, *Census of Population: 1950,* vol. 2, *Characteristics of the Population, Part 1, United States Summary* (Washington, D.C.: GPO, 1953), tables 59, 145.

32. "Why Do Arkansans Vanish?" *Business Week,* April 12, 1958, 96–97.

33. Phillips H. Brown and John M. Peterson, "The Exodus from Arkansas," *Arkansas Economist* 2 (winter 1960): 10–15.

34. Lee J. Alston and Joseph P. Ferrie, "The Bracero Program and Farm Labor Legislation in World War II," in *The Sinews of War: Essays on the Economic History of World War II,* ed. Geofrey T. Mills and Hugh Rockoff, 129–49 (Ames: Iowa State University Press, 1993).

35. Wayne D. Rasmussen, *A History of the Emergency Farm Labor Supply Program, 1943–47,* Agriculture Monograph No. 13 (Washington, D.C.: GPO, 1951).

36. Arkansas Employment Security Division, *Arkansas Agricultural Labor Report 1954* (Little Rock: Employment Security Division, 1955), 5.

37. *Arkansas Farm Labor Report 1962* (Little Rock: Employment Security Division, 1963), 10.

38. Arkansas Department of Labor, Employment Security Division, *Arkansas Farm Labor Report 1964* (Little Rock: Employment Security Division, 1965), 13.

39. R. Douglas Hurt, "Cotton Pickers and Strippers," *Journal of the West* 30 (April 1991): 30–42.

40. Farm Placement Service, State Employment Service, *Louisiana Farm Labor Bulletin* (Baton Rouge, La.: 1959–60), No. 17, July 17, 1959; No. 27, September 25, 1959; No. 30, October 16, 1959; No. 34, November 13, 1959, No. 28, October 28, 1960.

41. Mississippi Employment Security Division, *Mississippi Farm Labor 1961,* 34; Mississippi Employment Security Division, *Mississippi Farm Labor 1962* (Jackson, Miss.: Employment Security Division, 1963), 8.

42. *Arkansas Agricultural Report 1956,* 5; *Arkansas Agricultural Report 1958,* 4. See Craig Heinicke, "The Federal Soil Bank, the Decline of Cotton, and the Demise of the Southern Plantation in the 1950s," a paper prepared for the ASSA Meeting/Cliometric Society, New Orleans, January 1997.

43. Roger L. Burford, "The Federal Cotton Programs and Farm Labor Force Adjustments," *Southern Economic Journal* 33 (October 1966): 223–36.

44. James C. Cobb, *The Most Southern Place on Earth: The Mississippi Delta and the Roots of Regional Identity* (New York: Oxford University Press, 1992), 205, 253, 255.

45. Maier, "An Economic Analysis of Adoption of the Mechanical Cotton Harvester," 11, 57.

46. Leland DuVall, "Arkansas—The Agricultural Revolution," *Little Rock Arkansas Gazette,* April 6, 1969.

47. Ronald E. Seavoy, *The American Peasantry: Southern Agricultural Labor and Its Legacy: A Study in Political Economy, 1850–1995* (Westport, Conn.: Greenwood Press, 1998), 512; Donald O. Parsons, "Racial Trends in Male Labor Force Participation," *American Economic Review* 70 (December 1980): 911–20; LeRay, Wilber, and Crowe, *Plantation Organization and the Resident Labor Force, Delta Area, Mississippi,* 23.

48. Cobb, *Most Southern Place on Earth,* 266.

49. Lee J. Alston and Joseph P. Ferrie, "Paternalism in Agricultural Labor Contracts in the U.S. South: Implications for the Growth of the Welfare State," *American Economic Review* 83 (September 1993): 852–76.

50. Ibid., 870. See Adam Smith [pseud.], "The City as the OK Corral," *Esquire* 104 (July 1985): 64.

51. Aiken, *Cotton Plantation South,* 223–25.

52. The minimum wage increased to $1.15 an hour in 1968 and to $1.30 in 1969. See Charles S. Aiken, "The Decline of Sharecropping in the Lower Mississippi Valley," *Geoscience and Man* 19 (June 30, 1978): 162–63.

53. Cobb, *Most Southern Place on Earth,* 256, 274.

54. *Statistics on Cotton and Related Data, 1920–1973,* 71.

55. Cobb, *Most Southern Place on Earth,* 274.

56. Ibid., 271.

57. Seavoy, *American Peasantry,* 512.

Chapter 9: The Great Migration and the Mechanical Cotton Picker

1. Clifton L. Taulbert, *Once upon a Time When We Were Colored* (Tulsa, Okla.: Council Oak Books, 1989); and *The Last Train North* (Tulsa, Okla.: Council Oak Books, 1992).

2. See James R. Grossman, *Land of Hope: Chicago, Black Southerners, and the Great Migration* (Chicago: University of Chicago Press, 1989), 100–101.

3. Alferdteen Harrison, ed., *Black Exodus: The Great Migration from the American South* (Jackson: University Press of Mississippi, 1991), vii, 10–11; U.S. Bureau of the Census, *The Social and Economic Status of the Black Population in the United States: An Historical View, 1790–1978* (Washington, D.C.: GPO, 1978), 13, 15, 17.

4. See Stewart E. Tolnay and E. M. Beck, "Racial Violence and Black Migration in the American South, 1890–1930," *American Sociological Review* 57 (February 1992): 102–16, for comparisons of black and white migration.

5. See William Cohen, *At Freedom's Edge: Black Mobility and the Southern White Quest for Racial Control, 1861–1915* (Baton Rouge: Louisiana State University Press, 1991).

6. R. Douglas Hurt, "Cotton Pickers and Strippers," *Journal of the West* 30 (April 1991): 39.

7. Cohen, *At Freedom's Edge,* xi, xvi; Robert Higgs, "The Boll Weevil, the Cotton Economy, and Black Migration, 1910–1930," *Agricultural History* 50 (April 1976): 335–50. The weevil provided a positive motivation for improvement. In 1919, for example, the people of Enterprise, Alabama, built a monument to the boll weevil as a tribute to the insect's contribution to agricultural diversification.

8. See Stewart E. Tolnay and E. M. Beck, "Racial Violence and Black Migration in the American South, 1890–1930," *American Sociological Review* 57 (February 1992): 102–16; and Tolnay and Beck, *A Festival of Violence: An Analysis of Southern Lynchings, 1882–1930* (Urbana: University of Illinois Press, 1995).

9. See also Stewart E. Tolnay and E. M. Beck, "Black Flight: Lethal Violence and the Great Migration, 1900–1930," *Social Science History* 14 (fall 1990): 347–70.

10. Daniel M. Johnson and Rex R. Campbell, *Black Migration in America: A Social and Demographic History* (Durham, N.C.: Duke University Press, 1981).

11. Nicholas Lemann, *The Promised Land: The Great Black Migration and How It Changed America* (New York: Alfred A. Knopf, 1991), 3–21. See also Lemann, "The Origins of the Underclass," *Atlantic Monthly* 257 (June 1986): 31–43, 47–55.

12. Pete Daniel, *Breaking the Land: The Transformation of Cotton, Tobacco, and Rice Cultures since 1880* (Urbana: University of Illinois Press, 1985), 242, 245; Jack Temple Kirby, "The Transformation of Southern Plantations, c. 1920–1960," *Agricultural History* 57 (July 1983): 257–76 (quotation is on p. 270); and "The Southern Exodus, 1910–1960: A Primer for Historians," *Journal of Southern History* 49 (November 1983): 585–600. See also Kirby's *Rural Worlds Lost: The American South, 1920–1960* (Baton Rouge: Louisiana State University Press, 1987); Richard H. Day, "The Economics of Technological Change and the Demise of the Sharecropper," *American Economic Review* 57 (June 1967): 427–49; James H. Street, *The New Revolution in the Cotton Economy: Mechanization and Its Consequences* (Chapel Hill: University of North Carolina Press, 1957); and Street, "The 'Labor Vacuum' and Cotton Mechanization," *Journal of Farm Economics* 35 (August 1953): 381–97.

13. Anthony Walton, "Technology versus African-Americans," *Atlantic Monthly* 283 (January 1999): 17.

14. Harry C. Dillingham and David F. Sly, "The Mechanical Cotton Picker, Negro Migration, and the Integration Movement," *Human Organization* 25 (winter 1966): 344–51. Apparently, Dillingham and Sly ran their analysis using the difference between tenants at two points in time; but in all counties analyzed the number of tenants dropped, so the relationship between the change in the number of tenants and the number of pickers was inverse. In other words, their data showed that when the number of mechanical pickers went up, the number of tenants declined.

15. Craig Heinicke, "African-American Migration and Mechanized Cotton Harvesting, 1950–1960," *Explorations in Economic History* 31 (October 1994): 501–20.

16. Willis Peterson and Yoav Kislev, "The Cotton Harvester in Retrospect: Labor Displacement or Replacement?" *Journal of Economic History* 46 (March 1986): 199–216.

17. Warren C. Whatley, "New Estimates of the Cost of Harvesting Cotton, 1949–1964," *Research in Economic History* 13 (1991): 199–225. The quotation is from page 200.

18. Frank Maier, "An Economic Analysis of Adoption of the Mechanical Cotton Picker" (Ph.D. diss., University of Chicago, 1969).

19. U.S. Department of Agriculture, Economic Research Service, *Statistics on Cotton and Related Data, 1920–1973*, Statistical Bulletin No. 535 (Washington, D.C.: USDA, 1974), 66.

20. D. Cochrane and G. H. Orcutt, "Application of Least Squares Regression in Relationships Containing Autocorrelated Error Terms," *Journal of the American Statistical Association*" 44 (1949): 32–61. See also Mark L. Berenson, David M. Levine, and Matthew Goldstein, *Intermediate Statistical Methods and Applications: A Computer Package Approach* (Englewood Cliffs, N.J.: Prentice-Hall, 1983), 410–14.

21. Whatley, "New Estimates of the Cost of Harvesting Cotton," 220.

22. Peterson and Kislev, "The Cotton Harvester in Retrospect," 215.

23. For the 1950 population data, see U.S. Bureau of the Census, *Census of Population: 1950,* vol. 2, *Characteristics of the Population, Part 4, Arkansas* (Washington, D.C.: GPO, 1952), table 41; U.S. Bureau of the Census, *Census of Population: 1950,* vol. 2, *Characteristics of the Population, Part 18, Louisiana* (Washington, D.C.: GPO, 1952), table 41; U.S. Bureau of the Census, *Census of Population: 1950,* vol. 2, *Characteristics of the Population, Part 24, Mississippi* (Washington, D.C.: GPO, 1952), table 41.

For 1960: U.S. Bureau of the Census, *Census of Population: 1960,* vol. 1, *Characteristics of the Population, Part 5, Arkansas* (Washington, D.C.: GPO, 1963), table 27; U.S. Bureau of the Census, *Census of Population: 1960,* vol. 1, *Characteristics of the Population, Part 20, Louisiana* (Washington, D.C.: GPO, 1963), table 27; U.S. Bureau of the Census, *Census of Population: 1960,* vol. 1, *Characteristics of the Population, Part 26, Mississippi* (Washington, D.C.: GPO, 1963), table 27.

For 1970: U.S. Bureau of the Census, *1970 Census of Population,* vol. 1, *Characteristics of the Population, Part 5, Arkansas* (Washington, D.C.: GPO, 1973), table 35; U.S. Bureau of the Census, *1970 Census of Population,* vol. 1, *Characteristics of the Population, Part 20, Louisiana* (Washington, D.C.: GPO, 1973), table 35; U.S. Bureau of the Census, *1970 Census of Population,* vol. 1, *Characteristics of the Population, Part 26, Mississippi* (Washington, D.C.: GPO, 1973), table 35.

24. Frank H. Maier, "An Economic Analysis of Adoption of the Mechanical Cotton Picker" (Ph.D. diss., University of Chicago, 1969), 11–12, 57–60.

25. $Y = a + bx_1 + bx_2$ represents the regression equation used in table 9.7. Inserting figures into the equation for 1950, the net black migration estimate is calculated as follows:

$$Y = 3320 - 17170(0.01) + 17842(0.01)$$
$$Y = 3320 - 172 + 178$$
$$Y = 3320 + 6$$
$$Y = 3326$$

Chapter 10: The Consequences of Cotton Mechanization

1. Pete Daniel, *Breaking the Land: The Transformation of Cotton, Tobacco, and Rice Cultures since 1880* (Urbana and Chicago: University of Illinois Press, 1985), 168–83.

2. Ronald E. Seavoy, *The American Peasantry: Southern Agricultural Labor and Its Legacy: A Study in Political Economy, 1850–1995* (Westport, Conn.: Greenwood Press, 1998), 516–17.

3. Pete Daniel, "The New Deal, Southern Agriculture, and Economic Change," in *The New Deal and the South*, ed. James C. Cobb and Michael V. Namorato (Jackson: University Press of Mississippi, 1984), 37–61.

4. U.S. Bureau of the Census, *1997 Census of Agriculture, Arkansas State and County Data*, vol. 1, *Geographic Area Series, Part 4* (Washington, D.C.: GPO, 1999), table 16, p. 24.

5. The 1959 agricultural census was the last one that enumerated "sharecroppers"; the census, however, continued to report tenants.

6. For developments in rice, see Pete Daniel, *Breaking the Land: The Transformation of Cotton, Tobacco, and Rice Cultures since 1880* (Urbana: University of Illinois Press, 1985).

7. Roberta Rawlins, "Soybeans—New Cash Crop," *Little Rock Arkansas Democrat Magazine,* March 12, 1950; Harry D. Fornari, "The Big Change: Cotton to Soybeans," *Agricultural History* 53 (January 1979): 245–53.

8. Arkansas Department of Labor, Arkansas Farm Labor Program 1961 (Little Rock: Department of Labor, 1962), 10.

9. Congressional Quarterly, *Congressional Quarterly's Guide to Congress,* 2d ed. (Washington, D.C.: Congressional Quarterly, 1976), 567.

10. "Why Do Arkansans Vanish?" *Business Week,* April 12, 1958, 96–97.

11. Louisiana lost a congressional district after the 1990 census.

12. *Arkansas Statistical Abstract, 1989* (Little Rock: State Data Center, 1989), 4.

13. James C. Cobb, *Industrialization and Southern Society, 1877–1984* (Lexington: University Press of Kentucky, 1984), 38–39, 150–51. See also Cobb, *The Most Southern Place on Earth: The Mississippi Delta and the Roots of Regional Identity* (New York: Oxford University Press, 1992), 206, 227, 254.

14. For the full quotation, see page 87. This quotation was reconstructed from "Rust Cotton Picker," Southern Tenant Farmers Union Papers, Microfilm edition, roll 6, and from Oliver Carlson, "Revolution in Cotton," *American Mercury* 34 (February 1935): 136. See also Kathryn Coe Cordell, "Mechanical Cotton Picker," *Arkansas Gazette Magazine,* June 30, 1935, 3.

15. M. G. Vaiden, J. O. Smith, and W. E. Ayres, *Making Cotton Cheaper: Can Present Production Costs Be Reduced?* Bulletin No. 290 (Starkville: Mississippi Agricultural Experiment Station, February 1931); and Making Cotton Cheaper: Can Present Production Costs Be Reduced? Bulletin No. 298 (Starkville: Mississippi Agricultural Experiment Station, June 1932).

16. See Charles S. Aiken, *The Cotton Plantation South since the Civil War* (Baltimore: Johns Hopkins University Press, 1998), 227.

17. Jay R. Mandle, *The Roots of Black Poverty: The Southern Plantation Economy after the Civil War* (Durham: Duke University Press, 1978), 118.

18. Ibid., 117–19.

19. Lee J. Alston and Joseph P. Ferrie, "Paternalism in Agricultural Labor Contracts in the U.S. South: Implications for the Growth of the Welfare State," *American Economic Review* 83 (September 1993): 852–76.

Epilogue: Where Are They Now?

1. John T. Schlebecker to John J. Dierbeck Jr., July 30, 1969, box 445, McCormick International Harvester Collection, 1881–1985, State Historical Society of Wisconsin, Madison. Hereafter cited as IHC Collection.

2. John T. Schlebecker to James B. Mayer, September 11, 1969, ibid.

3. Mayer to Schlebecker, September 26, 1969, ibid. The loan turned into a donation. Mayer later made Old Red a permanent gift in exchange for a tax write-off. J. B. Mayer to G. Terry Sharrer, October 29, 1969, P. P. Haring Papers, National Museum of American History, Smithsonian Institution, Washington, D.C.; H. W. Conner, memorandum to John J. Dierbeck, November 10, 1969, ibid. Sid Cox to John T. Schlebecker, March 27, 1974; Schlebecker to Cox, April 3, 1974, Smithsonian Institution Archives, RG 240, series 6, box 11, folder 29.

4. J. A. Aeschliman, memorandum to A. R. McQuiddy et al., February 9, 1970, Haring Papers.

5. "First Mechanical Cotton Picker Wins Spot in US Exhibition," *Fresno—Past and Present* 12 (March 1970): 2.

6. *Memphis (Tenn.) Commercial Appeal,* April 24, 1977. Remarks for J. W. Wegener, Works Manager, IH Memphis Works Cotton Picker News Conference, Holiday Inn—Rivermont, Memphis, February 17, 1970, IHC Collection.

7. Press release, February 17, 1970, ibid. H. P. Morgan to Roger Walburn, January 13, 1970, Smithsonian Institution Archives, RG 270, series 6, box 11, folder 29.

8. Ed Wilborn, "'Old Red' Is Now History," *Progressive Farmer* (Mississippi and West Tennessee edition) 85 (May 1970): 86.

9. Ed Wilborn to J. Robert Massey, May 14, 1970, with attached memorandum, IHC Collection.

10. J. Robert Massey to Ed Wilborn, May 19, 1970, ibid. Massey identified the machine as a M-12-H, but other officials stated that it was a M-10-H. John J. Dierbeck to A. R. McQuiddy, June 19, 1970, ibid.

11. C. R. Hagen to C. M. Albright, July 28, 1970, ibid.

12. John J. Dierbeck to A. R. McQuiddy, June 19, 1970, ibid.

13. Memorandum attached to Wilborn to Massey, May 14, 1970, ibid.

14. H. J. Fleming, memorandum to C. L. Walker, July 13, 1970, ibid.

15. John J. Dierbeck to A. R. McQuiddy, June 19, 1970, ibid.

16. Herb Fleming, "From the Pages of Cotton-Picking History," *International Harvester Farm* (winter 1970/1971): 3–5.

17. John J. Dierbeck to A. R. McQuiddy, July 15, 1970, IHC Collection; McQuiddy to J. W. Nance Jr., July 23, 1970, ibid. Schlebecker approved the wording but other officials rejected it for use in the cotton picker exhibit. While he planned to use his wording in the full cotton production display, that exhibit was indefinitely postponed because of budgetary problems. Dierbeck, memorandum to Quiddy, August 12, 1971, ibid.

Old Red, however, is on display today in the National Museum of American History. The machine is identified as Item 405, "Mechanical cotton picker, International Harvester Model H-10-H, single-row, spindle cotton picker of 1942. Gift of Producers Cotton Oil Co., Fresno, California, through International Harvester Corporation." John T. Schlebecker, *Agricultural Implements and Machines in the Collection of the National Museum of History and Technology* (Washington, D.C.: Smithsonian Institution Press, 1972), 48. The museum was renamed the National Museum of American History in 1980.

However, as of July 1999, the Old Red exhibit contained the following state-ment: "John and Mack Rust, brother inventors from Arkansas, were wary of replac-ing farmers with machines. Still, they developed a reliable spindle machine in the late 1930s. During World War II, International Harvester Company successfully developed a mechanical cotton picker on the Hopson plantation near Clarksdale, Mississippi, and by the end of the war had machines on the market. Within two decades hand-picking of cotton had virtually disappeared and millions of farmers were forced off the land." This revision omitted any mention of Producers Cotton Oil Company, while giving credit not only to the Hopsons but also to IH and the Rust brothers.

18. In 1979 Old Red was designated an American Society of Agricultural Engineers Historic Landmark. "Designate 'Old Red' as ASAE Historic Landmark," *Agricultural Engineering* 60 (March 1979): 17–18. J. W. Nance Jr. to Arthur R. McQuiddy, July 31, 1970, IHC Collection.

19. Daniel J. Boorstin, *The Americans: The National Experience* (New York: Random House, 1965), 57–58. See John Jewkes, David Sawers, and Richard Stillerman, *The Sources of Invention* (New York: St. Martin's Press, 1959).

20. Harris Pearson Smith and Lambert Henry Wilkes, *Farm Machinery and Equipment,* 6th ed. (New York: McGraw-Hill, 1976), 344–66.

21. For a comparison between smooth and barbed spindles, see Wesley F. Buchele, *Mechanized Production Cotton, II. Cotton Pickers and Wheel Fenders,* Mimeograph Series No. 4 (Fayetteville: Arkansas Agricultural Experiment Station, September 1950).

22. John Gunther, *Inside U.S.A.* (New York: Harper and Brothers, 1947), 793; "Mr. Little Ol' Rust," *Fortune* 46 (December 1952): 150–52, 198–205. Reprinted as "John Rust Brings Home the Cotton," *Readers' Digest* 62 (April 1953): 73–77; *Time* 63 (February 1, 1954): 70; *New York Times,* January 22, 1954; *Little Rock Arkansas Gazette,* January 21, 1954; *Pine Bluff (Ark.) Commercial,* January 21, 1954; James H. Street, *The New Revolution in the Cotton Economy: Mechanization and Its Consequences* (Chapel Hill: University of North Carolina Press, 1957), 123; Jewkes, Sawers, and Stillerman, *The Sources of Invention,* 286; Clarence F. Kelly, "Mechanical Harvesting," *Scientific American* 217 (August 1967): 56–57; Richard B. Morris, ed., *Encyclopedia of American History: Bicentennial Edition* (New York: Harper and Row, 1976), 799; *Dictionary of American History,* rev. ed. 8 vols. (New York: Charles Scribner's Sons, 1976), 1:35; *Concise Dictionary of American Biography,* 5th ed. (New York: Charles Scribner's Sons, 1997), 1111. Joseph Nathan Kane, *Famous First Facts: A Record of First Happenings, Discoveries, and Inventions in American History,* 4th ed. (New York: H. W. Wilson Co., 1981), 204. In the internet database version, *Famous First Facts* states that the "First mechanical cotton picker of importance was the Rust Cotton Picker, a horse-drawn picker built by John Daniel Rust in Weatherford, TX, in 1928." See http://vweb.hwwilsonweb.com/. See also David Halberstam, *The Fifties* (New York: Villard Books, 1993), 446.

23. Harris Pearson Smith and Lambert Henry Wilkes, *Farm Machinery and Equipment,* 6th ed. (New York: McGraw-Hill, 1976), 344–66. Gavin Wright, "Agriculture in the South," in *Encyclopedia of American Economic History: Studies of the Principal Movements and Ideas,* 3 vols., ed. Glenn Porter (New York: Charles Scribner's Sons, 1980), 1:383; Gary Cross and Rick Szostak, *Technology and American Society: A History* (Englewood Cliffs, N.J.: Prentice Hall, 1995), 293; Wayne D. Rasmussen, "The Mechanization of Agriculture," *Scientific American* 247 (September 1982): 77–89; R. Douglas Hurt, *Agricultural Technology in the Twentieth Century* (Manhattan, Kans.: Sunflower University Press, 1991). R. Douglas Hurt, "Cotton Pickers and Strippers," *Journal of the West* 30 (April 1991): 30–42.

24. R. Douglas Hurt, *Agricultural Technology in the Twentieth Century* (Manhattan, Kans.: Sunflower University Press, 1991); and Hurt, "Cotton Pickers and Strippers," *Journal of the West* 30 (April 1991): 30–42.

25. Raymond Arsenault, "The End of the Long Hot Summer: The Air Conditioner and Southern Culture," *Journal of Southern History* 50 (November 1984): 597–628.

26. David C. Roller and Robert W. Twyman, eds., *Encyclopedia of Southern History* (Baton Rouge: Louisiana State University Press, 1979); and Charles Reagan Wilson and William Ferris, eds., *Encyclopedia of Southern Culture* (Chapel Hill: University of North Carolina Press, 1989).

27. See Gilbert C. Fite, *American Farmers: The New Minority* (Bloomington: Indiana University Press, 1981).

28. On J. I. Case, see Stewart Hall Holbrook, *Machines of Plenty: Pioneering in American Agriculture* (New York: Macmillan, 1955).

29. *Implement and Tractor* 104 (March 1989): 22; *Commercial Appeal,* July 18, 1997, February 22, 1998; "Big News for Farmers: Six-Row Cotton Picker," *Memphis Business Journal* 19 (August 18, 1997): 6; "John Deere Introduces World's First 6-Row Production Cotton Picker," PR Newswire, August 13, 1997.

30. Frank H. Maier, "An Economic Analysis of Adoption of the Mechanical Cotton Harvester" (Ph.D. diss., University of Chicago, 1969), 5, 260.

31. Ibid., 100.

32. Charles H. Wendel, *The Allis-Chalmers Story* (Sarasota, Fla.: Crestline Publishing, 1988), 90–91; and Norm Swinford, *Allis-Chalmers Farm Equipment, 1914–1985* (St. Joseph, Mich.: American Society of Agricultural Engineers, 1994), 354–63.

33. Interview with G. E. Powell, chairman of the board, Ben Pearson, Inc., Pine Bluff, Arkansas, June 5, 1992.

34. *Commercial Appeal,* March 13, April 26, 1970; *Delta Farm Press,* April 9, September 10, 1970; *California-Arizona Cotton,* November 1970, 14; Ed Wilborn, "Ideas—for Cutting Cotton Costs," *Progressive Farmer* 8G (January 1971): 8a.

35. These schools included the University of Arkansas at Fayetteville; Arkansas A & M College, now the University of Arkansas at Monticello; Arkansas AM & N College, a predominately black school known today as the University of Arkansas at Pine Bluff; and Mississippi A & M College, now called Mississippi State University.

36. J. D. Rust to Marshall and Marie [Wingfield], June 1, 1953, Marshall Wingfield Collection, box 1, folder 3, Special Collections, University of Memphis Library, Memphis, Tennessee. Thelma Rust to Marshall and Marie [Wingfield], June 21, 1954, Marshall Wingfield Collection, box 1, folder 3, ibid. See also *Pine Bluff (Ark.) Commercial,* October 8, 1952; *Memphis (Tenn.) Press-Scimitar,* June 15, 1953; *Little Rock Arkansas Gazette,* May 25, 1953, June 10, 1954. On his suit against Ben Pearson, see Ben "Pearson, Inc. v. The John Rust Company," *Arkansas Reports, Cases Determined in the Supreme Court of Arkansas, January 1954—July 1954,* vol. 223 (Little Rock: Democrat Printing and Lithographing Co., 1955), 697–705.

37. *Pine Bluff Commercial,* January 21, 1954; *New York Times,* January 22, 1954. He is buried in Graceland Cemetery at Pine Bluff, Arkansas.

38. *Who Was Who in America, 1961–1968* (Chicago: Marquis-Who's Who, 1968), 4:821.

39. For recent views, see Anthony P. Dunbar, *Delta Time: A Journey through Mississippi* (New York: Pantheon Books, 1990); and Anthony Walton, *Mississippi: An American Journey* (New York: Knopf, 1996).

40. Merle C. Prunty Jr., "The Renaissance of the Southern Plantation," *Geographical Review* 45 (October 1955): 459–91; Charles S. Aiken, "The Decline of Sharecropping in the Lower Mississippi Valley," *Geoscience and Man* 19 (June 30, 1978): 151–61. For a similar view, see Harald A. Petersen and Arthur F. Raper, *The Cotton Plantation in Transition,* Bulletin No. 508 (Starkville: Mississippi Agricultural Experiment Station, January 1954).

41. Charles S. Aiken, *The Cotton Plantation South since the Civil War* (Baltimore: Johns Hopkins University Press, 1998), 374–75.

42. David L. Cohn said, "The Mississippi Delta begins in the lobby of the Peabody Hotel in Memphis and ends on Catfish Row in Vicksburg." See James C. Cobb, ed., *The Mississippi Delta and the World: The Memoirs of David L. Cohn* (Baton Rouge: Louisiana State University Press, 1995), xi. Cohn referred to only the Mississippi Delta, overlooking the Arkansas and Louisiana deltas.

43. Benjamin and Christina Schwarz, "Mississippi Monte Carlo," *Atlantic Monthly* 277 (January 1996): 67–82.

44. Ibid., 74.

45. U.S. Bureau of the Census, *County and City Data Book: 1994* (Washington, D.C.: GPO, 1994), item 85, p. 303.

46. Jack E. White, "The Poorest Place in America," *Time* 144 (August 15, 1994): 34–36. See also Damon Nash, "Lake Providence, Louisiana: Long Road Back," *Louisiana Life* (spring 1993): 57–62.

47. *Little Rock Arkansas Democrat-Gazette,* January 4, 1998.

48. *Little Rock Arkansas Gazette,* February 25, May 10, 13, 14, October 13, 1990. For political reasons, the commission defined the Delta as consisting of most of Arkansas, Louisiana, and Mississippi, not the alluvial land on either side of the river.

49. Schwarz, "Mississippi Monte Carlo," 67–82.

50. James C. Cobb, *The Most Southern Place on Earth: The Mississippi Delta and the Roots of Regional Identity* (New York: Oxford University Press, 1992), 273.

51. Schwarz, "Mississippi Monte Carlo," 78.

52. Roger Beardwood, "The Southern Roots of Urban Crisis," *Fortune* 78 (August 1968): 80–87, 151–52, 155–56, 158. The quotation is from page 156. See also Ben H. Bagdikian, "The Black Immigrant," *Saturday Evening Post* 240 (July 15, 1967): 25–29, 64–68 and "When Negroes Move North," *U.S. News and World Report* 40 (April 13, 1956): 29–33.

53. Quoted in Charles S. Aiken, "The Decline of Sharecropping in the Lower Mississippi River Valley," *Geoscience and Man* 19 (June 30, 1978): 164.

54. Nicholas Lemann, "The Origins of the Underclass," *Atlantic Monthly* 257 (June 1986): 31–43, 47–55. The quotation is from page 35.

55. William Julius Wilson, *The Truly Disadvantaged: The Inner City, the Underclass, and Public Policy* (Chicago: University of Chicago Press, 1987), 55. See his appendix, "Urban Poverty and Migration," 165–87.

56. David Whitman, "The Great Sharecropper Success Story," *Public Interest* 104 (summer 1991): 3–21.

57. *Report of the National Advisory Commission on Civil Disorders* (New York: Bantam, 1968), 111.

58. See David L. Langford, *Going Home: Blacks Migrate from Northern Cities to Southland* (New York: Beacon, 1994).

59. *Arkansas Democrat-Gazette,* March 19, 1998.

60. Robert Palmer, *Deep Blues* (New York: Viking, 1995).

61. William Alexander Percy, *Lanterns on the Levee: Recollections of a Planter's Son* (Baton Rouge: Louisiana State University Press, 1985). A. A. Knopf originally published this volume in 1941. On Percy, see William F. Holmes, "William Alexander Percy and the Bourbon Era in the Yazoo-Mississippi Delta," *Mississippi Quarterly* 26 (winter 1973): 71–87. See Willie Morris, *North toward Home* (New York: Houghton Mifflin, 1967). On David L. Cohn, see "Lament for the South That Is No More," *New York Times Magazine,* January 22, 1950; *The Life and Times of King Cotton* (New York: Oxford University Press, 1956); *The Mississippi Delta and the World: The Memoirs of David L. Cohn* (Baton Rouge: Louisiana State University Press, 1995); and *Where I Was Born and Raised* (Boston: Houghton, Mifflin Co., 1948).

62. John B. Currie, Wilmot, Arkansas, interview with the author, December 17, 1996. A 1983 study of Texas tenants "revealed that farmers who rented most or all of their farmland had the largest and most productive farms, used better farming practices, and were more involved in community affairs" than farm owners. Don E. Albrecht and John K. Thomas, "Farm Tenure: A Retest of Conventional Knowledge," *Rural Sociology* 51 (spring 1986): 18–30.

63. Paul H. Williams, "The Rise and Fall of the Great Plantations," *Arkansas Times* 9 (July 1983): 86–93.

64. *Arkansas Gazette,* April 23, 1990.

Appendix

1. Everett S. Lee et al., *Population Redistribution and Economic Growth, United States, 1870–1950: Methodological Considerations and Reference Tables.* 3 vols. (Philadelphia: American Philosophical Society, 1957).

2. Ibid., 1:15–16.

3. Neil Fligstein, *Going North: Migration of Blacks and Whites from the South, 1900–1950* (New York: Academic Press, 1981), also uses this method to estimate black migration from 1900 to 1950. However, he uses state survivor ratios rather than national survivor ratios. For the period 1950–70, Arkansas, Louisiana, and Mississippi cannot be considered closed populations. As a result, national survivor ratios are used in the present analysis.

Selected Bibliography

Manuscript Collections

Ben Pearson, Inc., Scrapbooks, Quest Corporation, Pine Bluff, Ark.

Cash, William, Oral History No. 197, Delta State University Archives, Cleveland, Miss.

Cox, Allen Eugene, Papers, Special Collections Department, Mitchell Memorial Library, Mississippi State University, Starkville, Miss.

Deere Archives, Deere and Company, Moline, Ill.

Delta and Pine Land Company Records, Special Collections Department, Mitchell Memorial Library, Mississippi State University Library, Starkville, Miss.

Harring, P. P., Papers, National Museum of American History, Washington, D.C.

McCormick International Harvester Collection, 1881–1985, State Historical Society of Wisconsin, Madison, Wis.

Record Group 16, Records of the Office of the Secretary of Agriculture, National Archives, Washington, D.C.

Record Group 83, Records of the Bureau of Agricultural Economics, National Archives, Washington, D.C.

Record Group 211, Records of the War Manpower Commission, National Archives, Washington, D.C.

Record Group 224, Records of the Office of Labor (War Food Administration), National Archives, Washington, D.C.

Record Unit 240, Division of Agriculture and Mining Records, Smithsonian Institution Archives, Arts and Industries Building, Washington, D.C.

Rust, John, Papers, 1933–1953, Mississippi Valley Collection, University of Memphis Library, Memphis, Tenn.

Southern Tenant Farmers Union Papers, 1934–1940, Microfilming Corporation of America, 1971.

Wingfield, Marshall, Papers, 1939–1963, Mississippi Valley Collection, University of Memphis Library, Memphis, Tenn.

Newspapers

Little Rock Arkansas Gazette
Jackson (Miss.) Daily News
Memphis (Tenn.) Commercial Appeal

Pine Bluff (Ark.) Commercial
Pine Bluff (Ark.) Daily Graphic

Privately Printed Pamphlets

"50 Seasons of Growing Cotton Pickers." Ankey, Iowa: John Deere Des Moines Works, 1999.

"Growing Prosperity: The Story of the South's Best Known Farmer." Wilson, Ark.: Breeding and Research Division, Lee Wilson and Co., 1930.

Hopson, Harold H., Jr. "Mechanization of a Delta Cotton Plantation as Applied to Hopson Planting Company." Clarksdale, Miss.: Hopson Planting Company, 1944.

"International Harvester's Great New Cotton Picker: Now in Quantity Production." Chicago, Ill.: International Harvester Company, ca. 1949.

"A Pictorial History of the Development of the Ben Pearson Rust Cotton Picker." [Shreveport, La.]: Ben Pearson, Inc., [1962].

"The Rust Cotton Picker: Its Origin and Development." Pine Bluff, Ark.: John Rust Co., 1951.

"30 Seasons of Better Picking with John Deere." Moline, Ill.: Deere and Company, 1979.

Interviews

Ayres, Stanley, Leland, Miss., January 7, 1997.
Currie, John B., Wilmot, Ark., December 17, 1996.
Frizzell, J. T., Star City, Ark., March 2, 1977.
Frizzell, Steve, Star City, Ark., December 12, 1996; by telephone, February 19, 1997, August 26, 1999.
Nash, Jere, Jr., Greenville, Miss., January 7, 1997.
Powell, G. E., Pine Bluff, Ark., June 5, 1992.
Santucci, James, Leland, Miss., May 19, 1999.

Theses and Dissertations

Brannen, Claude O. "The Relation of Land Tenure to Plantation Organization with Developments since 1920." Ph.D. diss., Columbia University, Fayetteville, Ark., 1928.

Dong, Zhengkai. "From Postbellum Plantation to Modern Agribusiness: A History of the Delta and Pine Land Company." Ph.D. diss., Purdue University, 1993.

Ganger, David Wayne. "The Impact of Mechanization and the New Deal's Acreage

Reduction Programs on Cotton Farmers during the 1930s." Ph.D. diss., University of California, Los Angeles, 1973.

Heinicke, Craig W. "Black Migration from the Rural American South and the Mechanization of Agriculture." Ph.D. diss., University of Toronto, 1991.

Maier, Frank H. "An Economic Analysis of Adoption of the Mechanical Cotton Picker." Ph.D. diss., University of Chicago, 1969.

Musoke, Moses Senkumba. "Technical Change in Cotton Production in the United States, 1925–1960." Ph.D. diss., University of Wisconsin, Madison, 1976.

Whatley, Warren C. "Institutional Change and Mechanization in the Cotton South: The Tractorization of Cotton Farming." Ph.D. diss., Stanford University, 1983.

Wilmans, Lucy. "The AAA and the Arkansas Cotton Farmer," seminar thesis, no. 25, University of Arkansas School of Business, Fayetteville, 1935.

State Government Publications

Arkansas Employment Security Division. *Arkansas Agricultural Report, 1954–1978.* Little Rock, Ark., 1955–79.

Louisiana Employment Service. *Louisiana Farm Labor Bulletin, 1954–1961.* Baton Rouge, La., 1954–1961.

Mississippi Employment Security Commission. *Mississippi Farm Labor, 1953–1961.* Jackson, Miss., 1954–62.

Books and Articles

Aiken, Charles S. "The Decline of Sharecropping in the Lower Mississippi River Valley." *Geoscience and Man* 19 (June 30, 1978): 151–65.

———. *The Cotton Plantation South since the Civil War.* Baltimore: Johns Hopkins University Press, 1998.

Albrecht, Don E., and John K. Thomas. "Farm Tenure: A Retest of Conventional Knowledge." *Rural Sociology* 51 (spring 1986): 18–30.

Albrecht, Don E., and Steve H. Murdock. *The Sociology of U.S. Agriculture: An Ecological Perspective.* Ames: Iowa State University Press, 1990.

Alexander, Donald Crichton. *The Arkansas Plantation, 1920–1942.* New Haven: Yale University Press, 1943.

Alston, Lee J. "Tenure Choice in Southern Agriculture, 1930–1960." *Explorations in Economic History* 18 (July 1981): 211–32.

Alston, Lee J., and Joseph P. Ferrie. "Labor Costs, Paternalism, and Loyalty in Southern Agriculture: A Constraint on the Growth of the Welfare State." *Journal of Economic History* 45 (March 1985): 95–117.

———. "Paternalism in Agricultural Labor Contracts in the U.S. South: Implications for the Growth of the Welfare State." *American Economic Review* 83 (September 1993): 852–76.

———. "The Bracero Program and Farm Labor Legislation in World War II." In *The Sinews of War: Essays on the Economic History of World War II*, ed. Geofrey T. Mills and Hugh Rockoff, 129–49. Ames: Iowa State University Press, 1993.

Alston, Lee J., and Kyle D. Kauffman. "Agricultural Chutes and Ladders: New Estimates of Sharecroppers and 'True Tenants' in the South, 1900–1920." *Journal of Economic History* 57 (June 1997): 464–75.

Alston, Lee J., and Robert Higgs. "Contractual Mix in Southern Agriculture since the Civil War: Facts, Hypotheses, and Tests." *Journal of Economic History* 42 (July 1982): 327–53.

Arsenault, Raymond. "The End of the Long Hot Summer: The Air Conditioner and Southern Culture." *Journal of Southern History* 50 (November 1984): 597–628.

Bagdikian, Ben H. "The Black Immigrants." *Saturday Evening Post* 240 (July 15, 1967): 25–29, 64–68.

Baldwin, Sidney. *Poverty and Politics: The Rise and Decline of the Farm Security Administration.* Chapel Hill: University of North Carolina Press, 1968.

Bealle, James S. "Dixie Needs No Cotton Picker." *Forum* 97 (April 1937): 224–29.

Bertrand, Alvin L. "Some Social Implications of the Mechanization of Southern Agriculture." *Southwestern Social Science Quarterly* 31 (September 1950): 121–29.

Biles, Roger. *The South and the New Deal.* Lexington: University Press of Kentucky, 1994.

Bode, Frederick A., and Donald E. Ginter. *Farm Tenancy and the Census in Georgia.* Athens: University of Georgia Press, 1987.

Bogue, Allen G. *From Prairie to Corn Belt: Farming on the Illinois and Iowa Prairies in the Nineteenth Century.* Reprint, Ames: Iowa State University Press, 1994.

Brandfon, Robert L. *Cotton Kingdom of the New South: A History of the Yazoo Mississippi Delta from Reconstruction to the Twentieth Century.* Cambridge, Mass.: Harvard University Press, 1967.

Brown, Harry Bates, and Jacob Osborn Ware. *Cotton.* 3d ed. New York: McGraw Hill, 1958.

Brown, Phillips H., and John M. Peterson. "The Exodus from Arkansas." *Arkansas Economist* 2 (winter 1960): 10–15.

Bruton, Paul W. "Cotton Acreage Reduction and the Tenant Farmer." *Law and Contemporary Problems* 1 (June 1934): 275–79.

Bryan, Jack. "The Rust Foundation." *Southern Workman* 67 (December 1938): 361–66.

Burford, Roger L. "The Federal Cotton Programs and Farm Labor Force
    Adjustments." *Southern Economic Journal* 33 (October 1966): 223–36.
Calavita, Kitty. *Inside the State: The Bracero Program, Immigration, and the I.N.S.*
    New York: Routledge, 1992.
Carlson, Oliver. "Revolution in Cotton." *American Mercury* 34 (February 1935):
    129–36. Reprinted in *Readers' Digest* 26 (March 1935): 13–16.
Cobb, James C. "'Somebody Done Nailed Us on the Cross': Federal Farm and
    Welfare Policy and the Civil Rights Movement in the Mississippi Delta." *Journal
    of American History* 77 (December 1990): 912–36.
———. *Industrialization and Southern Society, 1877–1984.* Lexington: University
    Press of Kentucky, 1984.
———. *The Most Southern Place on Earth: The Mississippi Delta and the Roots of
    Regional Identity.* New York: Oxford University Press, 1992.
Cobb, James C., and Michael V. Namorato, eds. *The New Deal and the South.*
    Jackson: University Press of Mississippi, 1984.
Cohen, William. *At Freedom's Edge: Black Mobility and the Southern White Quest for
    Racial Control, 1861–1915.* Baton Rouge: Louisiana State University Press, 1991.
Cohn, David L. "Lament for the South That Is No More." *New York Times
    Magazine,* January 22, 1950, 14–41.
———. "White Shadow over Dixie: Too Much Cotton." *New York Times Magazine,*
    November 13, 1955, pp. 17, 42, 44, 47.
———. *The Life and Times of King Cotton.* New York: Oxford University Press, 1956.
———. *The Mississippi Delta and the World: The Memoirs of David L. Cohn.* Baton
    Rouge: Louisiana State University Press, 1995.
———. *Where I Was Born and Raised.* Boston: Houghton, Mifflin Co., 1948.
Conrad, David Eugene. *The Forgotten Farmers: The Story of Sharecroppers in the
    New Deal.* Urbana: University of Illinois Press, 1965.
Cross, Gary, and Rick Szostak. *Technology and American Society: A History.*
    Englewood Cliffs, N.J.: Prentice Hall, 1995.
Crown, William H., and Leonard F. Wheat. "State Per Capita Income Convergence
    since 1950: Sharecropping's Demise and Other Influences." *Journal of
    Regional Science* 35 (November 1995): 527–52.
Daniel, Pete. "Going among Strangers: Southern Reactions to World War II."
    Journal of American History 77 (December 1990): 886–911.
———. "The Transformation of the Rural South, 1930 to the Present." *Agricultural
    History* 55 (July 1981): 231–48.
———. *Breaking the Land: The Transformation of Cotton, Tobacco, and Rice
    Cultures since 1880.* Urbana and Chicago: University of Illinois Press, 1985.
Daniels, Jonathan. *A Southerner Discovers the South.* New York: Da Capo Press,
    1970. Originally published in 1938.

Day, Richard H. "The Economics of Technological Change and the Demise of the Sharecropper." *American Economic Review* 57 (June 1967): 427–49.

Drucker, Peter F. "Exit King Cotton." *Harper's* 192 (May 1946): 473–80.

Dunbar, Anthony P. *Delta Time: A Journey through Mississippi.* New York: Pantheon Books, 1990.

Dunn, Read P. *Mr. Oscar: A Story of the Early Years in the Life and Times of Oscar Johnston and of His Efforts in Organizing the National Cotton Council.* Memphis, Tenn.: National Cotton Council of America, 1991.

Dunnahoo, Patrick. *Cotton, Cornbread, Cape Jasmines: Early Day Life on the Plantations of the Arkansas River Delta.* Benton, Ark.: P. Dunnahoo, 1985.

Eldridge, Hope T. "Internal Migration in Peace and War." *American Sociological Review* 12 (February 1947): 27–39.

Eldridge, Hope T., and Dorothy S. Thomas. *Population Redistribution and Economic Growth,* vol. 3. Philadelphia: American Philosophical Society, 1964.

Farley, Reynolds. *Growth of the Black Population: A Study in Demographic Trends.* Chicago: Markham, 1970.

Ferleger, Louis. "Sharecropping Contracts in the Late-Nineteenth-Century South." *Agricultural History* 67 (summer 1993): 31–46.

———, ed. *Agriculture and National Development: Views on the Nineteenth Century.* Ames: Iowa University Press, 1990.

Fite, Gilbert C. "Mechanization of Cotton Production since World War II." *Agricultural History* 54 (January 1980): 190–207.

———. "Recent Changes in the Mechanization of Cotton Production in the United States." *Agricultural History* 24 (January 1950): 19–28.

———. "Southern Agriculture since the Civil War: An Overview." *Agricultural History* 53 (January 1979): 3–21.

———. "Voluntary Attempts to Reduce Cotton Acreage in the South, 1914–1933." *Journal of Southern History* 14 (November 1948): 481–99.

———. *Cotton Fields No More: Southern Agriculture, 1865–1980.* Lexington: University of Kentucky Press, 1984.

Fleisig, Heywood. "Mechanizing the Cotton Harvest in the Nineteenth Century South." *Journal of Economic History* 25 (December 1965): 704–6.

Fligstein, Neil. *Going North: Migration of Blacks and Whites from the South, 1900–1950.* New York: Academic Press, 1981.

Fornari, Harry D. "The Big Change: Cotton to Soybeans." *Agricultural History* 53 (January 1979): 245–53.

Frey, Fred C., and T. Lynn Smith. "The Influence of the AAA Cotton Program upon the Tenant, Croppers and Laborer." *Rural Sociology* 1 (December 1936): 483–505.

Garrett, Martin A., Jr. "The Mule in Southern Agriculture: A Requiem." *Explorations in Economic History* 50 (December 1990): 925–30.

Grubbs, Donald H. *Cry from the Cotton: The Southern Tenant Farmers' Union and the New Deal.* Chapel Hill: University of North Carolina Press, 1971.

Hagen, C. R. "Twenty-Five Years of Cotton Picker Development." *Agricultural Engineering* 32 (November 1951): 593–96, 599.

Hamburger, Tom. "Dramatic Population Reduction Inspires Technological Changes." *Arkansas Gazette,* May 19, 1977.

———. "Thousands Forced to Leave Land." *Arkansas Gazette,* May 16, 1977.

Hamilton, C. Horace. "The Negro Leaves the South." *Demography* 1 (May 1964): 273–95.

———. "The Social Effects of Recent Trends in the Mechanization of Agriculture." *Rural Sociology* 4 (March 1939): 3–19.

Hammond, Matthew B. "Correspondence of Eli Whitney Relative to the Invention of the Cotton Gin." *American Historical Review* 3 (October 1897): 90–127.

———. "Southern Farmer and the Cotton Question." *Political Science Quarterly* 12 (September 1897): 450–75.

Harrison, Alferdteen, ed. *Black Exodus: The Great Migration from the American South.* Jackson: University Press of Mississippi, 1991.

Heinicke, Craig. "African-American Migration and Mechanized Cotton Harvesting, 1950–1960." *Explorations in Economic History* 31 (October 1994): 501–20.

———. "The Federal Soil Bank, the Decline of Cotton, and the Demise of the Southern Plantation in the 1950s." Paper prepared for the ASSA Meeting/Cliometric Society, New Orleans, La., January 1997.

———. *John Deere Tractors, 1918–1987.* St. Joseph, Mich.: American Society of Agricultural Engineers, 1987.

Henderson, J. Lewis. "In the Cotton Delta." *Survey Graphic* 36 (January 1947): 48–51, 108–11.

Higgs, Robert. "The Boll Weevil, the Cotton Economy, and Black Migration, 1910–1930." *Agricultural History* 50 (April 1975): 335–50.

———. *Competition and Coercion: Blacks in the American Economy, 1865–1914.* Cambridge: Cambridge University Press, 1977.

———. *The Transformation of the American Economy, 1865–1914: An Essay in Interpretation.* New York: Wiley, 1971.

Hoffsommer, Harold. "The AAA and the Sharecropper." *Social Forces* 13 (May 1935): 495–502.

Holbrook, Stewart Hall. *Machines of Plenty; Pioneering in American Agriculture.* New York: Macmillan, 1955.

Holley, Donald. "The Second Great Emancipation: The Rust Cotton Picker and How It Changed Arkansas." *Arkansas Historical Quarterly* 52 (spring 1993): 44–77.

———. *Uncle Sam's Farmers: The New Deal Communities in the Lower Mississippi Valley.* Urbana: University of Illinois Press, 1975.

Holmes, William F. "Whitecapping: Agrarian Violence in Mississippi, 1902–1906." *Journal of Southern History* 35 (May 1969): 165–85.

Holt, James S. "Labor Market Policies and Institutions in an Industrializing Agriculture." *American Journal of Agricultural Economics* 64 (December 1982): 999–1006.

Hon, Ralph C. "The Rust Cotton Picker." *Southern Economic Journal* 3 (April 1937): 381–91.

Honeycutt, Tom. "The Second Great Emancipator: Eccentric Inventor John Rust Changed the Face of Modern Agriculture." *Arkansas Times* 11 (February 1985): 76–78, 81–82.

Hughes, Thomas P. *American Genesis: A Century of Invention and Technological Enthusiasm, 1870–1970.* New York: Viking, 1989.

Hurley, F. Jack. *Portrait of a Decade: Roy Stryker and the Development of Documentary Photography in the Thirties.* Baton Rouge: Louisiana State University Press, 1972.

Hurt, R. Douglas. "P. P. Haring: Innovator in Cotton Harvesting Technology." *Agricultural History* 53 (summer 1979): 300–307.

———. "Cotton Pickers and Strippers." *Journal of the West* 30 (April 1991): 30–42.

———, ed. *The Rural South since World War II.* Baton Rouge: Louisiana State University Press, 1998.

Jamieson, Stuart. "Labor Unions in American Agriculture." *Monthly Labor Review* 62 (January 1946): 25–36.

Jaynes, Gerald David. *Branches without Roots: Genesis of the Black Working Class in the American South, 1862–1882.* New York: Oxford University Press, 1986.

Johnson, Charles S., Edwin R. Embree, and Will W. Alexander. *The Collapse of Cotton Tenancy: A Summary of Field Studies and Statistical Surveys, 1933–35.* Chapel Hill: University of North Carolina Press, 1935.

Johnson, Daniel M., and Rex R. Campbell. *Black Migration in America: A Social Demographic History.* Durham: Duke University Press, 1981.

Johnson, H. Thomas. *Agricultural Depression in the 1920s: Economic Fact or Statistical Artifact?* New York: Garland Publishing Co., 1985.

Johnston, E. A. "The Evolution of the Mechanical Cotton Harvester. *Agricultural Engineering* 19 (September 1938): 383–85, 388.

Johnston, Oscar. "Will the Machine Ruin the South?" *Saturday Evening Post* 219 (May 31, 1947): 36–37, 94–95, 98.

Kester, Howard. *Revolt among the Sharecroppers.* New York: Covici-Friede, 1936.

Kirby, Jack Temple. "The Southern Exodus, 1910–1960: A Primer for Historians." *Journal of Southern History* 49 (November 1983): 585–600.

———. "The Transformation of Southern Plantations, c. 1920–1960." *Agricultural History* 57 (July 1983): 257.

———. *Rural Worlds Lost: The American South, 1920–1960.* Baton Rouge: Louisiana University Press, 1987.

Lange, Dorothea, and Paul Schuster Taylor. *An American Exodus: A Record of Human Erosion.* New York: Reynal and Hitchcock, 1939.

Langford, David L. *Going Home: Blacks Migrate from Northern Cities to Southland.* New York: Beacon, 1994.

Leach, Henry Goddard. "Humanizing Machines: The Rust Cotton Picker." *Forum* 96 (August 1936): 49–50.

Leahy, Michael. "A Drain on the Delta." *Little Rock Arkansas Democrat-Gazette,* December 31, 1995.

Lemann, Nicholas. "The Origins of the Underclass." *Atlantic Monthly* 257 (June 1986): 31–43, 47–55.

———. *The Promised Land: The Great Black Migration and How It Changed America.* New York: Alfred A. Knopf, 1991.

Leveritt, Mara. "Losing Ground: The Farm Crisis Hits Home in East Arkansas." *Arkansas Times* 11 (May 1985): 50–56, 68–72.

Lewis, E. E. "Black Cotton Farmers and the AAA." *Opportunity* 13 (March 1935): 72–74.

Maharidge, Dale, and Michael Williamson. *And Their Children after Them: The Legacy of Let Us Now Praise Famous Men, James Agee, Walker Evans, and the Rise and Fall of Cotton in the South.* New York: Pantheon Books, 1989.

Mandle, Jay R. *The Roots of Black Poverty: The Southern Plantation Economy after the Civil War.* Durham: Duke University Press, 1978.

Marks, Carole. "Black Workers and the Great Migration North." *Phylon* 46 (June 1985): 148–61.

———. *Farewell—We're Good and Gone: The Great Black Migration.* Bloomington: Indiana University Press, 1989.

Mathewson, R., and R. Mathewson. "Cotton Picker Opens a Revolution in the South." *Science Illustrated* 2 (March 1947): 86–89.

Mertz, Paul E. *New Deal Policy and Southern Rural Poverty.* Baton Rouge: Louisiana State University Press, 1978.

Metzler, William H. "Population Movement in Arkansas." *Arkansas Gazette Sunday Magazine,* April 7, 14, 21, 1940.

Mezerik, A. G. "Dixie in Black and White: King Cotton Strikes Again." *Nation* 164 (June 21, 1947): 740–741.

Mitchell, H. L. *Mean Things Happening in This Land: The Life and Times of H. L. Mitchell, Co-Founder of the Southern Tenant Farmers Union.* Montclair, N.J.: Allanheld, Osmun, 1979.

Moneyhon, Carl H. *Arkansas and the New South, 1874–1929.* Fayetteville: University of Arkansas Press, 1997.

———. *The Impact of the Civil War and Reconstruction on Arkansas: Persistence in the Midst of Ruin.* Baton Rouge: Louisiana State University Press, 1994.

Morse, J. Mitchell. "Revolution in Cotton." *New Republic* 115 (August 19, 1946): 192–94.

Musoke, Moses Senkumba. "Mechanizing Cotton Production in the American South: The Tractor, 1915–1960." *Explorations in Economic History* 18 (October 1981): 347–75.

Musoke, Moses Senkumba, and Alan L. Olmstead. "The Rise of the Cotton Industry in California: A Comparative Perspective." *Journal of Economic History* 42 (June 1982): 385–412.

Nelson, Lawrence J. "Oscar Johnston, the New Deal, and the Cotton Subsidy Payments Controversy, 1936–1937." *Journal of Southern History* 40 (August 1974): 399–416.

———. "Welfare Capitalism on a Mississippi Plantation in the Great Depression." *Journal of Southern History* 50 (May 1984): 225–50.

———. *King Cotton's Advocate: Oscar G. Johnston and the New Deal.* Knoxville: University of Tennessee Press, 1999.

"New Gin May Be Missing Link between Mechanical Cotton Picker and Spinning Mill." *Business Week,* January 22, 1938, 52.

"New Models of the Rust Cotton Picker." *Business Week,* September 3, 1938, 24.

Nourse, Edwin G., Joseph S. Davis, and John D. Black. *Three Years of the Agricultural Adjustment Administration.* New York: DaCapo Press, 1971. Originally published in 1937.

Novak, J. L., et al. "The Effects of Mechanical Cotton Harvesting Technology on Southern Piedmont Cotton Production, 1896–1991." *Agricultural History* 69 (spring 1995): 349–66.

O'Hare, William. "Report on a Multiple Regression Method for Making Population Estimates." *Demography* 13 (August 1976): 369–79.

Page, Arthur W. "A Cotton-Harvester at Last." *World's Work* 21 (December 1910): 13748–13760.

Patterson, Ruth Polk. "Movin' on up the Road: Black Migration from Fordyce, Arkansas, to Las Vegas, Nevada." Little Rock: R. P. Patterson, 1984.

Peterson, Willis, and Yoav Kislev. "The Cotton Harvester in Retrospect: Labor Displacement or Replacement?" *Journal of Economic History* 46 (March 1986): 199–216.

Petrie, John Clarence. "Rust Foundation to Aid Labor." *Christian Century* 55 (October 5, 1938): 1210.

Pritchett, Merrill R., and William L. Shea. "The Afrika Korps in Arkansas, 1943–1946." *Arkansas Historical Quarterly* 37 (spring 1978): 16–22.

Prunty, Merle C., Jr. "The Renaissance of the Southern Plantation." *Geographical Review* 45 (October 1955): 459–91.

Pursell, Carroll W., Jr. "Government and Technology in the Great Depression." *Technology and Culture* 20 (January 1979): 162–74.

Pursell, Carroll. *The Machine in America: A Social History of Technology.* Baltimore: Johns Hopkins University Press, 1995.

Rankin, Allen. "King Cotton Gets a Hotfoot: Flame Cultivator Destroys Weeds." *Collier's* 123 (March 12, 1949): 46, 72–73.

Ransom, Roger L., and Richard Sutch. *One Kind of Freedom: The Economic Consequences of Emancipation.* Cambridge: Cambridge University Press, 1977.

Raper, Arthur. *Machines in the Cotton Fields.* Atlanta, Ga.: Southern Regional Council, 1946.

Rasmussen, Wayne D. "The Mechanization of Agriculture." *Scientific American* 247 (September 1982): 77–89.

Ratcliff, J. D. "Revolution in Cotton." *Collier's* 116 (July 21, 1945): 24, 40–42.

Richards, Henry I. *Cotton and the AAA.* Washington, D.C.: Brookings Institution, 1936.

———. *Cotton under the Agricultural Adjustment Act: Developments up to July 1934.* Washington, D.C.: Brookings Institution, 1934.

Roger, Biles. *The South and the New Deal.* Lexington: University Press of Kentucky, 1994.

Royce, Edward. *The Origins of Southern Sharecropping.* Philadelphia: Temple University Press, 1993.

Russell, Albert R. *The First 40 Years: The National Cotton Council, 1939–1979.* Memphis, Tenn.: National Cotton Council, 1980.

———. *U.S. Cotton and the National Cotton Council, 1938–1987.* Memphis: National Cotton Council, 1987.

Rust, John. "The Origin and Development of the Cotton Picker." *West Tennessee Historical Society Papers* 7 (1953): 38–56.

———. "The Rust Cotton Picker." *Southern Workman* 67 (December 1938): 366–70.

Saloutos, Theodore. *The American Farmer and the New Deal.* Ames: Iowa State University Press, 1982.

Saunders, Dero A. "Revolution in the Deep South." *Nation* 145 (September 11, 1937): 264–66.

Sayre, Charles R. "Cotton Mechanization since World War II." *Agricultural History* 53 (January 1979): 105–24.

Schlebecker, John T. *Agricultural Implements and Machines in the Collection of the National Museum of History and Technology.* Washington, D.C.: Smithsonian Institution Press, 1972.

Schmookler, Jacob. *Patents, Inventions and Economic Change, Data and Selected Essays.* Edited by Zvi Griliches and Leonid Hurwicz. Cambridge: Harvard University Press, 1972.

Schulman, Bruce J. *From Cotton Belt to Sunbelt: Federal Policy, Economic Development, and the Transformation of the South, 1938–1980.* New York: Oxford University Press, 1991.

Schweninger, Loren. "A Vanishing Breed: Black Farm Owners in the South, 1651–1982." *Agricultural History* 63 (summer 1989): 41–60.

Seavoy, Ronald E. *The American Peasantry: Southern Agricultural Labor and Its Legacy, 1850–1995: A Study in Political Economy*. Westport, Conn.: Greenwood Press, 1998.

Sheridan, Richard C. "Chemical Fertilizers in Southern Agriculture." *Agricultural History* 53 (January 1979): 308–18.

Simon, Charlie May. "Retreat to the Land: An Experiment in Poverty." *Scribners* 93 (May 1933): 309–12.

Simpich, Frederick. "Arkansas Rolls up Its Sleeves." *National Geographic Magazine* 90 (September 1946): 273–313.

Skates, John R., Jr. "World War II as a Watershed in Mississippi History." *Journal of Mississippi History* 37 (May 1975): 131–42.

Smith, Adam [pseud.]. "The City as the OK Corral." *Esquire* 104 (July 1985): 62–64.

Smith, Harris Pearson, and Lambert Henry Wilkes. *Farm Machinery and Equipment*. 6th ed. New York: McGraw-Hill, 1976.

Snyder, Robert E. "Huey Long and the Cotton-Holiday of 1931." *Louisiana History* 18 (spring 1977): 133–60.

———. "The Cotton Holiday Movement in Mississippi, 1931." *Journal of Mississippi History* 40 (February 1978): 1–32.

———. *Cotton Crisis*. Chapel Hill: University of North Carolina Press, 1984.

Straus, Robert Kenneth. "Enter the Cotton Picker: The Story of the Rust Brothers' Invention." *Harper's* 173 (September 1936): 389–95. Reprinted in *Readers Digest,* 29 (October 1936): 43–47.

Street, James H. "The 'Labor Vacuum' and Cotton Mechanization." *Journal of Farm Economics* 35 (August 1953): 381–97.

———. *The New Revolution in the Cotton Economy: Mechanization and Its Consequences*. Chapel Hill: University of North Carolina Press, 1957.

Stryker, Roy E. *In This Proud Land: America, 1935–1943 as Seen in the FSA Photographs*. Greenwich, Conn.: New York Graphic Society, 1973.

Taylor, Paul S. "Power Farming and Labor Displacement in the Cotton Belt, 1937, Part 1, Northwest Texas." *Monthly Labor Review* 46 (March 1938): 595–607.

———. "Power Farming and Labor Displacement, Part 2, Southwestern Oklahoma and Mississippi Delta." *Monthly Labor Review* 46 (April 1938): 852–67.

Temin, Peter. "The Postbellum Recovery of the South and the Cost of the Civil War." *Journal of Economic History* 36 (December 1976): 898–907.

Tindall, George B. *Emergence of the New South, 1913–1945*. Baton Rouge: Louisiana State University Press, 1967.

Tolnay, Stewart E. "Structural Change and Fertility Change in the South, 1910 to 1940." *Social Science Quarterly* 77 (September 1996): 559–76.

Tolnay, Stewart E., and Patricia J. Glynn. "The Persistence of High Fertility in the American South on the Eve of the Baby Boom." *Demography* 31 (November 1994): 615–31.

Tolnay, Stewart E., and E. M. Beck. *A Festival of Violence: An Analysis of Southern Lynching, 1882–1930.* Urbana: University of Illinois Press, 1995.

Vance, Rupert B. *All These People.* Chapel Hill: University of North Carolina Press, 1945.

Webb, Pamela. "By the Sweat of the Brow: The Back-to-the-Land Movement in Depression Arkansas." *Arkansas Historical Quarterly* 42 (winter 1983): 332–45.

Wehrwein, George S. "Changes in Farms and Farm Tenure, 1930–1935." *Journal of Land and Public Policy Utility Economics* 12 (May 1936): 200–205.

———. "How Many Farmers Do We Require?" *Land Policy Review* 3 (September 1940): 3–7.

Welch, Frank J. "Some Economic and Social Implications of Agricultural Adjustments in the South." *Journal of Farm Economics* 29 (February 1947): 192–208.

Welch, Frank J., and D. Gray Miley. "Mechanization of the Cotton Harvest." *Journal of Farm Economics* 27 (November 1945): 928–46.

Weybright, Victor. "Two Men and Their Machine." *Survey Graphic* 25 (July 1936): 432–33.

Whatley, Warren C. "A History of Mechanization in the Cotton South: The Institutional Hypothesis." *Quarterly Journal of Economics* 100 (November 1985): 1191–1215.

———. "Labor for the Picking: The New Deal in the South." *Journal of Economic History* 43 (December 1983): 905–29.

———. "New Estimates of the Cost of Harvesting Cotton: 1949–1964." *Research in Economic History* 13 (1991): 199–225.

———. "Southern Agrarian Labor Contracts as Impediments to Cotton Mechanization." *Journal of Economic History* 47 (March 1987): 45–70.

Whatley, Warren C., and Gavin Wright. "Black Labor in the American Economy since Emancipation: What Are the Legacies of History?" In *The Wealth of Races: The Present Value of Benefits from Past Injustices,* ed. Richard F. America, 67–90. Westport, Conn.: Greenwood Press, 1990.

Whayne, Jeannie M. *A New Plantation South: Land, Labor, and Federal Favor in Twentieth-Century Arkansas.* Charlottesville: University Press of Virginia, 1996.

Whayne, Jeannie M., and Willard B. Gatewood. *The Arkansas Delta: Land of Paradox.* Fayetteville: University of Arkansas Press, 1993.

Wheat, Leonard F., and William H. Crown. *State Per-Capita Income Change since 1950: Sharecropping's Collapse and Other Causes of Convergence.* Westport, Conn.: Greenwood Press, 1995.

White, B. S., Jr. "Shrinking Foreign Market for United States Cotton." *Quarterly Journal of Economics* 54 (February 1940): 255–76.

Whitman, David. "The Great Sharecropper Success Story." *Public Interest* 104 (summer 1991): 3–21.

Wilcox, Walter W. *The Farmer in the Second World War.* Ames: Iowa University Press, 1947. Reprint: New York: DaCapo Press, 1973.

Williams, B. O. "The Impact of Mechanization on the Farm Population of the South." *Rural Sociology* 4 (September 1939): 300–313.

Williams, Paul H. "The Rise and Fall of the Great Plantations." *Arkansas Times* 9 (July 1983): 86–93.

Williams, Robert C. *Fordson, Farmall, and Poppin' Johnny: A History of the Farm Tractor and Its Impact on America.* Urbana: University of Illinois Press, 1987.

Woodman, Harold D. "Decline of Cotton Factorage after the Civil War." *American Historical Review* 71 (July 1966): 1219–36.

Woodruff, Nan Elizabeth. "Mississippi Delta Planters and Debates over Mechanization, Labor, and Civil Rights." *Journal of Southern History* 60 (May 1994): 263–84.

———. "Pick or Fight: The Emergency Farm Labor Program in the Arkansas and Mississippi Deltas during World War II." *Agricultural History* 64 (spring 1989): 74–85.

———. *As Rare As Rain: Federal Relief in the Great Southern Drought of 1930–31.* Urbana: University of Illinois Press, 1985.

Woodward, C. Vann. *Origins of the New South, 1877–1913.* Baton Rouge: Louisiana State University Press, 1951.

Wrenn, Lynette Boney. *Cinderella of the New South: A History of the Cottonseed Industry, 1855–1955.* Knoxville: University of Tennessee Press, 1995.

Wright, Gavin. *Old South, New South: Revolutions in the Southern Economy since the Civil War.* New York: Basic Books, 1986.

Experiment Station Bulletins

Baker, J. A., and J. G. McNeely. *Land Tenure in Arkansas: I. The Farm Tenancy Situation.* Bulletin No. 384. Fayetteville: Agricultural Experiment Station, January 1940.

Blalock, H. W. *Plantation Operations of Landlords and Tenants in Arkansas.* Bulletin No. 339. Fayetteville: Agricultural Experiment Station, 1937.

Bryant, Ellen S. *Population Growth and Redistribution in Mississippi, 1900–1970.* Bulletin No. 790. State College, Miss.: Agricultural and Forestry Experiment Station, 1971.

Engler, Kyle, W. F. Buchele, and J. C. Newell. *Mechanized Production of Cotton: I. Effect of Seedbed Preparation, Planting, and Cultivation on Mechanical Harvesting of Cotton.* Mimeograph Series No. 3. Fayetteville: Arkansas Agricultural Experiment Station, April 1950.

LeRay, Nelson L., George L. Wilber, and Grady B. Crowe. *Plantation Organization and the Resident Labor Force, Delta Area, Mississippi.* Bulletin No. 606. State College: Mississippi Agricultural Experiment Station, October 1960.

LeRay, Nelson, Jr., and Grady B. Crowe. *Labor and Technology on Selected Cotton Plantations in the Delta Area of Mississippi.* Bulletin No. 575. State College: Mississippi Agricultural Extension Station, April 1959.

Lessley, Billy V., and James H. White. *Crop Enterprises on Cotton Farms in Southeast Arkansas.* Report Series No. 111. Fayetteville: Arkansas Agricultural Experiment Station, June 1962.

McComas, Paul S., and Frank J. Welch. *Farm Labor Requirements in Mississippi.* Bulletin No. 387. State College: Mississippi Agricultural Experiment Station, June 1943.

McNeely, J. G., and Glen T. Barton. *Land Tenure in Arkansas: II. Change in Labor Organization on Cotton Farms.* Bulletin No. 397. Fayetteville: Agricultural Experiment Station, June 1940.

McNeely, J. G., Glen T. Barton, and Trimble R. Hedges. *Land Tenure in Arkansas: III. Income and Changes in Tenure Status of Share Renters, Share Croppers, and Wage Laborers on Cotton Farms.* Bulletin No. 438. Fayetteville: Agricultural Experiment Station June 1943.

Metzler, William H. *Population Trends and Adjustments in Arkansas.* Bulletin No. 388. Fayetteville: Arkansas Agricultural Experiment Station, May 1940.

Osgood, Otis, and John W. White. *Land Tenure in Arkansas: IV. Further Changes in Labor Used on Cotton Farms, 1939–1944.* Bulletin No. 459. Fayetteville: Agricultural Experiment Stations, August 1945.

Pedersen, Harald A., and Arthur F. Raper. *The Cotton Plantation in Transition.* Bulletin 508. State College: Mississippi State College, Agricultural Experiment Station, January 1954.

Tarver, James D. *Changes in Arkansas Population.* Report Series 21. Fayetteville: Arkansas Agricultural Experiment Station, December 1950.

Vaiden, M. G., J. O. Smith, and W. E. Ayres. *Making Cotton Cheaper: Can Present Production Costs Be Reduced?* Bulletin No. 290. State College: Mississippi Agricultural Experiment Station, February 1931.

———. *Making Cotton Cheaper: Can Present Production Costs Be Reduced?* Bulletin No. 298. State College: Mississippi Agricultural Experiment Station, June 1932.

Welch, Frank J. *The Plantation Land Tenure System in Mississippi.* Bulletin No. 385. State College: Mississippi State Experiment Station, June 1943.

U.S. Government Publications

Cooper, Martin R., Glen T. Barton, and Albert P. Brodell. *Progress in Farm Mechanization.* Miscellaneous Publication No. 630. Washington, D.C.: U.S. Department of Agriculture, 1947.

Farm Tenancy: Report of the President's Committee. Washington, D.C.: GPO, 1937.

Holley, William C., and Lloyd E. Arnold. *Changes in Technology and Labor*

Requirements in Crop Production: Cotton. National Research Project Report No. A-7. Philadelphia, Pa.: Works Progress Administration, September 1938.

Horne, Roman L., and Eugene G. McKibben. *Changes in Farm Power and Equipment: Mechanical Cotton Picker.* Report No. A-2. Philadelphia, Pa.: Works Progress Administration, August 1937.

Langsford, E. L. and B. H. Thibodeaux. *Plantation Organization and Operator in the Yazoo-Mississippi Delta Area.* Technical Bulletin No. 682. Washington, D.C.: U.S. Department of Agriculture, May 1939.

McKibben, Eugene G., and R. Austin Griffin. *Changes in Farm Power and Equipment: Tractors, Trucks, and Automobiles,* National Research Project Report No. A-9. Philadelphia, Pa.: Works Progress Administration, December 1938.

Rasmussen, Wayne D. *A History of the Farm Labor Supply Program, 1943–1947.* Monograph No. 13, 1951. Washington, D.C.: U.S. Department of Agriculture.

Technology on the Farm, a Special Report by an Interbureau Committee of the Bureau of Agricultural Economics, U.S. Department of Agriculture. Washington, D.C.: GPO, August 1940.

United States Bureau of the Census. *Historical Statistics of the United States, Colonial Times to 1970.* Washington, D.C.: GPO, 1975.

———. *Plantation Farming in the United States.* Washington, D.C.: GPO, 1916.

———. *Sixteenth Census of the United States: 1940. Population. Internal Migration, 1935–1940.* Washington, D.C.: GPO, 1943.

U.S. Congress. *Payments under Agricultural Adjustment Program.* 74th Congress, 2d sess., S. Doc. 274, 1936.

U.S. Department of Agriculture, Economic Research Service. *Statistics on Cotton and Related Data, 1920–1973.* Statistical Bulletin No. 535. Washington, D.C.: USDA, 1974.

U.S. House of Representatives. *Committee on Agriculture: Study of Agricultural and Economic Problems of the Cotton Belt.* 80th Cong., 1st sess., pt. 1 and 2, 1947.

Woofter, T. J., Jr. *Landlord and Tenant on the Cotton Plantation.* Research Monograph 5. Washington D.C.: Works Progress Administration, 1936.

Index